FROM TIRED

TO

Inspired

MARY KIM
SCHRECK

FRESH
STRATEGIES
TO ENGAGE
STUDENTS IN
LITERACY

Solution Tree | Press

a division of
Solution Tree

555 North Morton Street
Bloomington, IN 47404

800.733.6786 (toll free) / 812.336.7700
FAX: 812.336.7790

email: info@solution-tree.com
solution-tree.com

Visit **go.solution-tree.com/literacy** to download the reproducibles in this book.

Printed in the United States of America

16 15 14   2 3 4 5

Library of Congress Cataloging-in-Publication Data
Schreck, Mary Kim, author.
  From tired to inspired : fresh strategies to engage students in literacy / Mary Kim Schreck.
     pages cm
  Includes bibliographical references and index.
  ISBN 978-1-936764-37-2 (perfect bound) 1. Language arts (Elementary) 2. Language arts (Secondary) 3. Active learning. 4. Motivation in education. I. Title.
  LB1576.S3267 2013
  372.6--dc23
                          2012037489

Solution Tree
Jeffrey C. Jones, CEO
Edmund M. Ackerman, President

Solution Tree Press
President: Douglas M. Rife
Publisher: Robert D. Clouse
Editorial Director: Lesley Bolton
Managing Production Editor: Caroline Wise
Senior Production Editor: Edward Levy
Copy Editor: Tara Perkins
Proofreader: Sarah Payne-Mills
Text Designer: Amy Shock
Cover Designer: Rian Anderson

Acknowledgments

Solution Tree Press would like to thank the following reviewers:

Mary Baker
Instructor
School of Education, Lindenwood University
St. Charles, Missouri

Linda Beal
Reading Specialist
Portsmouth School District
Portsmouth, New Hampshire

Britton Gildersleeve
Director
Oklahoma State University Writing Project
Oklahoma State University
Stillwater, Oklahoma

Tiffany Holliday
English Teacher
Pinole Valley High School
Pinole, California

Erin Knoll
Director of Literacy
Schaumburg School District 54
Schaumburg, Illinois

Anne Namuth
Language Arts Teacher
Westlake Middle School
Broomfield, Colorado

Aaron Thiell
First-Grade Teacher
Tamarac Elementary School
Troy, New York

Solution Tree Press also wishes to thank Breona Banks, Jason Bergeland, Carol Brown, Steven Buback, Chris Carroll, Jenny Egger, Nick Heston, Benjamin McAlpin, and Chris Scofield for their contribution of student work and Keagan Shock for her drawings.

Visit **go.solution-tree.com/literacy** to download the reproducibles in this book.

Table of Contents

Reproducible pages are in italics.

Chapter Seven

Outrageous Teaching 107

Chapter Eight

Mixing Complexity and Integration Into Planning 119

Chapter Nine

Standards and Assessments Fostering Literacy Growth 137

About the Author

MARY KIM SCHRECK serves as an education consultant, author, and speaker across the United States. Over the years, thousands of teachers have attended her motivating, fast-paced workshops and keynotes, which blend current, research-based information on student literacy, engagement, creativity, and effective teaching practices into seamless messages. Her professional books are both reader-friendly and practical guides to helping teachers move theory into classroom practice. She is a firm believer that what you learn with pleasure you never forget, and her books and workshops are a living testament to this belief.

Mary Kim has worked with school districts throughout the United States, as well as with the National Writing Project and National Education Association. She has been an instructor for the Literacy Academies—a partnership between the Missouri National Writing Project and the State Department of Education, and for the I Can Do It Beginning Teachers Assistance Program. She has thirty-six years of classroom experience in environments ranging from an all-girls private academy, to a 270-student rural school that serves grades 6–12, to a public school of more than four thousand students. Most of her teaching career has been spent with the Francis Howell School District in St. Charles County, Missouri, where she experienced the challenges of a rural district forced to quickly become a suburban one.

For years, Mary Kim has been helping teachers in urban as well as suburban settings recognize and activate purposeful ways to challenge and motivate students. She has shared methods to get students to read more thoughtfully, speak and discuss with more articulation, and above all write and think with a sense of focus, control, and maturity. She has been following the fundamental blueprint for the Common Core State Standards since before it was formally written—specifically because she knows these fundamentals are, above all, good teaching.

Mary Kim published four books of poetry before focusing her attention on professional development. Her book *Transformers: Creative Teachers for the 21st Century* defines creativity as it appears in the classroom, while giving teachers concrete suggestions about how to better access their own personal creativity. *You've Got To Reach Them To Teach Them*, which was nominated for the Delta Kappa Gamma International Educator's Book Award, moves teachers from the topic of creativity to an examination of what they can do to engage their students and set an atmosphere for greater achievement. Mary Kim has served as editor of *Missouri Teachers Write* and has written articles for national and state education journals.

To book Mary Kim for professional development, contact pd@solution-tree.com.

Introduction

From Tired to Inspired is a baseline book for improving literacy in upper elementary through secondary classrooms. It does not deal with the mechanics of reading or writing acquisition, as do the materials written for lower grade levels. In fact, the lion's share of this book is dedicated to exploring the subtitle, *Fresh Strategies to Engage Students in Literacy*—how the ideas and tenets of literacy instruction play out every day for teachers and their students.

Author, speaker, and trainer Robyn Jackson (2011) always asks herself certain questions as she visits a classroom, including:

1. Who is primarily doing the thinking—the students or the teacher?

2. What level of instruction or stage of rigorous learning is involved?

3. How are the students engaged in the instruction? That is, do they understand the purpose of the work, or do they simply comply?

These three areas of concern are represented in the purpose and process of this book. First, literacy is a hollow set of skills if it is not enlivened by active, precise, and creative thinking on the part of the students. Without it, there is no comprehension, no articulating of ideas, and no conversation of any depth or breadth. The goal of all the exercises and instructional structures suggested here is to make better, independent thinkers of our students.

Second, instruction should be rigorous. We see this word used frequently but seldom see it pinned down to a workable concept or definition. Myths abound when discussing what a rigorous curriculum or activity should be. *Rigor*, as it is used in this book, refers to a high-level quality of effort, instruction, thinking, products, and expectations held by teachers and students alike. Rigor should be accessible to everyone, not only a select few. Rigor means challenging rather than difficult, quality rather than quantity, questioning rather than answering. Rigorous work results in products that are not predictable and, above all, are characterized by an attitude of self-motivated effort and ultimate satisfaction. Rigorous instruction stretches students' minds rather than burdening or boring them with tedious low-level work.

Third, woven through all the lessons, activities, and ideas for presenting curriculum suggested here is the assumption that they must be engaging to children. By engaging, I mean interesting and appealing to young minds. Challenging and rigorous instruction, if it is not appropriately balanced with support and materials that are of interest to students, can lead students to become overwhelmed and frustrated and to give up prematurely. To be successful, rigorous instruction must also take place in a supportive, engaging environment. Engagement breeds success, leading to an increase in motivation that in turn builds confidence. Confidence opens the gates for a student to exert effort and focus attention on the tasks assigned. As aptly stated by Peter Johnston (2012) in *Opening Minds*, the goal of engagement "has been neglected in the rush to standardize outcomes. When children are fully engaged in an activity, they press into service all of their resources and stretch themselves as necessary. Children are more engaged when they have choice, a degree of autonomy, and when they see the activity as relevant" (p. 125).

Little children walk into classrooms after having been lured for years into learning numbers and letters by using song and colorfully costumed big birds, purple dragons, pirates, and all manner of narrators. Now they are seated at desks and subtly told that the days of feathered narrators and dancing to lessons are over. They are introduced to testing procedures, timed performance requests, and walking single file with arms crossed and fingers on their lips. They are socialized into our schoolroom expectations. For more students than we would like to admit, this is a saddening transition that moves them into a frame of mind that is eventually labeled as unmotivated, reluctant, underachieving, restless, or inattentive—all byproducts of an institutionalized process that simply isn't attractive to them.

For every age, the gentle reminders of what we love—music, color, dreams of what is possible, being proud of ourselves for succeeding, playing with ideas, laughing, experiencing the joy of losing ourselves in projects we have chosen, trying again and again, changing our minds—can all be reawakened within the institutionalized process of the classroom by teachers injecting creative planning and a nurturing execution of instruction.

To engage students in this way, teachers need to have what are known as soft skills—skills that students react to intuitively. These soft skills that successful teachers possess involve relationships, emotions, humor, confidence, motivation, expectations, nurturing, hope, shaping the classroom environment, creativity, body language, and what can be called "withitness"—that state of awareness that enables a teacher to scan the room at all times for everything from potential behavior problems to misunderstanding of material.

To be successful in our efforts at bringing all students to a state of literacy competency that will serve them in our complex world, we must have more than book knowledge; we need to have a full palette of these soft or "people" skills at our disposal. The research substantiates the relationship between teachers' soft skills and their effect on the acquisition and mastery of literacy—especially in the case of reluctant learners. One study in particular, "Discovering Emotion in Classroom Motivation Research" (Meyer & Turner, 2002), reports that with all other things being equal, between two teachers, both of whom "appeared to cognitively scaffold understanding and provide opportunities for student autonomy effectively," the teachers' "patterns of affective support differed remarkably. In the classroom with higher student self-reports of negative affect and self-handicapping, the frequency of positive teacher responses was lower and the frequency of negative responses was higher" (p. 111).

This study, which covers motivation research over a ten-year period, goes on to explore what kind of emotional support from teachers helps students to activate self-motivation and increase their engagement in material—especially those students who are most reluctant to take risks or sustain motivation. Some of these supports include emphasizing that mistakes are a natural part of learning, modeling enthusiasm and interest, and creating opportunities for student choice. Other common characteristics among teachers who provide emotional support were a tendency toward seeing humor and an obvious love of learning. Teachers who are able to give explicit responses, share personal positive emotions with their students, and exhibit their own motivation as learners seem to be most effective in raising students' personal emotional responses to the class in general and the subject matter in particular. This combination of teacher behaviors results in higher student achievement. The connection between emotion, motivation, and achievement is so strong that it seems impossible to consider student motivation without considering the impact of the emotional context a teacher supplies (Meyer & Turner, 2002).

Marc Tucker (2011) writes:

> One may be good at physics and still be a poor physics teacher. To be good at teaching, one has to be able to connect with students, to engage them, inspire them, communicate easily with them, get inside

their heads and figure out what they don't understand and find a way to help them understand it. And it is not all about conveying "content." It is also about helping students to understand what the right thing is and why it is important to do it when doing it is not easy. It is about persuading a student that she has what it takes to go to college or stay in high school when her dad just went to jail and she is living on the sidewalk. It can be about being a friend, a mentor, and a guide. (p. 10)

When a teacher displays soft skills, students know instinctively—after just a few minutes—that they will enjoy the class, feel safe enough to take risks, laugh, be themselves, ask questions, and be emotionally as well as intellectually supported. They might not be able to articulate this immediately, but it's apparent to them on a deep level. This attitude sets the stage for effective learning (Barsade, 2002; Goleman, 1995; Jenson, 2003; Turner & Stets, 2005).

A fundamental precept of teachers who own and effectively utilize their innate soft skills in the classroom is that what we learn with pleasure we never forget. Elaborating on this concept, the best way to ensure that students are going to learn what we are teaching is to always make sure that the first time new material is introduced it is under pleasant conditions and never with words alone. That is why using props for any content area or age group is important!

The choice of topics in this book has been made carefully. The chapter topics align well with the Common Core State Standards (CCSS) in their emphasis on developing independent thinkers capable of dealing with complex texts and assignments in ample reading, writing, speaking, and listening opportunities that should constitute the bulk of the instructional period.

As of this publication, forty-five states have signed on to adopt the Common Core State Standards as the educational "law of the land" for their students. Because these standards are focused on more authentic development of thinking skills through deeper reading and more meaningful writing, speaking, and listening opportunities, they challenge educators to stretch themselves to provide a more rigorous and rewarding learning experience for their students. The appearance of these standards at this time in history provides a dramatic opportunity for American education to renew itself, to re-evaluate and realign itself to a more vigorous vision of what is possible to accomplish in the classroom. This book is meant to help teachers meet this challenge while enhancing their sense of empowerment and self-satisfaction in their careers. Since the Common Core State Standards are basically a blueprint for good, effective teaching, hopefully this book will help teachers to recognize those elements they are already doing well and focus attention on what still needs to be emphasized and embedded in their classroom lessons for optimal effectiveness.

Many of this book's reproducible examples and exercises (which can also be found online at **go.solution -tree.com/literacy**) can serve as durable templates for teachers to use with other material from multiple fields of instruction. It is my hope that teachers in the field will bookmark many of these activities once they see how readily they can be translated for use in their own classrooms. *From Tired to Inspired* has also been written for preteachers and teacher preparation institutions, so that teachers in training can see what fundamental tenets of literacy instruction look like in the upper-grade classrooms.

Chapter 1, "Close Reading and Close Writing," invites students to slow down their normal reading speed and shows how we can train and empower students to once again learn how to see. By seeing, here I mean to become aware of the small details that fill our vision but are often ignored because our minds are filled with so many other competing thoughts. Small children tend to be in the moment and focus on what is immediately before them. That quality is what we want to enhance in our students.

Chapter 2, "The Core of Literacy," examines the reality that we are all storytellers, that our brains use stories to make sense of information coming in through our senses.

Building on these themes, chapter 3, "Reteaching Strategies," deals with the necessity of thoughtfully weaving reteaching experiences into lessons throughout the year.

Chapter 4, "Cognitive Conversations," emphasizes how important it is for students to be orally engaged in their own learning and to be question makers as well as responders.

Chapter 5, "Using Novelty for Reluctant Learners," looks at how we can coax our less eager students into losing themselves in assignments by playing on their curiosity, their loves and interests, and their immediate need to see value and personal ability melded together in what we offer them to learn and do.

Chapter 6, "Creative and Critical Thinking Approaches to Literacy," offers teachers a primer in convergent and divergent thinking, processes that are necessary if students are to be strong thinkers able to use both sides of their brains effectively.

Chapter 7, "Outrageous Teaching," serves to continue the conversation on blending engagement with literacy-building techniques by spotlighting how teachers can use their "stage" to pull out all the stops and create a setting for learning in which difficult-to-understand material comes alive and remains in the memory indefinitely.

Chapter 8, "Mixing Complexity and Integration Into Planning," addresses the challenge of making the work we ask our students to do genuinely meaningful.

We draw together all aspects of nurturing literacy in chapter 9, "Standards and Assessments Fostering Literacy Growth." Here we take a few of the main guideposts of the Common Core State Standards and see how they play out in specific lessons.

In "Final Thoughts," I share a few concluding remarks.

We all are aware that education is considered serious business. We all feel the pressure of tests, evaluations, requirements, and measured outcomes inside and outside the areas of our control. If we are to keep our equilibrium and balance, we must teach from a position of joy and an authentic motivation that always keeps our students' welfare in the forefront. This has been my overriding goal in writing this book.

Chapter One

Close Reading and Close Writing

Close reading entails a critical analysis and examination of any content, whether it is print, film, music, painting, math, design, nonfiction or fiction, speeches, plays, and so on. Close reading is slow reading. It is reading that ratchets up attention to detail. In this chapter, we look at how teachers can foster a sensitivity to detail and word choice in order to promote more attentive thinking habits. We also look at using visualization as an effective comprehension tool when attempting to decode complex material.

Close reading is essentially a more text-centered method of moving students to deeper comprehension. Often, it entails multiple passes over the text with a different purpose guiding each reading. Students might read the material the first time for the main idea and overall meaning. The teacher's questions and consequent activities will reflect this purpose. The next reading might revolve around what choices the author has made regarding, for example, point of view or tone, and require students to analyze the implications of those choices. The third reading might then move to how this text relates to other texts or to the reader's life, values, and experiences. The product of this reading would be close writing—a critical analysis using a compare and contrast structure. This close writing moves in tandem with the purposes set by the teacher for each consequent reading. Here the connection between reading, writing, and thinking is most authentic. Both close reading and close writing are the doorways to building students' capacity for sustained rigorous practice and robust comprehension.

The Need for Rigor

Richard Strong, Harvey Silver, and Matthew Perini (2001) write that rigor is what is required of students for understanding content that is "complex, ambiguous, provocative, and personally or emotionally challenging" (p. 57). Much of what occurs in classrooms that is referred to as rigor doesn't come close to fitting this definition, however. Instead, we often see teachers laboring under the misconception that rigor means giving out more worksheets or assigning more problems, that learning next year's material a year sooner is rigor, or that rigor means giving writing assignments for a select few students. But as Barbara Blackburn (2008), author of the book *Rigor Is Not a Four-Letter Word*, explains:

> True rigor does more with less, preferring depth over breadth. Next, rigor is not just for your advanced students. Rigor is for every student you teach. That includes your students who are at risk of failure, your students with special needs, and your students for whom English is not their native language. . . . [T]he heart of authentic rigor is learning, not punishment. It is about growth and success, not failure. (p. 15)

I've found that to be able to plunge into rigorous work with a class, there must be both adequate preparation on my part and the existence of a warm, supportive environment. If a teacher believes the student holds the lion's share of responsibility for learning and therefore is at fault for failing to progress adequately, the student senses this and shuts down. When teachers establish instructional strategies with literacy as a primary focus in an enriched environment, however, the outcome is an atmosphere where risk-taking does not result in high stress and responses of fight or flight. According to Marian Diamond and Janet Hopson

(1998), reading and writing depend on a set of cognitive skills that thrive in environments that are rich in positive emotional support; stimulation of the senses; absence of undue pressure or stress; pleasure; novel challenges; opportunities to use whole-child range of skills; opportunities for choice, personal assessment, and modification; fun; and active participation. All of these elements need to be in place for a truly nurturing environment to exist and for cognitive learning to result in the freedom for students to take risks and not close down.

When teaching is rigorous, students are up to their elbows in higher-order thinking experiences, in analyzing and evaluating as well as creating. And they love it! When we invite students to think and act like artists, engineers, historians, politicians, doctors, scientists, lawyers, and CEOs, when our students play intellectual dress-up and rehearse for real-time careers, they are developing and strengthening the brain—preparing themselves to function in an unpredictable future.

How a teacher nudges students into exercising their latent thinking processes makes all the difference between a feeling of success and a refusal to even try. Many children would rather be considered trouble-makers than seen as "dumb" in front of their peers. They refuse to take educational risks for fear of experiencing possible failure and humiliation. Too often, as well, teachers feel that rigorous instruction is out of the reach of those who don't possess a firm foundation in basic skills. Year after year, these students are subjected to the drudgery of reams of worksheets and rote learning. The teacher must therefore function as a kind of artist, carefully planning a sequence of experiences to guarantee students a series of first successes that will serve to fuel motivation and effort.

As Richard Jones (2008) of the International Center for Leadership in Education observes, instruction must be not only rigorous but relevant:

> While it is essential that students acquire fundamental skills before they proceed to more complex work, teachers should not keep students hostage by requiring that they complete all the isolated basics before they have the opportunity to engage in challenging and applied learning experiences. Relevance is just as critical as rigor. Relevance can help create conditions and motivation necessary for students to make the personal investment required for rigorous work or optimal learning. (p. 5)

In the end, there is no linear, clear-cut alignment of skill acquisition that can be prescribed to all students. Real learning is always messier than most manuals and logic-driven explanations would lead us to believe. We emphasize rigor because most students pick up the basics as their innate hunger for higher-order thinking experiences are fed. Jones (2008) warns us that "teachers should not keep students hostage by requiring that they complete all the isolated basics before they have the opportunity to engage in challenging and applied learning experiences" (p. 5). The entryway into this state of grappling with complexity, ambiguity, provocation, and personally challenging material begins with close reading.

Slowing Down the Eye

For years, students have equated speed with competency, and this glorification of speed is reinforced by the fast-paced culture that surrounds us. We all know students are extremely proud of themselves when they can indicate with a swiftly raised hand that they have finished before anyone else. When we teach students how to intentionally slow down their normal reading pace, we are sometimes met with surprise. The very word *slow* has negative connotations for many. Students placed in the "slow group" in early grades later find that stigma difficult to remove. Of course, the need for building fluency in reading and writing legitimately pushes this quest for speed, yet it should be balanced by the recognition that speed isn't the only indicator of reading competency.

Close reading promotes a rediscovery and awakening of sensitivity to the power of words. Wordplay should be a staple of every teacher's literacy backpack—one of those strands embedded into the delivery of all content and instruction. Wordplay is not simply vocabulary study; it has a much more whimsical energy about it that runs on the fuel of curiosity, experimentation, and playfulness and is supported by a non-judgmental environment. A great outlet for a teacher's creativity is to devise as many short, novel wordplay mini-activities as possible that serve to punctuate the normal flow of instruction. In creating wordplay, I urge teachers to work with passages from books they are currently reading or with books that will be used later in the school year. Here are a few examples.

A Princess of Mars

The Walt Disney movie *John Carter* (Stanton, Andrews, & Chabon, 2012) celebrates the near centennial of the debut of Edgar Rice Burroughs' (1917) main character of the same name. The film is based on the first of his Barsoom series of science fantasy books, *A Princess of Mars*. Filled with tremendous action and swordplay scenes, this book is perfect for expanding our students' understanding of how authors vary their word choice. We ask the class to describe the actions that are found in a typical fight scene and reduce their responses to a short list—one that can be further reduced to the two words *hit* and *move*. Then we discuss why the author wouldn't just use these two words all the time.

Now we photocopy the passage we are working with. Because the written word alone is only half-alive—our students need to *hear* it as well as see it, building a picture in their minds so it can come to full, robust life for them—we invite them to go back over the passage and highlight the substitutes this author uses for *hit* and *move*, using one color for the *hit* words and another color for the *move* words. Using the reproducible How Authors Pick Their Words on page 154 (and online at **go.solution-tree.com/literacy**), they write their selected substitute words in the columns on the right-hand side of the paper. Figure 1.1 (page 8) shows what a typical student product might look like. After ten minutes of hunting, highlighting, sorting, and debating just how far to stretch the meaning of *hit* and *move*, we discuss with students how effective they find this technique to be. Finally, students circle their favorite substitutes, jot them down in their notebooks under a title like *My Choice* (or, *Cool Words* or *Curious Word Finds*), and share with each other.

Choosing the Words Ourselves

Linked to this activity is a flip-side activity in which students substitute more vivid words. We take a few short, plain sentences and use an online or print thesaurus or a photocopied list to provide possible additions and substitutions—chiefly for the verbs, but also for the nouns, adjectives, and adverbs. We do this with three or four short sentences at most. Core sentences (with the corresponding thesaurus entries to look up) might be:

1. An old person is walking down the street (*old, walk*).

2. A boy takes off his stinky socks (*take off, stink*).

3. Loud music is coming from a passing car (*loud, passing*).

4. A waitress clumsily drops a tray of food (*clumsy, drop*).

How Authors Pick Their Words:

My beast had an advantage in his first hold, having sunk his mighty fangs far into the breast of his adversary; but the great arms and paws of the ape . . . had locked the throat of my guardian and slowly were choking out his life, and bending back his head and neck upon his body. . . . In accomplishing this the ape was tearing away the entire front of its breast, which was held in the vise-like grip of the powerful jaws. . . . Presently I saw the great eyes of my beast bulging completely from their sockets and blood flowing from its nostrils. . . . Suddenly I came to myself and, with that strange instinct which seems ever to prompt me to my duty, I seized the cudgel, which had fallen to the floor at the commencement of the battle, and swinging it with all the power of my earthly arms I crashed it full upon the head of the ape, crushing his skull as though it had been an eggshell.

Without more ado, therefore, I turned to meet the charge of the infuriated bull ape. He was now too close upon me for the cudgel to prove of any effective assistance, so I merely threw it as heavily as I could at his advancing bulk. It struck him just below the knees, eliciting a howl of pain and rage, and so throwing him off his balance that he lunged full upon me with arms wide stretched to ease his fall. Again, as on the preceding day, I had recourse to earthly tactics, and swinging my right fist full upon the point of his chin I followed it with a smashing left to the pit of his stomach. The effect was marvelous, for, as I lightly sidestepped, after delivering the second blow, he reeled and fell upon the floor doubled up with pain and gasping for wind.

List Words That Mean *Move*:

sunk	advancing
bending	throwing (him off)
bulging	lunged
flowing	swinging
fallen	reeled
swinging	fell
turned	doubled up
charge	

List Words That Mean *Hit*:

locked (the throat)	threw
sunk (fangs)	struck
choking	swinging fist
tearing away	smashing
crashed	delivering
crushing	blow

Figure 1.1: How authors pick their words.

Source: A Princess of Mars by Edgar Rice Burroughs (1917). Kindle Edition, p. 16.

Neither of these exercises takes long. After the second one, we ask students to read their newly minted sentences, and we show approval for their elegant substitutions and additions. This is wordplay. We don't sully the feeling with a heavy layer of judgment. We don't deduct points if a student uses a word incorrectly while reshaping the sentences or if a student placed a wrong word for *hit* or *move* in one of the columns. The exercise is a direct attempt at both dampening the fear of failure many carry into the classroom and showing them that risk taking is welcome. This is not the time for assessment but for revelation about how words work.

Choosing the Actions and Words

An important follow-up to these two short exercises is to ask students to decide on an action scene they will write themselves. We brainstorm a large pool of possibilities together and pick two or three words that are the most dominant action words, like *hit* and *move* in the previous exercise. They then make a word bank of alternate words. The fact that the students know they are going to use the word bank they develop for a specific purpose gives the activity even more meaning and relevance.

Students now begin writing. After they finish the drafts of this short action piece, they exchange them with a neighbor or read them aloud in their three- to four-person writing group, asking their peers to guess the core words for which they exchanged substitutes. Another approach is to have students write the core words on the bottom of the paper and ask a partner to find the substituted words in the written scene. Basically, we are mimicking the previous wordplay assignment we completed, but this time with student-produced texts.

Working With a More Difficult Text

After these activities, we want to see what taking on a more difficult text can be like. In doing this, we always start small. Nothing closes down the enthusiasm for trying to figure out a hard-to-read text like assigning one that is too long too soon. This activity is based on a passage from the novel *Iron Council* by China Miéville (2004), the winner of myriad literary awards. Miéville describes himself as a fantasy geek who writes weird fiction. The activity, Puzzling Out Meaning (reproducible page 155 and online at **go.solution-tree.com/literacy**), involves reading the following evocative but somewhat obscure passage a few times to discern what it's about, answering a few simple questions, and guessing from context the meaning of unfamiliar words.

> Rudewood teemed. Birds and ape-things in the canopy spent the morning screaming. In a zone of dead, bleached trees, an ursine thing, unclear and engorged with changing shapes and colors, reeled out of the brush toward them. They screamed, except Pomeroy who fired into the creature's chest. With a soft explosion it burst into scores of birds and hundreds of bottleglass flies, which circled them in the air and recongealed beyond them as the beast. It shuffled from them. Now they could see the feathers and wing cases that made up its pelt.

> "I been in these woods before," said Pomeroy. "I know what a throng-bear looks like." (Miéville, 2004, pp. 13–14)

Students generally do a better job on this task than adults because of their closer access to the worlds of fantasy and imagination. When they are successful at deciphering the text, they are immensely proud of themselves! These types of short passages serve as great training wheels for longer, more complex texts they will encounter later.

Exercising Our Close-Seeing Abilities

When teachers introduce vocabulary and literary terms as the first part of a lesson, students' first experience with new material is often as scribes—copying down what a teacher has written or typed on the SMART Board or computer screen. But any vocabulary word or subject-specific term is an abstraction of experience. If we are concerned with and interested in having our students involved in close reading that is sensitive to detail and yields a deeper understanding before dipping into close reading itself, I suggest training them in the act of close seeing. Exercises that do this by calling on more of students' senses will yield far faster results when we move their attention to print.

For this activity, we need the help of play money in five denominations. This can be found in the toy section of most stores or purchased online. Each student is given a paper-clipped set of five bills, one of each denomination ($1, $5, $10, $20, and $50). Students can work in pairs or separately. Their first task is to see what they can see—to find as many ways as they can that these bills are alike or different and write down their findings. The reproducible on page 156, An Exercise in Close Seeing, contains a sample sheet for this purpose.

A key element in this activity is the metacognitive discussion that follows. Here are just a few of the questions you could ask using these five bills: What did you notice the *first* time you looked at the bills? How long did it take before you began to really see some of the differences and likenesses? How many times did you go over the bills—re-*viewing* the material? When inviting students to report to the whole group, ask them to circle one or two of the findings they think no one else will have noticed. When a student really does mention something no one else saw, pour on the congratulations! Praise that student as a detail finder! Explain how important that trait of observation will be later in both reading and writing.

A Cross-Curricular Close Reading

Teachers often despair at the lack of transfer students make with skills and content they have been taught. We have compartmentalized our thinking as a result of separating one subject from another in our schedules, our buildings, and our thought processes. To make matters worse, we have developed terms in each area that differ from those of our neighbors for the very same mental activities.

Take a close look at the terms we use in communication arts (column one) and science (column two). Can you think of any terms that could be added to this set? If you teach in another area, could you add a column that would fit your subject area?

We Say . . .	They Say . . .
Predicting	Estimating, hypothesizing
Evidence from narrative details	Data
Narrative writing	Story, word problems
Symbols, metaphor	Unknowns
Prompts	Questions
Visual sense	Spatial awareness
Writing process	Scientific method
Correct mechanics	Correct computation

Mixing in material and procedures from subjects other than our own discipline can help students overcome the tendency toward overly compartmentalizing learning. It can also show them how terms used in one area of learning can benefit their understanding of another. A word problem like the following, for example, which demands comprehension along with computation, serves as a great little exercise to use in a communication arts class: How many buses does the army need to transport 1,128 soldiers, if each bus holds 36 soldiers?

Cognition expert Alan Schoenfeld (1987) points out that this was one of the problems on the National Assessment of Educational Progress secondary mathematics exam, which was administered to a stratified sample of forty-five thousand U.S. students. Seventy percent of the students who took the exam set up and performed the long division correctly. Of those, 9 percent said the answer was 31 with a remainder of 12, 18 percent said the answer was 31, and 23 percent said it was 32. Thirty percent did not do the computation correctly. It's frightening that less than one-fourth of the students got the right answer (32). Even more frightening is that almost one out of three students said that the number of buses needed is 31 with a remainder of 12 (Schoenfeld, 1987).

We begin this exercise by telling students that over one-third of eighth graders didn't get the right answer and that the problem they ran into was one of comprehension rather than computation. We invite them to figure out what those students did wrong and write it on a piece of paper. We then have them make a drawing of their solution—to show what this problem looks like as a picture. If they made the same mistake as one-third of previously tested students, the drawing should look something like figure 1.2.

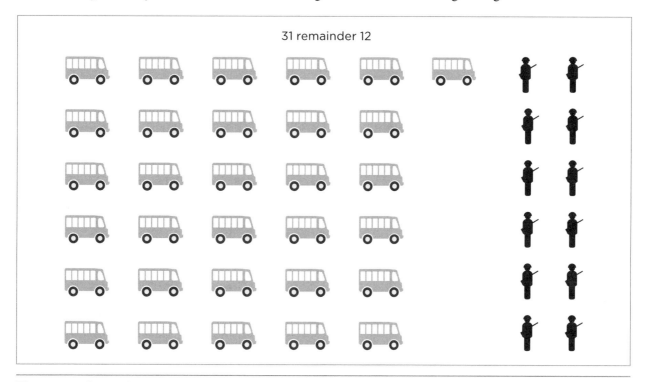

Figure 1.2: A word problem demanding comprehension along with computation.

Once the correct answer is clear to everyone, we talk about how comprehension is as important to a word problem in math as it is to a communication arts class. And to show off our students' newfound comprehension skills, we try one more exercise: If a cruise ship carries two hundred passengers and crew, and each of its lifeboats carries thirty people, how many lifeboats will the ship need?

Again, the best assessment will be the formative one we make as students try their luck at creating their own problems by mimicking the two they have already solved.

A Close Look at Fine Print

One of the most notorious ploys adults are subject to in daily life is found in the fine print to which companies, banks, and sales departments relegate their advertising materials. As teachers, we are always interested in broadening our students' literacy skills beyond their textbooks and equipping them with a little more practical understanding for negotiating the world of print outside the classroom. They offer a gold mine of possibilities.

While working as a consultant in an urban St. Louis high school, I was asked by a young teacher to help develop literacy stations for his juniors that would (a) be interesting and filled with good practice mini-assignments, (b) utilize relevant material, and (c) cover a wide spectrum of literacies. This was quite a tall order but very appropriate, and it was a wonderful challenge for me. I returned to his classroom a few days later with arms filled with plastic shoeboxes, colorful labels, directions for each box, and a wide variety of activities to fill them. One of the stations was the fine-print station, where I had placed a set of index cards. Taped to them were samples of information in fine print from credit card companies, newspaper ads, bank solicitations, and so on. On the back of each card were one or two questions that required the student to read the print more carefully—for example, to see what the terms of purchase really were, what the payment plan would be, just how many extra fees were being attached, how long the offer would be valid, or what the penalties would be if the client were to default on the payment. These are the kinds of things that we as adults have learned over the years to be wary of when confronted with offers that look too good to be true. Figures 1.3 and 1.4 contain a slightly modified form of a letter sent out from a credit card company in September 2011 (personal information has been omitted).

STP Bank

Your Card: STP Dividend Card
Your Account Ending In: 3791
Invitation Number: 789.880.9894
Credit Line: $20,000 as of June 24, 2011

GAIN

20% Bonus on Eligible Cash Back*

Bonus cash back on eligible purchases until 11/30/11.

- Enroll now for a 0.2% bonus cash back on the 1% you earn on eligible purchases. That's 20% additional cash back! Bonus cash back on your purchases means faster cash in your pocket just for using your STP Dividend Card.

- And remember, as a cardmember, you can enjoy:

  ➢ 1% cash back on all your purchases. And an average of 5% additional cash back at the 400+ retailers when you shop through STP Bonus Cash Center.

To enroll in this offer, respond by 09/23/11, and use Invitation Number 789.880.9894.

(1.877.555.5555   OR   ⌲ specialoffers.STPcards.com

Figure 1.3: The large-print offer from a fictitious credit card company.

In this exercise, our focus is on the large-print offer (figure 1.3) and the explanation of it (figure 1.4). Any asterisk next to a great offer, like the one next to "Cash Back," should be enough to set off alarm bells! Realizing this is itself a giant step toward fiscal literacy.

GAIN

20%
Bonus on
Eligible
Cash Back*

*   The 20% bonus cash back is gained on your 1% base earnings of purchases and excludes any other bonus or additional cash back you earn. Eligible purchases exclude transfer of balances, cash advances, items returned for credit, interest charges, and fees. The promotion starts within 7 business days of when you accept this offer and will end on 03/31/2013. The cash back you gain under this offer will be credited toward the $5,000 annual maximum accumulation.

    In order to participate in this promotion, your STP account must be current and open during the time of the promotion. You will no longer be eligible if you close your account.

Figure 1.4: Reading the fine print.

As an exercise in close reading, we pass out copies of the ad and ask students what the offer seems to be at first glance. Most look at the 20 percent—the largest bit of information on the sheet with the exception of the company's logo—and read "gain 20 percent bonus on eligible cash back." Most interpret that to mean that they will get back 20 percent of what they charge on the card. We create a mock-up situation. Suppose we buy a new computer that costs $525 and use our new charge card. We think we will be getting $105 back. But being the perceptive consumers that we are, we check out the fine print under the asterisk! This says that the "20% bonus cash back is gained on your 1% base earnings." That means that first of all we get 1 percent of the $525, which is $5.25, and now we get the added 20 percent bonus on this amount, which is a whopping $1.05. Add that to the $5.25 and we end up with $6.30 total cash back. You can practically hear the companies whispering "Gotcha!" as they send us our bonus checks.

None of us likes to be taken for a ride! I've found most students actually love to read into the fine print to see the real deal after all the misinformation is scoured away. This is a wonderful life skill to have our young people master before they learn the hard way. Reading into the fine print to see the real deal is also the essence of the second close-reading focus: What is the author's purpose and means at arriving at that purpose? For the final pass over this miniature close-reading text, we discuss how often commercials are deceptive, what experiences we have had of being taken in by such practices, and the problem of truth in advertising. We can move our analysis into the area of food and medicine labeling or to almost any other area where the object of the text is to persuade you to buy or use a product. The possibilities are endless.

Another interesting exercise in financial literacy relating to fine print involves cell phone rates. Deciphering what cell phone bills mean and comparing the costs of different companies' services provides another important life skill, evokes levels of interest, and leads to real savings for most teens.

Try This

Just for a week or so, avoid the urge to toss out most of the advertisements and changes in policy announcements and other pieces of mail we often ignore. Be a fine-print hunter for a while, and see if you can collect samples of fine print that seem to contradict the bulk of the message. Get your class excited about uncovering the truth behind the ad, and perhaps start a "truth in advertising" bulletin board to collect samples students can find with the help of their parents.

Reading Older Prose

Any teacher who sets out to provide rigorous material for students will have to smooth the way and mark the path with warning signs. It isn't only our English learners who have to grapple with unfamiliar words, dialects, and syntax. All our students need help. They must be taught how to read older forms of English prose that differ dramatically from what they are accustomed to reading. Sentence structure, grammatical devices, and vocabulary that were used in earlier eras present a very real stumbling block for students who have never had to tackle such challenges. Often, students become frustrated with sentences that are consistently longer and more involved than those found in contemporary English. As teachers of reading at every level and in every content area, our challenge is to give them tools to make sense of writing that can sometimes seems like it's in a foreign language. The payoff is well worth the effort.

We don't have to take on this task alone. Helpful suggestions for teachers attempting to teach the classics to today's learners can be found in Carol Jago's works, especially in her (2004) book *Classics in the Classroom: Designing Accessible Literature Lessons*.

Unlocking Hawthorne

Before beginning a close reading of *The Scarlet Letter* (Hawthorne, 2011)—a book I loved to present to my 21st century, button-pushing contemporary teenagers—I teach them a few tricks for reading Hawthorne's complex sentences.

On a sheet of paper, the SMART Board, or the overhead projector, we copy two sentences from chapter 5—one a sentence of 56 words, and the other, a very long sentence with 127 words. These are typical examples of sentences that seem to bully our students into losing all concentration, effort, and sense of confidence in themselves as readers. We present them in large print, since the larger these sentences appear, the more formidable they become. As a close-reading text, students find them impossibly dense and unreadable. But these are exactly the kinds of sentences that can be unlocked with a simple key—an understanding of the use of the dash. Basically, the dash is a punctuation mark that is used especially to indicate a break in the thought or structure of a sentence. So before we dive into our attempts at understanding, we ask our students to underline everything in front of the opening dash and everything after the closing dash in each of the two sentences.

> <u>Thus the young and pure would be taught to look at her with the scarlet letter flaming on her breast</u>— at her, the child of honorable parents, at her, the mother of a babe, that would hereafter be a woman, at her who had once been innocent—<u>as the figure, the body, the reality of sin</u>. (Hawthorne, 2011, p. 32)

> <u>It may seem marvelous, that, with the world before her</u>—kept by no restrictive clause of her condemnation within the limits of the Puritan settlement, so remote and so obscure, free to return to her birthplace, or to any other European land, and there to hide her character and identity under a new exterior, as completely as if emerging into another state of being, and having also the passes of the dark, inscrutable forest open to her, where the wilderness of her nature might assimilate itself with the people whose customs and life were alien from the law that had condemned her—<u>it may seem marvelous, that this woman should still call that place home, where, and where only, she must needs be the type of shame</u>. (Hawthorne, 2011, p. 32).

Now we read aloud only that which is underlined in sentence one. We do this so that students might catch more of the intention of the writer through our tone of voice. We ask them to read these parts of the sentence again silently before we begin asking for interpretation. Instead of asking the whole class for a volunteer, we ask the students to pair up and for each of the pairs to come up with a possible explanation for the sentence's message. We see that Hawthorne is elaborating on what he has just said, giving us more examples. Total participation is necessary in this activity; we want everyone to go away comfortable with his or her ability to unpack a type of sentence that Hawthorne uses so liberally throughout the book.

Next, we take on the giant 127-word sentence and see if what we just learned can be duplicated. To note one of the warning signs in this sentence, we explain the older meaning of the word *marvelous* to our students. In Hawthorne's day, this word connoted "wonderful, astonishing, or extraordinary" more than "good or positive by nature," as it does today. We also point out that some editions of the book have another set of dashes within the dashes, making the reading even more confusing to those not trained in Hawthorne's "dashing" prose! Then we translate the core. The feeling of empowerment ripples through the room, as pair after pair come up with what they feel is the basic meaning of the sentence. Then they dive in to the elaboration. They usually come up with at least four options that this young woman had at her disposal, besides staying in the little community that was dead set on making her the poster girl for what not to do with your life!

At this point, we ask our students to open the book to the fifth chapter, "Hester and Her Needle," and see if they can find the sentences we have just examined. Then we ask them to find examples of similar sentence construction on the same or next page—there are two in the next paragraph and two more in the following paragraph. We ask them to write a sentence saying what they learned about Hawthorne's style using this construction themselves. These are fun to read aloud!

Close Reading Poe

Teachers have an automatic home-court advantage when choosing a selection from the father of the short story, Edgar Allan Poe. Most think they love Poe's work, until they try to unravel the vocabulary and untangle the prose. We can use students' motivation to read a good Poe story as a perfect opportunity to show the benefits of close reading.

Poe's (1845) "The Masque of the Red Death" is exceptional in many ways but especially because, unlike most short stories, its focus is heavily on setting—not theme, not character, not plot. If students can't visualize the setting, they don't have anything to work with while reading it. The plot is simple, and dialogue is practically nonexistent, consisting of three short sentences spoken by the prince close to the end of the narrative. He has tried to shield himself and his friends from the plague that is ravaging his country by locking them all within his castle. Yet, here in the middle of his magnificent masquerade ball, the Red Death appears and takes their lives, despite all their efforts to avoid him. We limit our close reading to paragraph four, which describes the seven rooms within the abbey:

> It was a voluptuous scene, that masquerade. But first let me tell of the rooms in which it was held. There were seven—an imperial suite. In many palaces, however, such suites form a long and straight vista, while the folding doors slide back nearly to the walls on either hand, so that the view of the whole extant is scarcely impeded. Here the case was very different; as might have been expected from the duke's love of the "bizarre." The apartments were so irregularly disposed that the vision embraced but little more than one at a time. There was a sharp turn at the right and left, in the middle of each wall, a tall and narrow Gothic window looked out upon a closed corridor of which pursued the windings of the suite. These windows were of stained glass whose color varied in accordance with the prevailing

hue of the decorations of the chamber into which it opened. That at the eastern extremity was hung, for example, in blue—and vividly blue were its windows. The second chamber was purple in its ornaments and tapestries, and here the panes were purple. The third was green throughout, and so were the casements. The fourth was furnished and lighted with orange—the fifth with white—the sixth with violet. The seventh apartment was closely shrouded in black velvet tapestries that hung all over the ceiling and down the walls, falling in heavy folds upon a carpet of the same material and hue. But in this chamber only, the color of the windows failed to correspond with the decorations. The panes were scarlet—a deep blood color. Now in no one of any of the seven apartments was there any lamp or candelabrum, amid the profusion of golden ornaments that lay scattered to and fro and depended from the roof. There was no light of any kind emanating from lamp or candle within the suite of chambers. But in the corridors that followed the suite, there stood, opposite each window, a heavy tripod, bearing a brazier of fire, that projected its rays through the tinted glass and so glaringly lit the room. And thus were produced a multitude of gaudy and fantastic appearances. But in the western or back chamber the effect of the fire-light that streamed upon the dark hangings through the blood-tinted panes was ghastly in the extreme, and produced so wild a look upon the countenances of those who entered, that there were few of the company bold enough to set foot within its precincts at all. (p. 32)

Visualizing the Setting

We provide students with a piece of butcher paper about two feet long. As we draw what is described in the story on the SMART Board or overhead, students draw their own rendition on their large paper. We remind them that—as the story explains—all seven rooms are connected, but so irregularly that no one can stand in one room and see into another. After drawing our seven connected rooms, we draw a corridor around them. Large stained-glass windows look out from the rooms onto these corridors. After finishing this sketch of the masque ball's setting, we are ready to read the rest of the story.

In preparation for this close reading, we make a strange homework request: we ask students to bring two small action figures or tiny dolls to class. One will represent Prince Prospero and the other will be the Red Death. As teachers, we have our own set of figures attached to the board with masking tape, and we will move them through the various rooms as we read.

Hunting for Symbols

As we finish reading, the story appears to be a letdown to students, who have worked so hard sketching their settings in preparation for the action to come. The letdown is probably due to the fact that this story is primarily one of setting and not character or action. Most students want more to happen than having the Red Death simply walk through the rooms leaving everyone to die in his wake. But then we tell them that the best part is just beginning! As noted earlier, this story is exceptional insofar as it is so strongly dictated by its setting. It is also exceptional for another reason—the symbolism. Point by point, we peel away the visible to reveal one shining symbol after another. We guide students with questions: The rooms are described from east to west; what else moves from east to west? What could the color sequence of the rooms represent? How many rooms are there? Does anyone know any significance of that number? Let's look at why the tripods of fire are outside the windows—what happens when light streams through stained glass? Light from fire is not steady but is uneven in intensity and is constantly in motion, so what would this look like as it reaches and washes over the waltzers?

Supplying a Piece From Shakespeare

To add to students' sketches, we hand out copies of the speech from Shakespeare's (2011 version) *As You Like It* that's come to be known as "The Seven Ages of Man":

> All the world's a stage,
> And all the men and women merely players;
> They have their exits and their entrances,
> And one man in his time plays many parts,
> His acts being seven ages. At first the infant,
> Mewling and puking in the nurse's arms;
> And then the whining schoolboy, with his satchel
> And shining morning face, creeping like snail
> Unwillingly to school. And then the lover,
> Sighing like furnace, with a woeful ballad
> Made to his mistress' eyebrow. Then a soldier,
> Full of strange oaths, and bearded like the pard,
> Jealous in honor, sudden and quick in quarrel,
> Seeking the bubble reputation
> Even in the cannon's mouth. And then the justice,
> In fair round belly with good capon lined,
> With eyes severe and beard of formal cut,
> Full of wise saws and modern instances;
> And so he plays his part. The sixth age shifts
> Into the lean and slippered pantaloon,
> With spectacles on nose and pouch on side;
> His youthful hose, well saved, a world too wide
> For his shrunk shank; and his big manly voice,
> Turning again toward childish treble, pipes
> And whistles in his sound. Last scene of all,
> That ends this strange eventful history,
> Is second childishness and mere oblivion,
> Sans teeth, sans eyes, sans taste, sans everything. (pp. 150–151)

As we read this passage to our students, we jot down each stage of life in one of our seven rooms beginning in the east. Now we ask them where the Red Death began his march toward the final room, where the prince dies, and what that march through the rooms could possibly signify. When we suggest they look again at the stages of man we have written down, it dawns on many of them at the same time that, despite the protection of the prince, no one is safe from death's touch, no one can cheat death. We tie this piece of the symbolic puzzle in with Poe's insistence that the rooms be irregularly formed, so that no one could see into the other rooms. Since so much of the symbolism we have been discovering deals with the theme of time, we try to connect this piece of information to that theme as well. Eventually, someone offers the idea that perhaps the rooms are built that way because we never can see into the next stage of our lives. We can only see where we are. We can *imagine* what the future room will be like, and we can *remember* what the last room was like, but we can only really *be present* in the room we are in. Now we go back and realize we can include in our collection of time symbols the ebony clock that stands against the far wall in the final room. The completed drawing is shown in figure 1.5 (page 18).

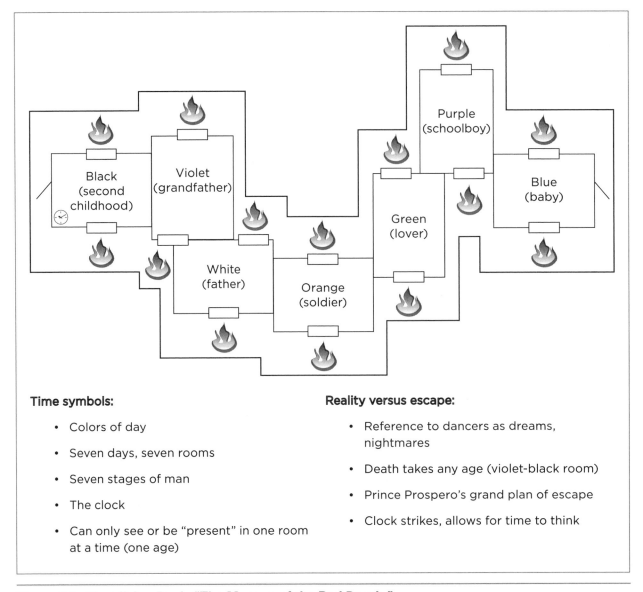

Time symbols:

- Colors of day
- Seven days, seven rooms
- Seven stages of man
- The clock
- Can only see or be "present" in one room at a time (one age)

Reality versus escape:

- Reference to dancers as dreams, nightmares
- Death takes any age (violet-black room)
- Prince Prospero's grand plan of escape
- Clock strikes, allows for time to think

Figure 1.5: Visualizing Poe's "The Masque of the Red Death."

Of course, those of you who know this story well are aware that we have not moved into the dream and masque symbols, which can also be mined to advantage. Later, we do return to look at other layers of the story, but for our purpose now, we're simply looking at the beauty of comprehension that a close study of the rooms themselves can afford our students. Such an experience will motivate many of them to want to have this same curiously satisfying experience repeated with another piece of literature later on. Students really love the richness in this discussion. For many, this is the first time they have ever keyed into symbolism in a comfortable, nonthreatening environment or examined how an author makes small pieces come together to take on a deeper dimensional life of their own.

First attempts at complex thinking skills need to be enjoyable and rewarding and offer a feeling of competency to young learners. At the backbone of this complexity is rigor. We can build on these positive experiences later and coax our learners to attempt even more demanding reading and thinking. Now, however, we must create an atmosphere of trust and confidence that leads them to say *yes* and feel they can indeed master the tasks we construct for them. Close reading that is carefully supported by opportunities for all members of the class to participate will be successful. Having each student draw and label the series of rooms guarantees that each student's attention is on the material, while providing a personal graphic organizer tailored to each child's ability and allowing an opportunity for students to interact with the story in a novel way.

Using a Complementary Piece for Comparison

There is a book of engaging—especially for boys—short stories edited by Jon Scieszka (2005) titled *Guys Write for Guys Read: Boys' Favorite Authors Write About Being Boys*. One story, by William Sleator (2005), is called, like Poe's story, "The Masque of the Red Death," and in it, Sleator tells about music based on Poe's story that he composed while in high school for a modern-dance ballet class. In Sleator's story, he gives a three-hundred-word rundown of what the original story is about and then proceeds to explain how the ballet went. Here's the challenge: students are to write the summary they think Sleator would write for Poe's story, also using three hundred words, with a five-word grace limit. After they complete their summaries, we compare them to Sleator's to see what they left out or added. We discuss the problems that a summary writer faces and what needs to be taken into account. We talk about the fact that many newspaper, magazine, script, and book writers are given a word count to abide by.

Then we discuss how Sleator decided to write a ballet from the Poe story line and challenge students to devise a product in another medium, using the same story as the base. Students are to come up with a proposal for their new product, provide a sample drawing of how it would look, and then pitch their ideas to the whole class. It would be easy to give students examples of ways this manipulation of the original story could be used, but it is best not to give them too many ideas; let them do the thinking. One suggestion is to give them the prompt *What if "The Masque of the Red Death" were a* _____? and have them fill in the line with as many possibilities as they can before converging on the one they ultimately choose to use.

The Magnificent 283-Word Sentence

Teaching literacy is the art of dipping our minds constantly into wells of words and lifting up buckets of sentences to examine, sip or gulp down, freeze or thaw, separate or combine—to play with. After years of such play, we come to the conclusion that rules and dictates are flimsy things in the hands of great writers and that, at times, we need to show students just how rules of writing are often bent and broken beautifully. The following sentence from Stephen Carter's (2002) novel *The Emperor of Ocean Park* is just such a sentence. It runs the entire page and is a hefty 283 words. Most of us would automatically consider such a heavy load a run-on sentence, but this elegant creation begs close reading and careful analyzing. It is indeed an example of a challenging, complex text the Common Core State Standards architects would embrace!

> The following Tuesday, twelve days after the death of my father, I return to my dreary classroom, populated, it often seems, by undereducated but deeply committed Phi Beta Kappa ideologues—leftists who believe in class warfare but have never opened *Das Kapital* and certainly have never perused Werner Sombart, hard-line capitalists who accept the inerrancy of the invisible hand but have never studied Adam Smith, third-generation feminists who know that sex roles are a trap but have never read Betty Friedan, social Darwinists who propose leaving the poor to sink or swim but have never heard of Herbert Spencer or William Sumner's essay on *The Challenge of Facts*, black separatists who mutter bleakly about institutional racism but are unaware of the work of Carmichael and Hamilton, who invented the term— all of them our students, all of them hopelessly young and hopelessly smart and thus hopelessly sure they alone are right, and nearly all of whom, whatever their espoused differences, will soon be espoused to huge corporate law firms, massive profit factories where they will bill clients at ridiculous rates for two

thousand hours of work every year, quickly earning twice as much money as the best of their teachers, and at half the age, sacrificing all on the altar of career, moving relentlessly upward, as ideology and family life collapse equally around them, and at last arriving, a decade or two later, cynical and bitter, at their cherished career goals, partnerships, professorships, judgeships, whatever kind of ships they dream of sailing, and then looking around at the angry empty waters and realizing that they have arrived with nothing, absolutely nothing, and wondering what to do with the rest of their wretched lives. (p. 109)

What can we do with this sentence? For one thing, we will *not* diagram it! Of course, there will be those who would like to give this a try. To these people, I say go for it! The rest of us will have more humble but still challenging ways to attack this prize, using, for example, the traditional guided questions often supplied to students after reading:

1. Read, then reread, then reread again. What is this sentence about? Can you summarize it?

2. Can you feel the sentence dividing into sections in your mind? Where are these divisions?

3. Remember the Hawthorne dashes? Read with those in mind. Can you go to your knowledge of punctuation for assistance? This should allow you to navigate the quote from the word *ideologues* to *all of them our students*, which will give you some indication of what the rest of the sentence focuses on.

4. Can you tease out the subject and verb? What is the bulk of the sentence talking about? (Now your class can be specific and point out the different types of students mentioned and note that they are being described according to their ideology.) Can you identify their various visions or ways of looking at things philosophically?

5. If you could ask for the definition of just one or two words, what would they be? (Here we are asking them to see if they can pick out the important words that make the comprehension of the entire sentence more likely. If we ask them for all the words that they need to have defined, the list would be too long and at this point really unnecessary for conveying the author's meaning.)

6. What does the speaker say will happen to his students? What are the apparent signs of their success? What great image does he use here? What are the likely results of their success?

7. How would you describe the tone of this sentence? How does the speaker feel about himself, his job, his students. What words gave you clues to help you figure out the tone?

8. Can you pick out any literary devices or specific word usage that made the sentence richer? Why do you think the author made this sentence so long? What effect does this have on the reader? Is that effect intentional?

Or, better yet, why not simply give your students the sentence and ask them to determine what would make good study questions to use as a reading guide, using the steps that follow. This would be far more satisfying for students than being given the questions—which end up as a cheat sheet if they read all the way through before answering them!

1. Read, then reread, then read once more. Can you feel the sentence dividing into sections in your mind? Where are these division? This piece never changes.

2. Write a couple of sentences on how you go about figuring out what this sentence means. What did you do first? Second? Write down your inner voice's chatter and your frustration and guesses.

3. Consult the dictionary for up to two words.

4. Translate the sentence into your own words—much fewer words, of course.

5. Write five to eight good study guide questions that would help a student navigate this sentence—the kind of questions that usually appear at the end of a chapter or exercise. Be sure to include one or two on literary devices or terms such as *tone, allusion, imagery, repetition, style, word choice, play on words, voice,* and so on.

6. Briefly but thoroughly answer your own questions!

7. Finish up your inner-voice chatter journal with regard to how you accomplished this task of untangling one of the longest sentences you may ever run into! (An inner-voice chatter journal is an exercise in recording the internal commentary a student goes through while trying to think through and solve a problem. By having students become aware of their own thinking—their metacognitive ability—they begin to refine their thinking and are able to more easily discuss how they solved a problem or where they got lost in the process.)

Try This

Look back on what material has been the most difficult for your students to grasp and retain. Where do they seem to lose the thread of understanding and start losing hope in their ability to figure out what is happening? Consider whether there is a visual activity they could do that might make more sense of the material. When we can locate the causes of misunderstanding and address them before we actually attempt to work the problem or read the text, we smooth the road and make for a much less stressful lesson.

Conclusion

As Anete Vásquez (2009) writes, "I see too many students, especially students in Title I schools, drowning from the fatigue of navigating a school day that offers too little academic rigor." We are the ones who show our students the doors they must pass through to come to grips with complex, challenging, ambiguous, and provocative material. If we not only show them the door but hold it open for them, greet them with a smile, and accompany them as they take those difficult first steps, we are more likely to be successful in stretching their resilience and increasing their effort. Attention to detail is the basic skill we build through close-reading exercises. It is one of the fundamental skills necessary for comprehension and making meaning. These types of exercises should punctuate our instruction throughout the year and supply a source of joy and support for our learners.

Chapter Two

The Core of Literacy

All communication is basically storytelling—we tell our story; we listen to yours; we compare ours to yours; we shape our thinking according to our internal story frames; we write from the baseline of our story and read what you write from that baseline. Our stories are our personal interpretations of reality. By sharing them with others, we begin to blend our perspective with that of others and more easily arrive at a richer understanding. It is this storytelling function, propelled by our various perspectives that forms the core of literacy.

A synonym for *story* is *narrative*, derived from the Latin verb *narrare* (to recount). As a constructive format—a work of speech, writing, song, film, television, video game, photography, or theater—a story recounts a sequence of nonfictional or fictional events. It is also considered the foundation of our thought-patterning mechanism and is woven throughout all our efforts at developing and mastering literacy. Story provides a framework for linking action and consequence, which gives us the ability to infer the intentions of others (Bruner, 1986).

Story also is a vehicle for determining value. Significant Objects is a fascinating literary and anthropological experiment created by Rob Walker and Joshua Glenn based on the hypothesis that stories are such a powerful driver of emotional value that the effect can actually be measured objectively (Glenn & Walker, 2012). These men buy cheap items at yard sales, from cat plates to ceramic hot dogs, have writers make up a short—couple of paragraphs—story about them, and then post the objects and stories on eBay. The results are amazing: the first stage of the project in 2009 consisted of items purchased for a total of $128.74 that ended up selling for a whopping total of $3,612.51—a 2,700% markup. Visit http://significantobjects.com for information on similar results from the next few stages of this experiment, plus samples of the stories. The book, *Significant Objects* (Glenn & Walker, 2012), is made up of the top one hundred items and stories featured in this experiment. This is the type of quirky experiment that makes a wonderful base for a writing assignment for students. After sharing some of the stories and pictures of items used in this project with the class, why not bring in a box filled with cheap, garage sale–type items, and have students pick one to write a story for it. The teacher can then make a small brochure of the items and their stories and have the school faculty "bid" on them as if they were being presented on eBay. Students could bring the brochures home to have parents participate as well.

Understanding Perspective

Narrative is intimately aligned with perspective, the lens through which a narrator conveys his or her unique connection with events, delivering the result through a distinct voice. The lens we look through shapes and informs us about the world we observe. Often, we quote the words attributed to Anaïs Nin, "We don't see the world as it is, we see it as we are" (Goodreads, n.d.) to show the importance of our individual perspective. Daniel Pink (2005) calls the essence of the aptitude of story "context enriched by emotion" (p. 101). When we examine the lens, or the story's context, we arrive at a richer truth beneath the facts.

Another equally viable metaphor for narrative was developed by David D. Thornburg (1999) in his paper "Campfires in Cyberspace: Primordial Metaphors for Learning in the 21st Century." Thornburg uses sitting around a campfire as the metaphor of choice for storytelling. He explains that "for thousands of years, storytelling was a mechanism for teaching. . . . Good stories have always embodied a blend of the cognitive and affective domains—in fact, in story, there is no separation between the two" (Thornburg, 1999, p. 1). Many of us have experienced the storytelling ritual of the campfire. Old and young gather around the flames, leaving their cell phones in tents or cars, and fall back on their own fund of stories to share and pass on.

Over thousands of years, we have learned best through the transmission of information wrapped in story. Marketers, politicians, advertisers, preachers—salesmen of all persuasions—know the power of blanketing their products in story. It is the mix of facts and emotional overtones that persuades, calls us to action, and cements information in our long-term memories. To be most effective at their trade, teachers, too, must hone and refine the art of storytelling to produce greater achievement and student understanding. Today's campfires are more virtual than carbon based. Social media such as Facebook and Twitter serve as a prime example of a virtual campfire where individuals tell their stories, comment on others, and produce that feeling of community. The book read by multiple students in the classroom provides this same communal effect, while generating a fund of narrative responses as well.

Adding Narrative to the Standards

One of the major changes in the CCSS from its early to its final draft deals specifically with the inclusion of narrative writing. The earlier drafts dealt predominately with what is known as the *paradigmatic* mode of human thought, with very little acknowledgment given to the role of narrative. The paradigmatic mode organizes the world into categories and concepts, explains natural phenomena, and seeks objective truth based on evidence and proof (Bruner, 1990). Through narrative, on the other hand, we make sense of those facts we accept to be true, showing how they affect people's lives and why people behave and think the way they do. "Narrative imagining . . ." cognitive scientist Mark Turner (1996) writes, "is our chief means of looking into the future, of predicting, of planning, and of explaining. . . . Most of our experience, our knowledge, and our thinking is organized as stories" (pp. 4–5).

The groundswell of criticism that prompted the writers of the CCSS to insert more balance into the standards by bolstering the role of narrative is far more than an academic footnote. Narrative requires the exercise of many of the skills held up as standards in the Common Core—it demands reflection and analysis and requires us to interpret and make meaning of a series of facts, to construct and order patterns of knowledge, to create both sequential and diachronic (developmental) order, and to make judgments. At every level of learning, our students need opportunities to employ the skillful use of narrative, both orally and in written form when required to manipulate information.

If we are serious about preparing our students for the needs of the 21st century, we will take the lead of business thinkers who have acknowledged that the mastery of narrative writing and thinking is a necessary attribute in growth management. In 1995, persuasion (and therefore narrative) accounted for 25 percent of the U.S. gross domestic product (McCloskey & Klamer, 1995), and it has only grown since then. "Marketers," writes Seth Grodin (2009) "didn't invent storytelling. They just perfected it."

Narrative may be not only important to business but to health as well. No one would contest the need for doctors to possess technical mastery in their selected fields, but today more and more medical schools are acknowledging the health benefits to patients when doctors pay attention to patient narratives. Today, courses in narrative medicine have doctors not simply asking diagnostic questions from checklist sheets, but asking patients to tell them their life stories. In some medical schools, students even learn to keep parallel charts—one with quantitative information, another with their patients' narratives and emotional reactions to treatment (Pink, 2005). Plainly, these practices demonstrate the need for equal attention to both of these modes of human thought for optimum achievement.

The use of narrative is not an end in itself but rather a vehicle to synthesize information coming from sources other than the student's own life. (This is the place where prior knowledge is best filled in for students lacking a broad background of information.) Stories serve as frames for making meaning and producing ideas derived from the study of various texts. Before we offer several predominantly text-driven exercises, let us suggest an activity that can prove to students just how embedded storytelling is in their nature and how easy it is to activate.

Constructing a Fable

I first came upon this activity for constructing a fable in the book *Beat Not the Poor Desk*, by Marie Ponsot and Rosemary Deen (1982). Although published decades ago, it still speaks articulately to the contemporary educational community.

We do not tell the students we are instructing them in the process of fable writing; in fact, we tell them very little about what they will be doing. We simply explain that we will be giving directions on writing a short dialogue under the guise of teaching the correct punctuation for such writing. We remind students that every time a new character speaks, a new paragraph starts. We also remind them to use quotation marks around any word, phrase, or sentence that a character utters. Then we read the following script (the material in brackets has been added):

> Imagine it is the middle of the night in the middle of the countryside through which a road runs. A horse is coming down the road. [Here, we abruptly stop and ask students what color and breed their horses are. This places everyone on the path of imagination. It also shows them that there is plenty of room for variety in whatever lens they decided to use. No one needs to see this the same way as others do.] The horse meets a bear. [Again, we stop and get information about the type of bears they each see in their mind's eye.] For your first paragraph, write what the horse says to the bear.
>
> After writing—and we too write, as always, whatever we ask students to write in class—we say, "Now for paragraph two, write what the bear says to the horse."
>
> That done, we say, "In paragraph three, write what the horse says to the bear."
>
> We then say, "All of a sudden a storm breaks out—lightning, thunder, rain. Write a sentence or two about that for paragraph four."
>
> We write, then say, "Now what does the bear say to the horse? Make that paragraph five."
>
> Having written, we say, "For one last paragraph, paragraph six, write what the horse says to the bear."
>
> Finally, we ask them to read over to themselves what they have written. Then we say, "Now skip a couple of lines, and write, 'The moral of this fable is.' Take a few minutes to think it over, and write the moral."
> (Ponsot & Deen, 1982, p. 15)

Students are amazed that they all come up with a legitimate little story. What they are experiencing is the brain's ability to pattern and construct a story on the basis of very little information. It's in our DNA to do this. Our brains strain to make meaning of what they encounter, and the narrative is our best means for doing so. I am always amazed each time I tell a group to write what the bear says to the horse, and everyone begins writing something down.

Using the Formula

It usually works to ask students to simply write an exposition based on the formula A speaks to B, B speaks to A, A speaks back to B, there is an interruption or disruption, B speaks to A, A to B, and there is a moral at the end. Ask them to do this as a homework assignment using two animals or any other living creatures. We show how this structure consists of two sides of the same coin: the narrative is the concrete, detailed portion, and the moral is the abstract aphorism. We talk of how these two elements leave the reader with a sense of completion.

Notice that the script mentions that we teachers also complete the exercise. Teachers who have been participants in National Writing Project courses often single out this one strategy—writing with their students—as having the most positive effect on the classroom climate and engagement. It sends a powerful message that writing is important. You also share your results, along with your frustrations, as you join them in drafting texts. Try doing this in your own classes and see what remarkable results it can yield.

In the following homework-generated attempt at the fable structure titled "The Two Clams," a tenth-grade student leads us into thinking we know what will happen—and then abruptly twists the ending.

Two clams were sitting in the ocean talking when they got into a heated argument.

"Hey, gimme some of that slime off the bottom of the sea, I'm hungry," said the first clam.

"Go find your own, you lazy bum!" exclaimed the second.

"Well, you don't have to be so *shellfish*!"

"Ah, *clam up*!"

Suddenly a wave went over them that sent them tumbling end over end.

"Hmmm, looks like the tide is going out. Time to burrow into the sand," said the second clam.

"Nah, I think I'm gonna sit up here and get a tan," the other one said.

"I wouldn't do that if I were you," said the second one. "All sorts of things . . ."

"Get off my shell, you old fuddy-duddy. Just 'cause you're four times as old as me you think you know more than me. You're probably already getting senile or something anyway."

An hour later the clam was still sitting on the sand enjoying the sun and the cool breeze. Suddenly a dune buggy came rolling down the beach and smashed the clam. The dune buggy rode off down the beach with a smashed clam stuck in its tire treads.

Moral: Listen to your elders.

Although we address the topic of discussion and listening in the fourth chapter, this exercise works here as a perfect example of how to train students to listen and respond to other students' shared work. The fact that all fables are presented orally cuts out the distraction that occurs when a student sees another's writing and notices mistakes in spelling, grammar, and punctuation. This is the beauty of the campfire telling—we hear the voice, intonation, and emphasis that the storyteller wants to convey. The ear is the primary sense involved and is listening with the purpose of being able to respond on what it is hearing. Students will remark on a piece's diction, use of similes or metaphors, or anything else that catches their attention. They will notice puns, other forms of wordplay, and repetition. They will all definitely comment on novelty, surprise, and humor in a piece. All comments are subtle teaching moments, as students silently file away what pleases the group about another's writing. What is being praised will eventually be duplicated. This is one of the strengths in such a practice.

Moving From Self to Text to Global Concerns

Now that our students see themselves as storytellers, they can read the stories others write from a new perspective—as fellow writers. One of the best instructional shifts being ushered in with the arrival of the Common Core State Standards is the emphasis on having students approach various subject areas through the lens of the creators of those disciplines—they are to think and act like scientists, historians, writers, and mathematicians. Instead of simply being consumers of information, they are being asked to respond and approach these various fields as fellow creators and manipulators of these disciplines. In the area of literature, we ask our students to consider worlds that are different than their own by examining the text itself for understanding.

When we set up situations in which poverty and inequity are going to be discussed with students who live under these circumstances, we find it easier to address these issues without linking the conversation to race or ethnicity. We study the circumstances of others by dipping into the well of empathy that our own life stories have afforded us, yes; but we are also examining the text itself more carefully to reveal truths that might not be as visible at first glance. Sherman Alexie's accounts of life on and off the Indian reservation make a powerful source of material for reading, writing, and discussing how others cope with situations similar to their own, even if they have never lived on a reservation.

A chapter of *The Lone Ranger and Tonto Fistfight in Heaven* (Alexie, 1993) titled "Indian Education" is a wonderful selection to use with all students, especially those from inner-city or rural environments. It traces the author's school years from first through twelfth grade in short single episodes. As we read each grade-level piece as a class, we determine its theme. For example, first grade: bullies; second grade: discrimination; third grade: censorship; and so on. After completing the chapter, students choose one of the twelve themes about which they can easily recount a personal experience. This is the personal narrative component. Then we widen our lens to embrace more global issues, using the detailed directions that follow for this process.

1. Read the selection from *The Lone Ranger and Tonto Fistfight in Heaven* by Sherman Alexie, titled "Indian Education," pp. 171–180.

2. On a sheet of paper, jot down the themes we come up with as a class for each of the different grade levels.

3. Next, choose one of the twelve grade levels and its theme to use for the basis of a paper.

4. On another sheet, write about a time or event when you experienced the same feelings or circumstances that the theme suggests. Place this freewrite aside to use later.

5. The opening paragraph of the final paper will introduce the universality of the theme—how all humans are affected by or aware of this theme at one time in their lives. An example would be how bullies aren't just on the playground; large companies can be bullies, countries can be bullies, and so on. This paragraph focuses on the broad ramifications of the specific theme you choose.

6. Next, discuss how Alexie experiences this theme himself. When writing this section, make sure to mention his name, quoting a line or two to back up assertions that this is evidence of the theme.

7. Now go to the more personal example of the theme. You have already written this freewrite. Reread it to see what sections you need to fill in with concrete examples. Your aim is to be specific and vivid in your details.

8. Now you are ready to tie all three pieces together with a final paragraph by repeating the fact that this is not an isolated experience but rather a universal one that many people experience in their lives.

9. Share your piece with a partner.

10. Both of you should comment, ask any questions about the pieces, and give suggestions for improving them.

11. Consider this feedback, make any necessary changes, and type the final draft.

This structure lends itself to good teaching about strong beginnings and endings and careful use of transitions to make the writing flow smoothly.

This structure also allows students to observe the consequences of a chosen theme as it moves from the wide perspective of the world situation down to the actual experience related in the text itself and finally to the personal narrative that gives it all meaning for the writer. A product from an inner-city student without much prior writing experience shows how this structure facilitates her logical arrangement and use of narration. This was also the first time she allowed herself the opportunity to verbalize her feelings:

> Every day thousands of people get their feelings hurt. What follows is all about how you handle being hurt. You could keep it all in and become depressed, or you could lash out and hurt the people that hurt you. If you look at the world today, there are lots of bad consequences from people getting their feelings hurt. In the news, you always see someone who got shot or stabbed because he or she did something or said something that hurt someone's feelings. You also see it in schools when kids end up fighting. The main reason they are fighting is because someone hurt their feelings.
>
> Sherman Alexie, in his autobiographical novel, *The Lone Ranger and Tonto Fistfight in Heaven*, also experienced getting his feelings hurt. He was in a basketball game, and he actually had the win in his hands. When he missed the last two free throws in the game, it devastated him. The next morning when he read the local sports page, it read "Indians lose again" in big, bold letters. Since Sherman was the only Indian playing on the basketball team, it really hurt his feelings for himself as a player and himself as an Indian. It seemed he was always losing and laughed at.
>
> I can really relate to what Sherman Alexie felt. When I was in the eighth grade, I got pregnant. I was so devastated, because my boyfriend denied both me and my baby. I was so hurt and left wondering why he would treat me like this. I felt so alone and a loser like Sherman must have felt.
>
> I feel that everything happens for a reason. When you get your feelings hurt, maybe God is trying to teach you a lesson. Maybe he is trying to show you the right path you should choose and not to do this

to someone else. Everyone alive gets their feelings hurt, what's important is how you choose to handle it. Just remember things will work out, hurt feelings will eventually go away.

This is an example of how literature allows students to enter into unfamiliar territory and yet find themselves and their own world reflected back to them. The common experience of being human is shared through the reading of literature but even more so by writing about literature: the writing allows the chemistry of internalization to kick in and enables the student to make sense of both worlds—the written and the experienced.

Bumping Up the Rigor

In order to highlight just how adherence to the CCSS can subtly shift what happens in the minds of our students, we can change how we frame our ordinary discussion questions. When you frame questions that require students to go into the text and pull out the meaning, you are making the shift from asking less of your students to asking more. The following selection is the first-grade vignette from this same chapter, "Indian Education."

> My hair was too short and my U.S. Government glasses were horn-rimmed, ugly, and all that first winter in school, the other Indian boys chased me from one corner of the playground to the other. They pushed me down, buried me in the snow until I couldn't breathe, thought I'd never breathe again.
>
> They stole my glasses and threw them over my head, around my outstretched hands, just beyond my reach, until someone tripped me and sent me falling again, facedown in the snow.
>
> I was always falling down; my Indian name was Junior Falls Down. Sometimes it was Bloody Nose or Steal-His-Lunch. Once, it was Cries-Like-a-White-Boy, even though none of us had seen a white boy cry.
>
> Then it was a Friday morning recess and Frenchy SiJohn threw snowballs at me while the rest of the Indian boys tortured some other *top-yogh-yaught* kid, another weakling. But Frenchy was confident enough to torment me all by himself, and most days I would have let him.
>
> But the little warrior in me roared to life that day and knocked Frenchy to the ground, held his head against the snow, and punched him so hard that my knuckles and the snow made symmetrical bruises on his face. He almost looked like he was wearing war paint.
>
> But he wasn't the warrior. I was. And I chanted *It's a good day to die, it's a good day to die*, all the way down to the principal's office. (Alexie, 1993, p. 171)

After reading this vignette with students, the difference between a question such as "What might the phrase 'My U.S. government glasses were horn-rimmed, ugly' say about the narrator's living conditions?" and "What fact in the text leads you to believe the narrator is poor?" is huge. The second question asks the students to find the proof in the text rather than having the question give them the evidence without requiring any interaction with the text. Even ordinary questions can entice students to think more deeply. This seek-and-find exercise should begin to punctuate the questioning routines in the classroom. Other possible questions requiring hunting in this short text might be:

- What probable incidents happened to the narrator in school that are revealed by the nicknames he was given?

- What connections can you make between the chant "It's a good day to die" and how the narrator describes himself in the final two paragraphs?

- What title would you give this section?
- What evidence in the text makes this title plausible?

Using Storyboard as a Narrative Tool

As a thinking tool, the storyboard helps us make connections between the information and ideas that we hold in our minds. It can be of any length—from two to even a thousand squares. It can be used in the simplest of forms with young students or as a dense, elaborate display of content for filmmakers. It has a naturally engaging hook for students because of its combination of logical sequencing and hands-on drawing. This medium involving pictures plus writing can be considered the origin of all written language used by ancient cultures, from the Egyptian hieroglyphs to the Chinese pictographs. By its nature, it combines both creative and analytical thinking in one context. Whether used to create new narratives or to summarize and replicate the texts being studied in class, the storyboard is an ideal tool for teachers to have in their toolboxes.

Figure 2.1 shows the first ten drawings of a storyboard constructed by a student over the short story: "Leiningen Versus the Ants," by Carl Stephenson (n.d.a.), first published in the December 1938 edition of *Esquire* magazine. This story can be heard on a podcast mimicking old-time radio shows (http://criticalpressmedia.com). It is also included in many textbooks and was the basis for both a *MacGyver* episode in the 1980s and a sequence from *The Naked Jungle*, starring Charlton Heston. A copy of the text can be found on the Classic Shorts website.

Go to page 157 (or **go.solution-tree.com/literacy**) to find a blank pictorial narrative organizer for your students to use to create either an original storyboard or one that serves to summarize another text.

Combining Facts With Emotion: Wiesel's *Night*

An autobiographical, nonfiction text that is often the subject of study in classrooms across the United States is Elie Wiesel's (1969) *Night*. This slim, moving volume captures the Holocaust in its stark, uncompromising reality through the eyes of a firsthand witness. With the dual goals of discovering the depths of their sense of empathy and sharpening their skills of blending fact and narrative to produce insight, we construct the work our students will be doing. This piece of writing will be strongly text based and couched within a self-created narrative.

The Record Sheet

As we read, we keep a record of all the factual data of places, persons, dates, and artifacts that we can pull from the text. This record will form the basis for the factual authenticity of the narrative students will create later. Nothing is more disengaging for students than continually taking notes that bear no relevance to assignments and are used for no purpose other than to regurgitate them on a test sheet. During this assignment, we make sure students are aware that this record will be invaluable for them as they begin to knit together their culminating paper.

A simple four-column sheet, with the columns marked *people*, *places*, *events*, and *things* is sufficient for this record-keeping activity (see reproducible page 158).

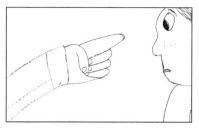

1. Leiningen is being told that he and his peons will never survive the ants.

2. Leiningen is telling his peons that they will remain at the plantation to protect it from the ants.

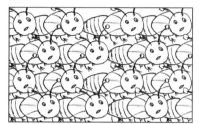

3. Twenty-square miles of hungry ants are coming.

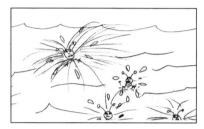

4. Many ants were washed away after trying to cross the moat without rafts.

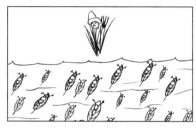

5. The ants decided to cut down leaves from neighboring woods and use them as rafts to sail across the moat.

6. The ferocious ants made it across the moat, attacked a peon, and begin to destroy the plantation.

7. Leiningen gathers his peons together and watches his plantation be destroyed by the ants.

8. Leiningen watches a naked Indian try to escape by jumping into the Amazon river where he gets torn apart by piranhas.

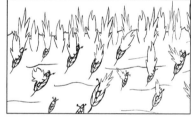

9. Ants try to get into the inner moat which is then filled with petrol and lit. They burn.

10. Leiningen becomes worried and fears that he and his peons will be eaten alive if he doesn't do something fast.

Figure 2.1: Beginning storyboard for "Leiningen Versus the Ants."

The Prompt

The overriding prompt is a variation of the RAFT format in which a student takes a *role*, decides on an *audience*, selects a *form*, and focuses on a specific *topic*. Students receive the following prompt, which serves as the basis for the class discussion on clarifying what is to be expected of them: You are Elie ten years after he was freed from the concentration camp. Decide how you receive a container with seven items from those days ten years ago. When you take out each item, tell:

- What emotion it brings out in you
- What the item actually is (describe it)
- What event in the book it is connected to (use names, places, and specifics to explain this)

The List of Items

Taking the time to make a good list of items in the story is important to the quality and enjoyment of following the prompt. We use the information from the charts that the students have updated after every chapter, and we create a new list. Figure 2.2 shows a sample of such a class-created list for *Night*.

rusty spoon	Star of David mirror	red coat	family picture
knife and spoon	gold pieces	nuts and bolts factory	gold crown
whip	Work Is Liberty signs	ashes	shoes
sheet music	piece of bread	hangman's noose	barbed wire
death squad report	shower head	Warning: Danger of Death	bullet casings
matches	map of Auschwitz	blanket	Eiffel Tower replica
broken violin	bell	cauldron	speaker
crematorium replica	striped shirt	needle	toy train car
selection list	Talmud	Torah	piece of paper
stopwatch			

Figure 2.2: Class-created list of items for *Night*.

Powerful Empathetic Products

One tenth-grade boy who followed the prompts was not usually one to participate or show much interest in many of the assignments he was given to do. Although he didn't say this to his teacher, he found the topic of the Holocaust and the account of Elie's experience in the concentration camp of intense interest. He shared his paper with his mother before turning it in, and his mother posted it online, where it made quite an impression on readers. One such reader—who lived in Germany—was himself a Holocaust survivor, and he responded with amazement that a young teenager from the United States could have such insight into how many feelings those memories could evoke. The locking together of emotion with facts in this tenth-grader's story is a powerful way to stretch and expand the empathy factor that is one of the benefits of narrative and one of the loftiest of human expressions. Following is an excerpt from his paper:

Ever since I met up with Elise, the French Jewish girl from Buna, we decided to have a reunion every year. We would meet in Paris at the Café du Canapé. Today I went and sat at our usual table, and when I arrived at the table a box with my name on it was just sitting there. In the box was a shiny silver bucket containing seven items all having a certain purpose.

Carefully observing the first object as I pulled it out I noticed it was a bloody blanket. A painful memory returned all the agony I felt while we were running from Buna to Buchenwald. The blanket was from when I had my foot operation at Buna. When we were about to leave, I needed a shoe or something large enough to wrap my foot in. All I could find was this blanket. This memory also brought back the emotional pain I went through. Watching my father struggle to keep up with the group while I myself struggled to keep going. Instead of staying behind in the hospital, we made the decision to run with the rest of the remaining inmates of the concentration camp. I wonder if my father would still be alive if we would have stayed behind.

Next, I admired a young girl's red overcoat. Its shiny gold buttons and black pockets reminded me of my beloved sister, Tzipora. All of the sorrow I felt for her, my family, and all the Jews rose in my chest. I still miss her, not a day goes by where I don't wish that she was still here. She will always be in my heart and there she will live on forever.

A bright yellow Star of David came next. This star brought out my anger as I thought back on how the Germans divided our town into ghettos, and how we were forced to wear this symbol of prejudice and inequality to everyone who saw us.

Hatred. This is what I felt as I pulled the rusty model train out of the bucket. I hated the Germans for putting us in those horrid cattle cars. Squished together like sardines, we battled at times over crumbs of bread just to stay alive. Madame Schatcter knew of our fate as she screamed and screamed. If only we would have listened. We ourselves were changed by the conditions of the camp. It changed our view and outlook on a person being punished or their actions. The experiences in the cattle cars were the first signs of this change in us.

When I pulled out those round, plastic yellow bullet casings, all of the fear rushed through my veins once again. As we were running in the snow I felt fear. Fear that I or my father may fall behind and be Shot! Killed! If we had not been strong enough or had the will to survive, one of those bullet casings would have belonged to one of us.

The framework we use to develop this paper seems very simple at first glance, but as a text-based exercise it is a powerful mechanism with which to elicit strong connections with the text and a deep sense of comprehension of the author's meaning and intent. Students use this short, three-pronged set of directions after choosing from a list of physical items mentioned in the book: explaining what emotion each brings out, describing what the item actually looks like or how it functions, and saying what event in the book it is connected to (using names, places, and specifics to do this). This framework allows the student a wide degree of choice when picking the items to be explained, giving the student an opportunity to focus the lens of his narrative on those areas that were most meaningful during the reading. It also provides for a product that resounds with an air of authenticity not only because of the inclusion of details and facts but even more so because of the inclusion of the emotional component. By moving the student from a third-person objective position as a reader to a first-person perspective as a writer, the product takes on a richer dimension and resonance.

Try This

Add a directive to include an emotional component in prompts that deal with people, places, events, and things, as in the *Night* prompt. Compare the papers students turn in with ones you had assigned in the past to see if they have a richer sense of depth and voice.

Activating Curiosity and Inference

One element of narrative that has always served to engage the reader is curiosity. What will happen next? Who is that person? Why do they all seem so worried? Curiosity is coated with questions—questions that stimulate the brain to be on alert and move into search mode. Curiosity coaxes the reluctant student out of his apathy even before he is aware that this is happening. Effective teachers realize this almost innately and work to introduce new material in ways that build their students' need for knowledge. This is not accomplished through the overscaffolded, teacher-centered oral lecture with PowerPoints on SMART Boards—a legitimate criticism that proponents of the CCSS raise. Rather, this is a lesson with independent practice focused directly on the text itself.

Teachers begin with the assumption that students can independently master text. Students are encouraged to give the text multiple readings, share interpretations, and arrive at a broader understanding than they had after a single reading. The classroom scenario in the next section is at the heart of practice geared toward reaching these standards. Because of the engaging force of curiosity, this activity is successful with any level of reader.

Sharing Random Quotations as an Opening Activity

Each student receives an index card with a couple of sentences from the text that he or she soon will be reading in its entirety. From simply reading these sentences, the student will take a stab at figuring out what the material on his or her card might mean and predict what the book might be about.

Students then are asked to move around the room and find someone with whom to share their card's information. After both share their cards and their interpretations, each finds another student to exchange information with, and then a third. Students then return to their chairs, and on the backs of their cards write what they have learned from the three sharings. Then we ask them to make another prediction. The whole class then discusses what it has learned or inferred from this experience.

With older emerging readers in a low-performing urban district, we used quotations from the first few chapters of the widely popular adolescent novel (now also a film), *The Hunger Games* by Suzanne Collins (2010). We chose more than twenty quotes in all so that none were duplicated during the sharing. Here are three:

> Tonight. After the reaping, everyone is supposed to celebrate. And a lot of people do, out of relief that their children have been spared for another year. But at least two families will pull their shutters, lock their doors, and try to figure out how they will survive the painful weeks to come. (Collins, 2010, p. 10)

> Whatever words they use, the real message is clear. "Look how we take your children and sacrifice them and there's nothing you can do. If you lift a finger, we will destroy every last one of you. Just as we did in District 13." (Collins, 2010, p. 19)

All forms of stealing are forbidden in District 12. Punishable by death. But it crossed my mind that there might be something in the trash bins, and those were fair game. Perhaps a bone at the butcher's or rotted vegetables at the grocer's, something no one but my family was desperate enough to eat. (Collins, 2010, p. 29)

Planting Seeds of Curiosity While Teaching Grammar

Another, subtler, way to allow a student's natural curiosity to bubble up to the surface before actually introducing a novel or other text to be studied is to use lines or short sections beforehand in other lessons. Students are given a sheet containing one of these quotes from *The Hunger Games* and instructed to quickly circle, for example, either all the prepositional phrases, pronouns, or nouns they find in the text they receive, then bring the sheet up to the teacher for correcting. Numbers typed before the sentences give them a hint as to how many of the selected part of speech are in the sentence, as shown in the following two exercises for prepositions and pronouns, respectively.

Quote #1: Circle the prepositions—

[1] The rules of the Hunger Games are simple. [3] In punishment for the uprising, each of the twelve districts must provide one girl and one boy, called tributes, to participate. [3] The twenty-four tributes will be imprisoned in a vast outdoor arena that could hold anything from a burning desert to a frozen wasteland. [3] Over a period of several weeks, the competitors must fight to the death. [0] The last tribute standing wins. (Collins, 2010, p. 18)

Quote #2: Circle the pronouns—

[5] I grit my teeth as Venia, a woman with aqua hair and gold tattoos above her eyebrows, yanks a strip of fabric from my leg, tearing out the hair beneath it. [2] "Sorry!" she pipes in her silly Capitol accent. [1] "You're just so hairy!" (Collins, 2010, p. 61)

The passages, especially the one for pronouns, elicit quite a few questions and a sense of curiosity regarding what this passage could possibly be about. When students reach these specific passages in the whole text later, there are many cries of delight as they remember having seen them before! Tiny formative assessments like these little challenges go a long way toward shedding light on who gets it and who doesn't, as well as planting seeds of curiosity in student minds.

As a side note, when using these challenges with students who had just spent weeks on their grammar unit, a teacher discovered that most of them still didn't have a clue what a pronoun was. As a suggestion, I told her to initiate a "banned pronoun day," where no one was allowed to use any pronouns at all. We told the students that they knew a lot more about pronouns than they even imagined. The teacher and I modeled how often we used pronouns in our everyday exchanges. When we tried to *not* use them in our speech, the entire class laughed at how clumsy our speech became. We had students pair up and try to talk without using pronouns. When one slipped in a pronoun, the other was to catch his partner and have him repeat the statement without the offending part of speech. It didn't take long for these students to realize just how valuable pronouns were to their conversations. Students began asking questions like, "Is *it* a pronoun?" "How do I talk without using *I* or *you?*" Then we tried it out in writing. The short assignment was for students to write a couple of paragraphs about their plans for the weekend without using pronouns! This really confirmed that we take for granted this humble part of speech. It also made the word itself— *pronoun*—more meaningful! Trying to speak or write without these small words was not only difficult and clumsy, it was tremendously more time consuming!

Using Narratives as Vehicles for Learning

Most literature teachers of quality know that any literary selection serves more as a vehicle than a destination. Memorization of facts about a piece we spend time with is not the end product we want our students to carry away with them. That approach to learning reflects an old, narrow, and inaccurate view of intelligence. Compounding this issue is our current emphasis on testing as a reliable measure of everything from teacher competence, to a student's level of achievement, to a school's ability to educate effectively. A reliance on single-test assessments to inform students about their success or failure leaves many students thinking they don't possess the intelligence to do well in the future and serves to indelibly mark them (Brown, Galassi, & Alos, 2004; Flores & Clark, 2003; Madaus, Russell, & Higgins, 2009; Paris & McEvoy, 2000). This unit is geared to help dispel the narrow notion that students' intelligence can be gauged by a single test. The teacher plays an important and valuable role in widening the scope of a student's view of what he or she is learning and in keeping the effects of a single test-taking experience in perspective. Showing students evidence of their learning in myriad ways throughout the year is a sensible goal for all teachers to aspire to.

The emphasis on how we choose, create, and focus our lessons has subtly changed from asking ourselves what we want students to *know* to asking ourselves what we want them to *do*, and finally to asking ourselves what we want them to *learn*. Choosing a piece of literature and then crafting the instruction so that we reach set purposes is the science and art of the teaching profession. The instructional unit described in the next section is just such an attempt at moving from knowing to doing to learning, using the narrative piece as the vehicle.

What We Want Them to Know and Do

There are two main pieces of text that we will be blending and accessing in order to work through the project-based assignments that compose this unit (I define *unit* here as a cluster of activities, materials, and lessons that revolve around a predetermined purpose and emphasis). The first is Arthur Costa's indicators of intelligent behavior (Costa, 2008). Costa's indicators are:

1. Persistence—I don't give up even when it's difficult to find the answer or solution. I keep trying.

2. Decreased impulsivity—I avoid acting without thinking. I consider the consequences to my possible actions. I make sure I understand the directions before beginning a task.

3. Listening—I am sensitive to the feelings, knowledge, and abilities of others. I can detect indicators of their emotional states through their body language. Others see me as understanding and empathetic.

4. Flexibility—I am open to the ideas of others even if they differ from mine or seem to be unusual. I do not judge others' ideas until I consider them carefully. I am more concerned about truth than being right.

5. Metacognition—I often examine how I came to conclusions. I can describe the steps I took to come to an answer. By thinking about my thinking, I improve.

6. Concern for accuracy—I pay close attention to detail. I check my work for errors; if I find any, I quickly correct them.

7. Questioning—I am not afraid to ask questions for fear of displaying ignorance. I am curious and want to find out how things work. When I notice discrepancies, I ask for clarification.

8. Drawing on and applying past knowledge—I can apply what I learned to new situations. I constantly make connections between what I've experienced and new information.

9. Precision of language and thought—My oral and written expression is more concise and descriptive. I don't name objects as "things." I don't use vague nouns or pronouns.

10. Use of all the senses—I know my senses are strong sources of information, and I try to stay alert, open, and aware of what is happening around me.

11. Ingenuity, originality, and insight—I use time and resources creatively to find different ways to do things. I am uneasy with the status quo and enjoy doing things differently than others. I am a risk taker and internally motivated.

12. Wonderment, inquisitiveness, curiosity, and the enjoyment of being a problem solver and thinker—I enjoy thinking and solving problems. I am beginning to display compassionate behavior toward other life forms and see the need to protect the environment. I experience the joy and awesomeness of being alive and able to explore ideas.

Although Costa's list has now expanded to sixteen habits of mind, we are concentrating on these twelve. We want students to know what these habits are and how they are exhibited in a person's behavior. Coupled with traditional course material, these indicators can spark curiosity, new insights into the course material, motivation, novelty, and a fresh approach to the structure of content delivery.

Our assignments are designed to put students through their paces and stretch them while building skills that are necessary to be successful as adults. We keep a balance in sustained difficulty between the material and the manipulation of that material. We ease that difficulty on one or the other as the students move toward a consistent frequency in proficiency. Neither rigor nor engagement exist without a challenge that is seen as both meaningful and doable, and that requires effort and energy.

One of the earliest activities students do to familiarize themselves with the twelve indicators is to choose five they feel they possess and give concrete examples of why. This exercise is a powerful look at how many more ways there are to rate one's intelligence than simply using a test grade or report card. It has the ability to give students a more positive look at themselves, and to relieve some of the stress that comes with the pressure to perform. Our literary vehicle for this activity is the young adult novel *Ender's Game* by Orson Scott Card (1994). The film version stars Harrison Ford, Ben Kingsley, and Asa Butterfield (of *Hugo* fame). The link to current popular culture isn't the reason for choosing the book, but it certainly doesn't hurt as a way to rope in a few more reluctant readers! Their final project follows.

This Is Your Mission

You have been chosen as the psychological evaluator who will make the final decision about whether or not Ender Wiggin is mentally capable of handling the position of battle commander. Your assignment is to study his complete file (the book *Ender's Game*) and determine whether he has exhibited intelligent behaviors of quality and breadth. After charting your evidence, you will write your formal report, choosing at least five of his strongest areas of intelligence in your estimation. You will provide ample evidence, including concrete examples from his file, to support your statements.

Your goal is to persuade the International Fleet Panel of the validity of your evidence and thus the validity of your recommendation. You will be informed as to the specific date and time you are to appear before the International Fleet Panel to present your findings. This appearance will be

CONTINUED →

videotaped for later consideration by the entire International Fleet Department if the panel deems your recommendation sound and complete.

Please bring the following items to this meeting:

- A written copy of your formal report, including all your observations and examples, as well as your professional interpretation of those observations

- Your raw data as found on your indicator sheet

- Labeled visuals of Ender during a specific battle room scrimmage as well as two additional visuals of his strongest observable behaviors in action

- Your recommendation sheet (a one-paragraph abstract) that summarizes your decision and the strengths upon which you chose to base your judgment

Bring all of these items in the folder marked with the number you have been assigned and turn them in to the head panelist after your presentation.

You are expected to explain your report as clearly as possible using your visuals to strengthen your statements. You are not to read your report but to make eye contact with all of the panel members. If time allows—you are to use no less than four minutes and no more than seven—you are free to solicit questions from the panel to clarify any information you have offered.

Thank you for the time and energy this assignment will demand. Remember, your role in the survival and safety of the world is critical and necessary.

What We Want Them to Learn

For this unit, one of our purposes is to have students experience and understand the difference between presenting their ideas orally and in writing. They will have the opportunity to do both of these using the same information. They will be expected to present their ideas and research in a way that is pleasing, comfortable, and not irritating for the listeners. No one enjoys being read to when receiving information in a presentation. Students typically come away from oral presentations like this with a sense of anxiety and concern, feeling that they had failed to explain their written points clearly.

These presentations are videotaped. Students are invited to view their presentations and then see if their concern and anxiety is still warranted. Usually it is not. Although they might not have felt at the time that their material was delivered as smoothly as they had wished, they come to realize it really was well presented. The presence of personality, voice, eye contact, and use of visuals all served to make the delivery as good as, if not better than, the written form.

A second purpose is for students to have abundant practice in gathering concrete evidence from the text, in sorting out and choosing the strongest evidence to back up assertions, and in organizing the material for optimal impact. We give students a sheet of removable dots that they can apply to the margins of the book as they find evidence to support the assertions they will be making. Later, they can go back and chart the evidence without having to reread everything. A similar strategy, if students are lucky enough to have access to digital books, is to mark their evidence as they go using the tracking and highlighting features found on most virtual devices and to return to these marks later to fill out their charts.

A third purpose, and one that will serve our students in later years, is for them to experience collecting far more information in their research than they will use in their final products. This, too, is always a surprise for most students. At first, they are frustrated that they have accumulated so much information but are not using a third of it. Learning that this is what happens in true research situations serves as a real eye-opener for these young researchers.

Our final purpose is for students to learn to recognize the indicators of intelligent behavior in their own lives, in the lives of others, and in the readings throughout the year. These indicators are not meant to be seen simply in the isolated textual material we are using for this direct investigation. This will be the responsibility of both the teacher and the students as the year progresses. The teacher—knowing that reteaching is best done by using different contexts and multiple opportunities over time—has the responsibility to plan specific instructional lessons that revisit these indicators and should allow the student to take the time for periodical reflection on and observation of their own personal growth.

The Harris Burdick Writing Challenge

If any teacher trying to motivate students to write hasn't yet discovered the Chris Van Allsburg (1984) book of illustrations titled *The Mysteries of Harris Burdick*, that teacher has a welcome surprise ahead! This is no ordinary book of illustrations. For each of the fourteen full-page drawings there is a story, a line from which is printed on the page opposite, along with the story's title, whetting the imagination. It is said that Harris Burdick left the portfolio with a publisher in hopes of interesting him in the book but never returned—and could not be found. The publisher decided to publish the drawings in hopes Burdick would surface—though he never did. Over the years, many popular authors have taken on the challenge of writing a story that would go with both the phrase and the illustration. And in 2011, the book *The Chronicles of Harris Burdick: Fourteen Amazing Authors Tell the Tales* was published with stories by such authors as Sherman Alexie, Gregory Maguire, Jules Feiffer, Walter Dean Myers, Lois Lowry, Stephen King, and Louis Sachar among others (Van Allsburg, 2011).

Teachers who have used these pictures with their students have reported to me on the success they have had in stimulating students of every type and skill level to write with enthusiasm and imagination. Over the years, many successful lessons and suggested activities using these pictures and aimed at beginning through more seasoned writers have been written and published. Many are easily accessible online. One of the wonderful websites available (www.hmhbooks.com/features/harrisburdick) helps teachers use these pictures in even more creative ways. With the addition of celebrated authors, we have an even wider range of options for using both the illustrations for writing activities and the published stories for reading. What student wouldn't be interested in reading what a "real" writer has written about the picture he or she also picked!

Options for Using the Harris Burdick Illustrations

When time is ample and our objective is to have students experiment with writing a full short story, we usually do this activity as a follow-up to our instruction on the elements of the short story. A short-story unit is a staple of the ninth-grade curriculum in most districts across the country. It is featured as unit one in the Common Core Curriculum Mapping Project guides (http://commoncore.org/maps). This high-quality resource offers seventy-six complete English language arts teaching units based upon the requirements of the CCSS, written by teachers for teachers, and available for a $20 membership fee. For those in the midst of developing curriculum that reflects the CCSS, this is a beneficial resource to have at your side.

The suggested objectives for this unit are stated as follows:

- Identify and explain plot structure (that is, exposition, rising action, crisis/climax, falling action, and resolution) in stories read.

- Understand and explain why plots in short stories usually focus on a single event.

- Analyze how authors create the setting in a short story.

- Define the concept of theme, and identify the theme or themes in stories read.

- Identify and explain characterization techniques in short stories.

- Identify and explain the use of figurative language in short stories.

- Analyze how authors create tone in short stories.

- Identify the point of view in a short story, and analyze how point of view affects the reader's interpretation of the story.

- Write a coherent essay of literary analysis with a clear thesis statement, at least three pieces of evidence from texts, and a strong introduction and conclusion.

Along with the need to instruct students in how to analyze and pull apart the stories of others, there is a need to instruct them in how to put together what they have been learning—to experiment in the "doing" of learning—by writing a story of their own from their unique lens of observation. How interesting it will be to use those CCSS-friendly objectives and have students apply them to one of their fellow classmates' stories. And how interesting it would be to apply those objectives to a story written for *The Chronicles of Harris Burdick* that used the very same prompt!

Teachers who are considering purchasing the set of pictures might want to order the portfolio version, since the pictures are larger and on separate sheets, so you won't be forced to tear your book apart.

A nice touch is to scan the pictures and ask students to paste the one they have chosen onto the final copy of their story. The need for choice in student work is also amply satisfied here, as students have fourteen very different illustrations to choose from. Having used this assignment over the years, we've found that at no time was one picture singled out and used more often than any other.

An important element in such assignments that is sometimes skipped over because of time constraints is the celebration of the products—the campfire experience. Students need to have an audience for their work that extends beyond the teacher. When the opportunity is given to share their work with their fellow classmates, the importance of that work is magnified in their eyes, as is the effort that goes into it. There are many ways one can set up the sharing sequence of these stories. One of my favorites is to have students move their chairs into a circle—reminiscent of the campfires of old—and with a blank page stapled to the back of their stories, pass them to their neighbor to read and add a comment. We explain what types of comments we are asking for: positive comments over ideas or writing style; things that surprise and delight; and questions and general observations. After allowing enough time to read and comment on a paper, we ask students to pass their story along to their neighbor and read a new one. Depending on the time available, we read and comment on as many as possible. Students are more interested in the comments made by their peers than any made by the teacher.

If time is too tight to spend on writing a full-blown story in class, an option is for students to choose a picture and write only the beginning of a story, including enough exposition to explain the conflict, introduce the main character or characters, describe the setting, and, with a "to be continued" at the end, leave the reader wanting more! Many times students ask if they may finish their stories, even though it is not part of the assignment. When these beginnings of stories are read aloud in class, students are urged to predict what might happen next, which in itself is a creative and entertaining exercise in problem solving.

More "Bumping Up" for More Rigor

As mentioned earlier, there is a definite benefit to keeping the strengths of the CCSS in mind while designing instruction. One such benefit is the opportunity to increase the rigor and to urge more student independence in academic behavior. In the past, I would explain the background of the fourteen Burdick illustrations and how these pictures were representative of the stories. I orally reconstructed the entire introduction to the book for them and jumped immediately into the assignment I had prepared. But on another occasion, I passed out copies of the introduction without any pep talk and asked students to read it. I asked them to underline important facts and statements that might give us a better understanding of what Chris Van Allsburg has in store for us. Students were invited to copy down five facts or statements that they found to be most important and share these with their neighbors. At this point—now with a better-informed class—I began the discussion about the assignment. As small as this shift in procedure might seem, it changed the class from a spoon-fed group to a more literate and informed one who were given the chance to consult the text first before being told what it says.

Conclusion

In many of the exercises and suggested products we have included here, students take on a role. In one, they become Elie Wiesel ten years after he was freed from the concentration camp; in another, they are psychological evaluators, studying a file and making recommendations based on evidence they accumulated. These roles create a need for the student to take on the perspective of people who lead very different lives than he or she does—to put on a different set of lenses to see the world.

Other exercises in this chapter have our students themselves acting as storytellers. This is fundamental to how we have learned and taught over the generations—sitting around the campfire. We tell not only our own stories but those of others. This is the foundation of literacy. All the threads of communication spin out from this inborn urge to make sense of the world by making sense of our stories.

Chapter Three

Reteaching Strategies

Basically, reteaching is simply teaching again—this seems self-evident. It's not the definition that needs clarifying, though; it's the reasons, the ways, and the timing of reteaching that need to be addressed. This chapter is grounded in the notion that it is necessary to shift away from the traditional view that reteaching is needed primarily for those students who don't fully understand or have failed to learn. Reteaching of major concepts and skills is needed for *all* students—even those who seem to have mastered the material on the first round of introduction. As Daniel Willingham (2006) writes, "Our brains retain information better when we spread learning over a longer period of time, say months or even a year, versus cramming it into a few days or weeks" (p. 50).

"But I taught you that!" "You knew how to do that problem two weeks ago—what happened?" "How can you say you don't remember this? You got a hundred percent on this just recently!" "I know your teacher taught you that last year; do I have to teach it all over again?" Statements like these are often heard from frustrated teachers who don't know what went wrong. Students who seemingly understood material as it was presented and practiced suddenly have no idea how to transfer the skill or recollect the content. This frustration is now more painful, since teachers are being rated and judged over how well their charges can perform on standardized tests. If their students do poorly, it becomes an accusation that the teacher hasn't been doing his or her job. Yet, the teacher is certain the material was taught, the curriculum was followed, and the students seemed to grasp it at the time.

We have all experienced the balancing act between spending too much time on a topic or not enough and having to speed through. We've all felt a kind of betrayal when we were sure students had mastered what we taught, only to have them look at us with blank stares or use the same wrong grammatical formation once again. I don't think this happens because we spent too long or too short a time teaching the concept, but rather because we didn't spend our planning time deciding how to weave that new concept or skill into our lessons *over the long run*. Nor did we plan how to present that concept or skill differently than we did the first time. This is where our Crazy 8s come in.

Crazy 8s

Many of us will remember the card game by this name. I began using this title for its name alone—*crazy* and *8s*—and not in conjunction with the game itself. Wong and Wong (2009) write, "A child needs to repeat something on the average eight times to learn it. To unlearn an old behavior and replace it with a new behavior, a child needs to repeat that new behavior on an average of twenty-eight times" (p. 70). We urge teachers to use the following plan for teaching and reteaching important concepts and skills.

Since we know students of all ages need to repeat information and behaviors before it can be cemented into their brains, we should actively plan how to accomplish this. First, teachers should carefully decide what new concepts or skills are most important for their students to firmly grasp. Not everything falls into this category. Much work has now been done on curriculum to designate these high-priority concepts and skills in all content areas. The CCSS initiative is certainly one of the most ambitious attempts to whittle down the number of standards and allow teachers to better focus on those we can all agree are most important for our students to master. Also, as teachers skilled in formative assessment, we can recognize what skill or information the group under our charge is having trouble grasping that needs reinforcement.

Once we designate an important concept or skill, we should prepare eight different ways of teaching and reteaching it and plan how we intend to weave that information into other lessons in the future. As we have noted, spaced recall has long been found to be effective in aiding retention (Reynolds & Glaser, 1964). A meta-analysis conducted in 2006 by Nicholas Cepeda, Harold Pashler, Edward Vul, John Wixted, and Doug Rohrer draws the following conclusion from a study of the literature on this subject:

> A primary goal of almost all education is to teach material so that it will be remembered for an extended period of time, on the order of at least months and, more often, years. The data described here reaffirm the view (expressed most forcefully by Bahrick, 2005, and Dempster, 1988) that "separating learning episodes by a period of at least 1 day, rather than concentrating all learning into one session, is extremely useful for maximizing long-term retention." (Cepeda et al., 2006, p. 370)

They continue to explain that for most practical purposes, since we desire retention that will last months or years, the interval for the spaced recall events should be well in excess of one day.

Studies show that the same kinds of efforts currently being employed by teachers to improve short-term performance—correct answers on high-pressure tests—are actually *reducing* students' long-term retention (Cepeda, Coburn, Rohrer, Wixted, Mozer, & Pashler, 2008). When teachers design material that mirrors the state tests—in formatting, phrasing, and examples of problems to be expected—there may be short-term gains in scores, but this same practice "increases knowledge loss from day to day, week to week, and year to year" (Bean, 2011).

Rohrer and Harold Pashler conclude the following in their study of conventional instructional strategies and human learning (Rohrer & Pashler, 2010):

> As the present review discloses, experimental research on human learning and memory is beginning to make a distinctive contribution to this enterprise, offering concrete advice about how the mechanics of instruction can be optimized to enhance the rate of learning and maximize retention. In some cases, the results reveal that study and teaching strategies that do not require any extra time can produce two- or threefold increases in delayed measures of learning. It is striking how often these strategies differ from conventional instructional and study methods. If educational practices (ranging from textbook layout and educational software design to the study and teaching strategies used by students and teachers) are adjusted to exploit the kinds of findings discussed here, it ought to be possible to significantly enhance educational and training outcomes. (p. 410)

Following is a summary of strategies to support retention (Rohrer & Pashler 2010):

- We need to purposefully place reviewing and reteaching events into other learning conditions. Instead of blocking new learning altogether and then moving to another topic, textbooks and instruction should interleave or lace the old into the new continuously. Current textbooks do nothing to purposefully help teachers weave older material into new material.

- Space needs to be made in the learning process to allow for mistakes to be made and accepted as a normal stage of learning, without punitive grading consequences. Students might make more

mistakes on the spaced reteaching reviews, but studies show they will end up with more retention and for longer lengths of time and more accuracy.

- Strategies that make for better short-term recall inhibit long-term retention. For those of us very concerned about the short-term results (standardized test results), a blending of both types of strategies may be the best recourse.

- When students reread material—the most common method of "studying"—and try to deter-mine how well they know the facts, their estimates of what they know show little relationship with their performance on the test. Formative testing, however, both enhances learning and inhibits forgetting by heightening attention and requiring the process of retrieval. Short-answer tests seem to enhance recall over their alternatives. Instructional practices would be more effec-tive if the proportion of learning time that learners spend retrieving information is increased.

These reteaching for retention strategies can be folded into our everyday instructional methodology without taking any more time and with less effort than we are already expending. By using more specific formative assessments during the instructional period and catching the errors early, instead of waiting for the final more inclusive test and then having to go back and repair whatever misunderstandings are appar-ent, teacher and student time and energy are indeed conserved. The result should be a dramatic increase in both learning and retention.

After spending most of my adult life teaching adolescents how to improve their reading and writing, thinking and creating, and articulating and listening, I've arrived at a few pragmatic, discrete skills that greatly propel writing and reading performances. I had the good fortune of showing these skills to a team of teachers and teaching them to a few of their students while serving as a consultant in St. Louis and Kansas City high schools. Grammar is always a sticky issue to bring up with teachers, who have mixed views of its importance, its function in writing instruction, and the methodology that should be employed for teaching it. When I told the teachers that I would be showing their low-performing, inner-city fifteen- and sixteen-year-olds how to accurately punctuate a transposed adverbial clause beginning a sentence, I saw their eyes roll. Some of them began telling me that these students didn't even know the difference between a noun and a verb. Others told me that it would be a waste of time, since they'd never get it anyway. Some asked me "Why? Why begin with that?" which I felt was a fair and necessary question. A few asked, "How?"—another fair and necessary question. While teaching their students how to execute this particular punc-tuation mark correctly with consistency, I would also be modeling to these teachers how to develop and play out a Crazy 8s format for retention.

Does Grammar Support Writing?

A student doesn't necessarily need to read the label inside his jacket to know how and when to wear it. Nor does he need to know the grammatical labels for each word he writes to be able to communicate effi-ciently. For over half a century, studies have shown that the relationship between a strong knowledge of grammar and one's ability to write well simply doesn't exist. In fact, in 1985 a resolution was passed by the National Council of Teachers of English (NCTE, 1985) stating:

> Resolved, that the National Council of Teachers of English affirm the position that the use of isolated grammar and usage exercises not supported by theory and research is a deterrent to the improvement of students' speaking and writing and that, in order to improve both of these, class time at all levels must be devoted to opportunities for meaningful listening, speaking, reading, and writing; and that

NCTE urge the discontinuance of testing practices that encourage the teaching of grammar rather than
English language arts instruction.

The resolution's proposers pointed to fifty years of evidence showing that the teaching of grammar in isolation does not lead to improvement in students' speaking and writing, and may in fact hinder the development of students' oral and written language (NCTE, 1985).

All those worksheets, underlined words, and arrows to other words really never translate into students' actual writing proficiency, and they definitely do not transfer to students' enthusiasm for writing. Nevertheless, I have found a handful of grammar necessities that do pragmatically transfer if taught correctly and functionally, and the comma after an adverbial clause beginning a sentence is one of them.

By being able to begin their sentences with adverbial clauses, students immediately give their writing a boost in maturity level. Their sentences sound more adult and less like halting students' language. Most high school students lacking written fluency simply hate how their writing sounds to them. We need to affirm the fact that we know they are much more intelligent than they currently sound on paper and that we also know a few simple ways to change that—for example, using complex sentences, varying the beginnings of their sentences, and being sensitive to word selection and detail. We begin with the complex sentence format—without using that label; there will be plenty of time to mention it to students after they are comfortable with its use.

Brainstorming to Get to Our Crazy 8s

It is my firm conviction that any new material must be delivered in an upbeat, pleasant manner and never by words alone. With this always in mind, we brainstorm around a dozen ways we can present and practice the specific concept we are targeting, and then keep only those that seem most productive.

Crazy 8s Brainstorming Sheet Example

Concept or content choice (a skill or content concept that is difficult for students to learn, remember, or understand): Formulation, recognition, and punctuation of subordinate clauses

Purpose: Improve writing maturity through sentence combining, revising, and punctuation of transposed adverbial clauses. Improve reading comprehension by an awareness of sentence structure.

1. Brainstorming: Write down as many ways that you can teach this concept as possible, even if they sound crazy or impractical! The following describes some of the ways you could teach and reteach the concept of properly punctuating the transposed adverbial clause starting a sentence.

   a. Use butcher paper to make two clauses each about six feet long—one dependent and one independent; designate Comma Man or Comma Lady to wear a huge comma, have students holding the two clauses switch positions to show when to use Comma Man and when he isn't needed. The sample I use to illustrate this with students and teachers consists of (dependent clause) "since I met you" and (independent clause) "I've never been the same."

   b. Videotape the students moving these clauses back and forth while you read the sentences with emphasis. Have Comma Man or Comma Lady turn around facing the back when the sentence reads, "I've never been the same since I met you," then turn back to show off his or her comma when the sentence reads, "Since I met you, I've never been the same."

   c. Give students cheat sheets of adverbial conjunctions; have them use one to start a sentence mimicking the butcher paper sample. Have them rewrite the sentence switching the position of the clauses. Monitor each student for correct use of the comma. Have him or her do this again with another conjunction. Have a neighbor check for accuracy of comma usage.

d.   Make baggies with cut-out clauses—one color for subordinates, another for independents—have commas in the baggies as well. In pairs, make sentences with the clauses and punctuate.

e.   On yet a different day, when writing a summary of another unrelated lesson, have students make sure that one of their sentences starts with an adverbial conjunction and has two clauses and a comma in the right place; remind them to use their cheat sheets.

f.   Copy a page from a current reading assignment they are working on, and have them underline the sentences that fit the construction they have been practicing.

g.   Ask students to take a slip of paper with two clauses on it from a fish bowl and put together the two clauses in two different ways, once using a comma and once not using the comma, and then bring it to you for individual inspection and a formative grade.

h.   While students are revising a paper on a different lesson, ask them to make sure they add at least a few sentences using a comma somewhere within the paper.

i.   Watch the videotape from the initial introduction of this concept.

j.   Write six conjunctions on the board numbered one to six. Each student throws a die and writes a sentence with a conjunction that matches the number.

k.   Start a story with one of these sentence constructions, then pass it down the row. The next student adds another sentence, moving the story along with the same kind of construction. Continue passing the papers and building the story.

l.   Have students bring in examples of this sentence construction from another class's written material.

2.   If you are doing this exercise with other teachers, now share your examples with them and add a few more ideas to your list. For example:

a.   Play Stump the Bell Ringer by having a volunteer ring a bell every time a student uses this construction to answer a question in class. Both the bell ringer and the student who answers get recognition.

b.   Go through old writing assignments (hopefully in folders), and see if you can find any sentences that begin with a conjunction. See whether they are punctuated correctly.

3.   From your two lists, choose the eight best ways to teach your selected material.

4.   Order your eight for the best possible effectiveness over time. For example:

a.   Day one—Do the butcher paper switch and the videotaping of this activity. (5 min.)

b.   Day one—Have students write two practice sentences from cheat sheets. (15 min.)

c.   Day two—Do the baggie activity in pairs. (5–10 min.)

d.   Day two—If applicable, have students find this type of sentence in material you are reading. (10 min.)

CONTINUED ➔

e. Days later—Ask students to be sure to add to their writing assignment a sentence of this type and underline it. (Adds no extra time to an already scheduled activity)

f. At least a week later—Students are to bring in a "sighting" of this construction in material from another class. Share these. (10 min.)

g. Before a test—Play back the film clip of students switching the butcher paper. (3–5 min.)

h. Much later in the year—Repeat the request to have them add two to three sentences in this construction to another writing assignment. (Adds no extra time)

5. Share your final list with someone.

6. Debrief: On a note card or scrap paper, write down what you think about this process and your final results. Were there any surprises? any new ideas? any questions still left unanswered? What will you take home with you from this exercise? Which strategy from your sheet would be new to your teaching methods?

7. After trying this out with your students, discuss with your fellow teachers what worked and what could be reframed for other material. If you felt you spent more time than usual, was it worth it? Was there any transfer to their writing that was not directly requested by you?

The reproducible on page 159 contains a blank worksheet for using this exercise in your classroom.

How Is This Teaching Unique?

Added up, the time spent on learning this concept was approximately one fifty-minute class period. In a traditional lesson, students would have spent about the same amount of time reading examples from a text, with the teacher asking volunteers to add in or take out commas from sample sentences when needed. Perhaps the teacher would also take time to write a few on the board. Students would be assigned a worksheet of similar sentences to do themselves as seatwork, and then perhaps go through them as a class, with each person taking one sentence and deciding whether it needs changing or not. Students would correct their worksheet and put a score on top. The teacher would collect the work and record the day's grade. The teacher and students alike would then agree that the material had been taught.

In contrast, in the Crazy 8s system, the time of review is staggered over days and weeks. Also, there is a lack of similarity in the learning method; students see exaggerated forms of the construction, write original examples, move sentence pieces around physically, search for like constructions in unrelated materials, examine the work of peers, and blend this construction into their own writing. The mantra *they have been taught* changes into *they are learning*.

Why is spending fifty minutes on this single grammatical construction worth the time? The reason is that after students understand how to write complex sentences of this type, it is much easier to begin asking them to make thoughtful decisions concerning the relationships between clauses. Too often students are required to memorize rules and formations that are still foreign to their working writing habits. Teaching these subtleties prematurely—before students are actually using them—is wasting time. As with any construction, it's the strength of the base that allows the structure to reach great heights.

In fact, most anything can be taught to most anyone if you:

1. Begin with a pleasant experience to strengthen the fragile confidence

2. Break it up into small bites

3. Keep attention focused by short segments of practice

4. Use novelty to change strategies

5. Remember that a nonjudgmental period of learning is essential

6. Always give instant constructive feedback

7. Keep it low on words and high on senses and student talk

8. Stagger the direct instruction and reteaching intervals

Necessity of Self-Monitoring

In one of the four classes I visited when going desk to desk checking each student's newly created sentences (immediately following the butcher paper exhibit with Comma Man or Comma Lady), I found a disturbing situation. Many of the students were punctuating their sentences not with commas but apostrophes. My first thought was that many of these students' backgrounds in English was minimal at best, and perhaps few had had any instruction in punctuation of any kind. I just kept going from student to student saying, "Good, that's the right place, but now *lower* that comma down out of the air!" That night I went home and reviewed the film clips I had taken of the classes I had visited. When I got to this particular class's clip, I saw the problem. I had chosen a tall boy to be Comma Man, and his comma was attached to the top of his shirt; and when observed through the eye of the camera as well as through the eyes of the students, he was looking more like Apostrophe Man! The fault was mine!

This incident made a lasting impression on me. I began to take a closer look at what students see while we teach. I examined pictures, drawings, artwork, and illustrations for textbooks and posters. I began comparing the illustrations in textbooks with illustrations for the same concept on websites. I discovered an appalling difference and range of visual interpretations. Soon I began collecting samples of visuals that could give students wrong ideas. It is far more interesting for them to be shown something that adults have done wrong and be asked to point out the irregularities than to simply do the problems. Students love to catch adults in mistakes!

A simple example of this is a set of stickers from an office supply store that represents the sun and its planets. I imagine students are supposed to take the stickers off the little sheet and make a solar system for themselves. The problem is that each planet and the sun itself are identical in size. What a distortion of a very real set of facts! I am reminded of a commercial for Jimmy Dean sausages where men are dressed up as planets and the spokesperson is the sun. They all need a good Jimmy Dean breakfast before they can revolve properly around Mr. Sun. Like the stickers, all are in costumes of approximately the same size. Showing this brief commercial, then asking students to point out what's wrong with this picture is great for sharpening their critical-awareness skills and correcting misinformational representation.

The X-Ray Machine

The X-Ray Machine is a method of analyzing and focusing students' attention on areas of their writing that need immediate work. In this instance, we focus on varying the beginnings of sentences. If students become aware of the necessity to vary the beginnings of their sentences, they will automatically become better writers. This specific habit needs a variety of practice opportunities that are well spaced out over a couple of months. This may sound easy, but it's not. Breaking a student's normal habit to start many sentences within a paper with the same construction or even the same words takes patience and concerted effort on the part of the teacher. But this effort pays off more than most other efforts a teacher puts into helping students write more maturely.

At the beginning of the school year, I assign an essay that students enjoy writing—about their favorite out-of-school pastimes or the top ten items they would buy if given an unlimited credit card to use, or what five places they would like to visit if they had no money concerns. I make it clear that I really need them to come back to class with that essay in hand, and I tell my classes that they will be putting this writing into the X-Ray Machine to see just what they need to be working on this coming semester.

When they arrive with their papers, the first thing students do is number the sentences. Then they copy the first four words of each numbered sentence onto the chart I give them and identify the number of verbs in each one of the sentences. I move around the room, helping them. The next column asks them to write down the number of words in each sentence. Students tend to like this activity, since they can do most of it without worrying that they are making a mistake. Everyone can copy words and count them! The last column has an asterisk on it. That can stand for anything the instructor wants to have students look for. On this initial piece, I want to know how many paragraphs they have in their work. So I ask everyone to count which sentences are indented in their papers. Most students' papers are written in longhand and an indention designates a new paragraph. In typed papers, students might have used the block style and skipped a line to show indention. We are checking for paragraphing and are not worried about the method of showing this. Some have one huge paragraph, others have too many paragraphs. This diagnosis takes, on average, about twenty minutes to do with a group of students.

A partially filled out X-Ray Chart is shown in figure 3.1. A blank, reproducible X-Ray Chart can be found on page 161.

Now I help them read their X-rays!

1. Do they have many sentences? Great! The first column is their fluency column. If they don't have very many, then I ask them to write "I need fluency" at the bottom of the page as a writing target they will need to work on this year.

2. Is there variety in how they begin their sentences? Often, their sentences will all start in a similar way: I am, there is, and so on. I ask them to circle the ones that are repetitious and on the bottom write the words "I need sentence variety," again as something they will need to improve.

3. We look at the verbs for repetition, but we also look at the verbs for action. I explain that mature writers choose their verbs very carefully in order to provide detail and energy.

4. Now we look at the number of words per sentence. I want them to know we are looking for variety. I want short, long, skinny, and fat sentences! If most of the sentences have about the same number of words, the paper will seem boring to the reader. If most sentences seem about the same, students write down "I need more variety in sentence length."

5. Here comes our most infamous disregard for correctness. If students have no indentions listed in the asterisk column other than the beginning one, we have them write the Schreck Rule of Indention (or "I need to make new paragraphs") on the bottom of their papers and use it until they figure out a better way. Here it is: Measure down your paper about two and a half inches, then indent. Keep going until you run out of writing. Chances are, most students have changed subjects about that often, and if they begin this way, they can adjust their paragraph breaks later to fit the meaning. The crazy truth is that this works: in my experience, students get the hang of figuring out when to indent thoughtfully *after* they get into the habit of indenting, not before.

X-Ray Chart Example

Number all the sentences in your essay. Then fill in this chart for the first ten sentences of your piece, one row at a time. Number and then write the sentences first, then add the first four words of each sentence, and so on. Remember that your verbs are not necessarily in the first four words of your sentence and that there might be more than one verb per sentence. The last column is where you designate that a paragraph is beginning; everyone should place an asterisk in the first row. After filling out the chart, we will diagnose our writing X-rays for strengths and weaknesses. Circle any sentences that start in a similar way. Mark your own targets for improvement at the bottom of the page and date it.

Number of Sentence	First Four Words in Each of My Sentences	Verbs Used in Each Sentence	Number of Words in Each Sentence	New Paragraph (*)
1	My name is Jennifer	is (1)	5	*
2	That isn't my real	isn't (1)	5	
3	My real name is	is (1)	6	
4	I'm in the witness	am (1)	6	
5	Before I was put	was put, lived (2)	10	
6	My father worked for	worked, manufacture (2)	10	
7	His name is now	is, is (2)	14	
8	My mother worked for	worked (1)	6	
9	Her name is Bambi	is, works (2)	14	
10	I used to go	used to go (2)	9	

My Writing Targets

I need sentence variety.
I need more action verbs.
I need more variety in sentence length.
I need to make new paragraphs.

Figure 3.1: Using an X-Ray Chart to teach how to vary sentence structure.

Like most teachers, we tell our students how valuable these writing skills are. Most students agree and decide right then and there that this is what they will do—they will watch for variety in their sentence lengths and verb choices, become aware of how they begin sentences, do more (or less) paragraphing, and in some cases, more writing about the topic. None of it sounds too difficult, and most students think this is a piece of cake to carry out. Everyone feels "taught."

How We Set Them Up for Failure—On Purpose!

Now for real subversive teaching! We haven't mentioned the vary-the-beginnings-of-your-sentences admonition for some time. We begin a writing lesson, the purpose of which we wrongly tell students is to practice letter writing. We set up the following situation.

We advise students to pretend that one of their teachers from another class will be moving soon and leaving her position. The principal comes to ask for their input on what the best teacher to replace her would be like, since he will be interviewing candidates shortly. He asks each member of the class to write him a letter explaining what qualities and personality traits he should be sure the new teacher possesses.

We brainstorm what our past experiences in school have taught us about the kind of teacher we would like to see fill this new position. We share examples of what characteristics or qualities we *don't* want this teacher to possess as well. After filling a board and their notebooks with personality traits, notes, and additional ideas, students then choose the traits that are most important and the ones for which they can easily give examples. We restate that the product they will be creating is a letter to the principal and remind them how to set up their letters so they contain a salutation, signature, date, and address. We set the date for bringing the rough draft of this letter to class, then give them class time to begin drafting.

Failure by Highlighter

To refresh your memory, the aim of this assignment is to get back to the original goal of catching students *not* varying the beginning of their sentences despite the goals they set the day we did the X-Ray Chart. It may seem a long, involved way to make a point, and I guess it is, but it really reinforces the original lesson and in my experience makes for the best learning moment that most of them will experience in the semester.

At this point in the process, we hand out highlighters and ask students to highlight any sentences that seem to begin with the same wording. Almost without exception, there is a whole-class gasp as each student rereads the paper from this vantage point. The letter format by its nature demands a first-person point of view, and the purpose of the letter is to state a number of qualities and traits that their new teacher should possess. This means that students could easily end up with a page of print that has many sentences beginning with *I want*, or *she should be*, or *she must have*, or *this teacher should not*. We walk around, telling them not to worry if their papers are all marked up—that's *good* and means they really will be learning something this hour! Only a couple of students end up with rough drafts that haven't been well-pinked or yellowed by the time we are ready for the next step.

Now is the most important part of the lesson. We tell them to change those sentences they highlighted. When they ask how, we suggest they flip a part of the end to the front and find another way to start—perhaps with a different subject, or by combining two sentences. Here is a section of a typical paper, before and after the exercise.

> Dear Principal Jones,
>
> My name is Kris Murr. I am in Mrs. Smith's history class, and I am sad that she will be leaving us. I thank you for giving all of us an opportunity to tell you what kind of teacher you should hire to take her place. I have a long list but will only write about a few.
>
> I find that I learn best with a teacher who is outgoing with a good sense of humor. I find I am, however, someone who needs a teacher who can discipline the class and not let kids get away with anything. I enjoy discussing and working with others in class and not filling out worksheets all the time. I want a teacher who is fair and doesn't pick favorites or pick on others she doesn't like.

I hope you will choose a teacher who knows lots about history and not just what is in our textbook. I like it when a teacher has us do interesting projects and not just read and take notes, and then tests us.

Sincerely,

Kris Murr

In ten sentences, this young lady has used the word *I* twelve times. We explore options: she combines the subjects in the first and second parts of the second sentence, dropping the second *I*, so the sentence now reads "I am in Mrs. Smith's history class and am sad that she will be leaving us." She also decides to begin the next sentence with just "Thank you." She continues weighing her words and changing them so the revision becomes much more than rewriting or retyping the same thing again after simply using spell-check.

Dear Principal Jones,

My name is Kris Murr. I am in Mrs. Smith's history class and am sad that she will be leaving us. Thank you for giving all of us an opportunity to tell you what kind of teacher you should hire to take her place. I have a long list but will only write about a few.

Like most people, I like a teacher who is outgoing, with a good sense of humor, but that teacher must also be able to discipline the class and not let kids get away with anything. Because I enjoy discussing and working with others in class, I don't want a teacher who has us just fill out worksheets all the time.

I hope you will choose a teacher who knows lots about history and not just what is in our textbook. Also, be sure that this teacher has us do interesting projects and not just read and take notes, and then tests us.

Sincerely,

Kris Murr

Most students really don't know how to dig into a draft and play with the wording. This experience helps them understand.

Reteaching like this is the heart of good instruction that has been thoughtfully planned, spaced, and folded into other lessons. As we walk around the room helping each student, we are at our finest as teachers. We are not assigning learning; we are teaching and nudging the learning into each student's literacy habits one person at a time. For many, this is also the first time they realize that editing a paper is not simply rewriting, not simply fixing the spelling problems—it's actually digging into the text and manipulating it for a better rhythm and feel, and above all for more precise meaning.

An Effective Follow-Up Using Cartoons

An additional exercise cements the importance of varying sentence beginnings for more variety and interest. For this assignment, we use either a book of single-frame cartoons or an old calendar of one-a-day cartoons. Suggestions of good ones to use might be *Teacher Cartoon-A-Day: 2012 Day-to-Day Calendar* by Jonny Hawkins (2011), which keeps on the good-teacher theme, or similar calendars based on sports or animals. To double-dip this assignment with vocabulary study, try using Marc Nobleman's (2005) *Vocabulary Cartoon of the Day* for elementary or *Vocabulary Cartoons: SAT Word Power* by Sam Burchers (2007). Copies of all these and similar sets can be found online at cut-rate prices at sites such as Amazon. Here are the directions: After students have torn out the cartoons they want to use, ask them to write a sentence explaining what is happening in each cartoon frame. If they are using the vocabulary cartoons, they are to write a sentence using the new vocabulary word. They should be ready to trade with other students for different cartoon pages. There is only one rule: they cannot start one of their sentences with a word they have already used. We give each student about four or five pages and listen as the giggles and gasps begin. Students can't wait to finish writing about the cartoons they have described so far so they can get another pile of cartoons. Around the tenth sentence, most students begin to run out of ways to vary the sentences. Now is when we begin giving suggestions: We ask them to take out their cheat sheet of adverbial conjunctions and pronouns to begin with. We suggest flipping parts of the sentence around. We propose as many suggestions as we can. Getting them to keep trying for twenty-five sentences is made a much smoother challenge by using cartoons!

Conclusion

Reteaching is teaching. None of us has much experience of learning something well the first and only time we were exposed to it. We all need repetition to absorb information and develop skills. The Crazy 8s device and tools such as the X-Ray Machine emphasize the need for novelty and newness in reteaching exercises. This takes planning ahead to establish how one can weave opportunities to repeat important concepts and revisit newly learned skills into other content and activities. Teachers who plan in this way have the satisfaction of seeing their students really remember and apply this information to other situations.

Chapter Four

Cognitive Conversations

To improve student literacy, we need a better quality of "talk" in the classroom—a change in who is doing the talking and how it is structured. We need to move away from simple interrogations, examine our questions, and urge thoughtful student questions and answers. An examination of what is said in the classroom by all participants moves us away from simply focusing on assignments and activities to grappling with the true complexity of the act of teaching.

Questioning, Conversing, and Listening

Questions, as we shall see in this chapter, belong to the student as well as the teacher. By shifting the opportunity and responsibility to pose questions to the student, we change the dynamics of the entire learning experience. Asking a question not only exposes a student's thinking processes but allows that student to open up to the ideas and opinions of others (Rosenshine, Meister, & Chapman, 1996). Talking in class, a punishable offense for as long as there have been classrooms full of students, is now being examined in an entirely new light. As conversation, elaboration, summary, repetition of content, and response to others' ideas and thoughts, talking is now considered a high-quality opportunity for deeper learning and understanding. Talking is also intimately integrated with questioning (Fisher, Frey, & Rothenberg, 2008).

Conversation and questions are the vehicles of thinking—the modes of transportation, so to speak, of cognitive communication. These vehicles need to be understood, polished, tuned up, and fueled so they can flow with opportunities to carry and share ideas. Our young charges need to be taught how to best drive, steer, accelerate, and use the brakes of these vehicles. They need to learn how to recognize and interpret the signs along the road and modify their conversation in response.

Rachel Billmeyer (2009) writes:

> All students can learn how to think, reflect, and question in a competent manner. Questions linking content to a reader's life provide connections when learning factual information. Training all students to generate high-level questions helps all students learn how to think effectively before, during, and after reading.

The goal of strategic reading is comprehension; strategic readers work actively to construct meaning, are independent, and read to learn by questioning and posing problems to enhance understanding. These readers and writers grow to become proficient in taking an active role in their relationship with the printed page and learn to articulate to others what they are experiencing in their interaction with text.

The third component of this triad interaction is listening. To be effective in the learning process, listening must be an active rather than passive experience. Students need to be able to examine and purposefully strengthen their ability to listen thoughtfully not only to the teacher but to their peers and to themselves as well. Direct instructional experiences in mindful listening can open minds and focus attention. A poster I read once made the point that most communication problems are due to the fact that we don't listen to understand, we listen to reply. A consistent interchange where there is authentic dialogue coming from thoughtful listening is much more difficult to attain in a classroom than it is to verbalize and write into standards. Following are sections of an email written to a literacy coach asking for help with classes in which students don't seem to have any desire to buy into this goal of actively working toward constructing meaning.

> There aren't really any behavior issues, just motivation issues. For the most part, everyone is there on a daily basis, but hardly any work gets done by the students. We do direct instruction and guided practice, and it seems to go fine, but then I get nothing out of them when they have to do something on their own. They won't read and they won't do homework. Even the simplest task in class won't get done. They just sit there and zone out. When I try to incorporate movement to wake them up, they complain and don't do it. I don't know what else to do. There was an assignment due today and out of thirty-two students, six turned it in.
>
> My second concern is my seniors. I think that they are just not being good students, specifically when it comes to any work or studying they have to complete on their own outside of school. When test time or essay time comes, many of them bomb it. It's disappointing when I do *so much* scaffolding but they still don't do their part. (T. Holiday, personal communication, December 8, 2011)

There is a great deal of frustration voiced in this teacher's email. The wonderful scenarios of students independently studying complex texts—formulating theses statements that are amply supported by evidence in those texts and then conversing with fellow students over the legitimacy of their reasoning—seem but a distant dream. For many, the day-to-day reality is more nightmare than dream. What do we do to turn this situation around? Where do we begin?

Let us look at more generalized solutions on how to begin the school year, so that we create an environment where that teacher's now unresponsive students wouldn't have the opportunity to entrench those habits of chronic disengagement.

If we want to see a specific behavior in our classrooms, we need to teach it. We cannot necessarily expect our students to act as we would like simply because we ask them to. Any preschool or kindergarten teacher and even teachers in upper grades know full well that telling students to line up and walk quietly to lunch won't guarantee that this will occur. They know telling isn't teaching. This holds true for the behaviors we would like our middle and high school students to adopt in our classes. If we want them to listen, we teach them how to listen; if we want them to discuss, we teach them how to discuss; if we want them to respectfully and thoughtfully respond to another's comment or work, we teach them how.

Those Precious First Few Days of School

Sadly, our first few days of classes are usually spent reading the school handbook, with all its rules, regulations, and punishments—the fine print of school regulations. Then we hand out books, go over our own classroom rules and regulations, and give an overview of our course. These are the days when students are taking the temperature of the room's environment, carefully reading the teacher's body language, and forging their opinions of other students—when patterns for the year, like newly poured cement, are beginning to set to stone. The job of the teacher is not so much to read rules and regulations and point to where homework should be deposited or hall passes should be obtained. Your job as the teacher during these few days is the following:

- Convince students how happy you are to have them in your class.

- Assure them that you intend to see that each one will do well and succeed in learning as much as possible.

- Create an atmosphere of positive, respectful joy and love for the subject matter.

- Build a feeling of confidence in your ability to demand kindness and respect for and from each member of the class.

- Ensure students that this class will challenge them without allowing them to fall behind, and will often be fun and filled with laughter along with bell-to-bell work.

- Explain to them that your first priority is to help them learn to think for themselves and be able to articulate their thinking and the reasons for their thinking to others.

This list could go on and on, but these are the basic principles that need to be voiced in the beginning of the year. Only then can we begin to teach the routines and behaviors that will serve to accomplish these goals.

Why am I including this topic and these admonitions in a book devoted to literacy? Why don't I leave these comments between the covers of my last book—*You've Got to Reach Them to Teach Them* (Schreck, 2011)—on student motivation and engagement? The reason is that there *is* no literacy instruction if there is no classroom management, mutual respect, or agreed-upon procedures for how literacy training will be accomplished. All the great literacy theory and all the strategies in the world are useless in a class devoid of the right atmosphere for learning.

Discussing First Assignments and Behaviors

From the very beginning of the school year, it is necessary to create an atmosphere of thoughtful conversation and student-initiated questions. It is in these early exchanges between teacher and students that the unwritten rules of the classroom—concerning what pleases or displeases the teacher and where the boundaries of talk and behavior are drawn, rules that are not always verbalized but conveyed intuitively—are picked up by the class.

With this in mind, I usually give an autobiographical piece for homework that first day of class. One of my favorites asks the students to put themselves in the role of someone who knows them well and, using this point of view, introduce themselves to the teacher and the class. How do we do this? We give multiple examples, since this is often confusing to students at the onset. We explain that they might choose a brother or sister and write about themselves as if they were that brother or sister. We offer that they might even use a pet as the speaker, or a parent, neighbor, good friend, or grandparent—anyone who knows a lot about their lives. We stipulate that this person must have known them at least for the last ten years in order to do justice to the paper. Using this persona, they should write about themselves. Areas to cover might be what they like to do, what their personality is like, what kind of students their teachers can expect them to be, and any past events that are important to know about so that we can best relate to them as a teacher. Keep the directions open, and invite them to add anything at all that might sound like something the speaker might really say.

In the next class period, we do not ask our students to turn in their papers. Instead, we call out the students one by one and ask them to tell us whom they chose to be the "speaker" of their introduction, and only then to put the piece on our desk. We all laugh together at the choices. Eventually, we will call out the name of a student who doesn't have his or her paper. We do not reprimand this student; we ask only that he put his name and the reason why the assignment was not completed on a piece of paper and walk to the front and turn that in. We don't have to say anything else; everyone in class is aware that this student didn't do his homework! Nicely, we tell him to be sure to bring it with him the following day or even at the end of this day if he has a chance to write it. We have planted the first seeds of both our expectations and the unwritten law concerning how to bring a smile to the teacher's face!

This walk to the front with homework ensures that students can't hide the fact that they haven't done their work from us or the other students. We replicate this procedure a couple more times, emphasizing how glad we are that those who brought in their work did so, since we need to have something to work with in class—to read, share, rewrite, and discuss. This is how we build and reinforce good behavior from the very beginning.

Students then immediately get their papers back and read their letters of introduction in groups of three or four. We ask them to see if they can tell if the chosen persona sounds authentic. Would a mother's letter sound like this? Would a letter written by a little brother sound like this? Would we have said all this if we had written in first person? We examine what we have written and question how the prompt might have been responsible for framing a response we might never have given if it had been worded differently.

After a few minutes of group sharing—and always with a clear purpose of what to listen for—we ask the class if anyone has heard a paper that sounds as though it really were written by someone besides the student. By doing this instead of simply asking for volunteers to share their papers, we are assured of getting papers that might be good examples but are written by students who would never volunteer to share on their own. Again, we offer each student the opportunity to read to the class, to pass, to have someone else read the paper, or to have the teacher read it. Respect and sensitivity with regard to not putting a student on the spot in the beginning of the year is essential—every student always has the right to decline when it comes to sharing out loud to the whole group.

Respecting the Reader

Before a student reads the paper to the class, we remind everyone how to listen. No one is allowed to speak to anyone else, and even wiggling in the desk is discouraged while a student is reading. This is one of the most important rules of our classroom etiquette. Along with this is the responsibility of the student who is reading to use enough volume and inflection that everyone in the room can easily hear. We practice this with the first volunteer. We suggest that the student read so softly that no one can understand her, which brings laughter. Then we have this student increase her volume until we are all satisfied.

Before the reading begins, we again instruct the class on what to listen for. This is always noted before anyone reads out loud. For this set of readings, students are to listen for specific details that make the paper sound like it really was written by a person other than the student. We tell the class that it will be invited to share these details after the reading.

Now the class is asked to tell us what details it heard that made the piece sound authentic. These might range from a mother introducing her son as a dear boy, or smart, or a perfect student, to a little brother sharing details of how much of a teaser his brother is, or how much trouble he gets in at school, or how he never does his homework when he's supposed to, and so on. This is the class's first introduction to the kind of conversation we will be having during the semester. We have set the ground rules, the need for the space for quiet reflection, for respectful listening, and for thoughtful responses and queries without a frantic hands-in-the-air sound-byte-type of shallow answer.

Embedding Academic Vocabulary

During each whole-class reading of student work—whether it be full papers or simply the best sentence chosen by each student to share with the class—we respond to the comments students make by reframing them in academic terms. While students are reading their introductory letters, we introduce the concept of tone and explain how different letters are written with a different tone of voice because of the persona or point of view that has been adopted. If you use concrete examples before making the connection to concepts like *simile* and *alliteration*, students will more easily understand the meaning of these terms. First the concrete, then the abstract—always!

In another example, when a student was reading a fable she had just written, a listening student remarked that he loved the phrase "the horse tiptoed down the road as if it were a prissy little girl afraid of getting her shoes muddy." We all agreed we liked the comparison and that it definitely fit the character. We noted that this kind of comparison is known as a simile. Later, in regard to another paper, a student commented that she liked the sound of the phrase "a flock of page-flapping book birds." Others said they, too, liked this description of a "flock" of open books with the wind ruffling their "wings." We asked if anyone remembered the academic term for words that begin with the same sound. Many recalled learning about alliteration in former classes and seemed thrilled to be able to apply their prior knowledge. By drawing attention to these terms that appear in their writing, we cement and add meaning that far surpasses a worksheet version of literary-term practice.

We do readings as a whole class in the beginning of the year for two reasons: first, we are teaching students not only how to read their pieces out loud for maximum understanding but more importantly how to listen to others' papers for the types of phrases and examples they might use later when they work in small groups. These whole-class readings set the template for careful listening and appropriate responding. Secondly, we are providing them with the academic vocabulary that they will use to explain what they hear in others' papers. We are showing on a large scale what we will expect them to do later in their small groups. We do not allow students to simply give us broad general comments, such as "I liked it" or "It was well written." We probe until they can be more specific and explain what they really mean, such as "The words the character is speaking really sound like the ones she would use when she's talking to someone."

To this I might respond, "You mean then that the *diction* the writer is using really fits the type of character described?"

Or, a student might say, "I really liked the ending; I didn't expect it to happen like that."

The teacher could then respond, "Yes, that *surprise ending* caught all of us off guard. What did we expect to happen? Why?" and, "O. Henry uses this technique often. What other story have you read that had a similar surprise ending?" Quickly, a student remembers "The Necklace" and confidently raises her hand.

"Can you think of any examples from films or other books that used this same technique equally well?"

A student might reply, "The movie *The Sixth Sense* was on cable the other night. That ending really was a surprise to me. I never saw it coming." And so the connections are made and information moves to understanding.

Who Does the Talking in Your Classes?

Studies have demonstrated that most classroom talk and questions belong to the teacher. In research undertaken in twenty-seven classrooms in six secondary schools in the United States by James T. Dillon (1988), an expert on questioning behaviors in education, only 1 percent of pupils asked questions. On the other hand, questions accounted for over 60 percent of the teachers' talk (Dillon, 1988). In Douglas Fisher, Nancy Frey, and Carol Rothenberg's (2008) book *Content-Area Conversations*, these educators and researchers counted the words in a typical teacher-class exchange over material that was not easily mastered by the entire class. The teacher spoke 190 words while the students spoke 11, or only 6 percent of the discourse. Teacher-student questioning dominates the exchange within the classroom but not for the purpose of initiating thinking as much as to establish procedures (30–60 percent) such as "Did you turn in your homework?" "Are you finished?" Only around 33 percent of teaching time is devoted to questions dealing with learning. Moreover, Trevor Kerry, a professor at Lincoln University, finds that 96 percent of these questions devoted to learning are all lower-order questions requiring students to remember, as opposed to 4 percent higher-order questions requiring them to think (Kerry, 2010).

It's no wonder then that the Common Core State Standards have devoted a strand to speaking and listening:

> Including but not limited to skills necessary for formal presentations, the Speaking and Listening standards require students to develop a range of broadly useful oral communication and interpersonal skills. Students must learn to work together, express and listen carefully to ideas, integrate information from oral, visual, quantitative, and media sources, evaluate what they hear, use media and visual displays strategically to help achieve communicative purposes, and adapt speech to context and task. (NGA & CCSSO, 2010b)

In other words, teachers need to move away from the front of the room, both figuratively and literally, and begin allowing students to ask the questions and to talk, listen, and respond to each other. For some, this is a huge shift in classroom behavior.

Shifting to Have Students Do More Talking

The smoothest step to active engagement is for students to have discussions with each other. With active engagement, the focus is on reasoning and evaluating evidence, collaborating with others to formulate and solve problems, elaborating ideas, and empowering students to have confidence in their ability to think and talk about their thinking. This can't happen in a room dominated by teacher talk with an emphasis on regurgitating right answers to already formulated questions. In many classrooms, a visitor would deduce that the purpose of education is to produce excellent *Jeopardy!* contestants.

So where do we start? First, a little active research on what actually is going on in your classroom might bring home these statements about teacher talk more profoundly. Perhaps try the following: ask a fellow teacher to chart your classroom's talk for around twenty minutes or more, using a stopwatch or timer to record when talking begins and ends, and noting on the reproducible Classroom Talk (page 162) who is doing the talking. Another chart might be used to record who is asking questions and the kinds of question being asked. Record your results using the reproducible Types of Questions Asked and by Whom on page 163.

Making Frequent Stops for Summary Checks

Another way to begin shifting the weight of talk from teacher to students is to stop during the presentation of material and ask students to turn to a neighbor, decide who will be A and who will be B, and then ask the As to summarize to the Bs what they have heard. Next, ask the Bs to add anything that might have been left out or to formulate a question about the information for A to answer. These stops should never be long—one minute for each speaker at the most—and should be inserted frequently throughout the class period, especially if the teacher is using direct instruction for transferring information.

Practicing With Sand Timers

For students to experience real listening, we set up the following exercise. Students decide on a topic that holds real interest to each of them—a topic that will be easy for them to talk about without running out of things to say. We brainstorm the types of topics they could possibly pick—their favorite sport or music or video game, a hobby or skill they spend a lot of spare time on, an interest in animals or cars or computers, a favorite vacation or place, thoughts on what makes them angry or happy or fearful. We keep throwing out ideas until everyone is satisfied with one he or she can easily talk about.

Then they pair up, and each pair is given a two-minute sand timer (many types are available online by the dozen for a few dollars). Student A will go first and talk about his topic for the entire two minutes. Student B is to listen, following these directives:

- Don't interrupt the speaker at all; keep silent.

- Be sure to show you are listening by using good body language (nodding head, keeping eye contact, showing interest).

- Listen carefully so that you can ask the speaker a question that pertains to something being said.

- If the speaker can't think of anything else to say, just sit quietly until he does think of something or the time runs out.

When the timer's sand runs out, student B should ask at least one question and listen to the response. The students then change roles. Student A becomes the listener and B the speaker. After B finishes and has answered the questions posed by student A, the two of them should discuss how it felt to be a listener who doesn't interrupt, whether this was difficult or easy to accomplish, and what it felt like to be able to speak without being interrupted. After everyone has finished the exercise and discussed it, we ask students to share with the whole class what they experienced in their pairs. Experiencing listening firsthand and being told to listen are two very different things! The most common response is the strange feeling of not being interrupted and of being allowed to keep talking. From students who are usually the more vocal ones in the group, we hear how much they learned about a student they didn't know before. When this is tried for the first time with a group, some students can't fill up the time talking and need to just stay still until the timer runs out. However, when this exercise is used later on in the year, many of those same students are able to fill up the time more easily. Much also depends on the interest in the topic.

Discussions Are Not Debates

An important area to cover with students before expecting them to participate in worthwhile discussions is the difference between a discussion and a debate. One of our goals when using small-group discussions is to focus students on reasoning and the evaluation of evidence. We use these small groups to empower students to be able to think when confronted with a difficulty and to help them practice conjecturing about problems and explore how they might best be approached. We want these group experiences to enable students to clarify and expand on the ideas of others, to feel comfortable providing evidence or reasons for their statements, and to weigh the reasonableness of their own and others' conclusions. Each of these goals requires that students talk with one another and are able to reflect upon their own thinking. This won't happen if students view these discussions as competitions to win or opportunities to force others to agree with their positions. When this mindset is in play, those not speaking are thinking only about what it is they will say when given the chance and how they intend to counter what is being said, and consequently are engaged in only surface listening.

The goal of communication within a discussion is the creation of something new from the mix of all the comments and ideas shared by the group. This is dialogue, not debate. Dialogue—according to physicist David Bohm (2004), widely recognized for his significant contributions to the discussion of the relationship between art and science—isn't like giving out a set of directions on how to get to one's house. Nor is it meant to convey information from one person to another as accurately as possible. Dialogue works "if the people are able freely to listen to each other, without prejudice, and without trying to influence each other. Each has to drop his old ideas and intentions, and be ready to go onto something different when called for" (Bohm, 2004, p. 3). We need to help our students master this essence of dialogue if we want our group discussions to be meaningful learning events. A simple exercise to show how discussions should look uses a balloon or beach ball. Students are to work together to keep the ball in the air, not let it hit the floor. In the same way, they are to keep the discussion going, not let it hit the floor.

Before setting up discussion groups in your room, it is important to hold a whole-class discussion on the differences between what is expected and desirable in a dialogue and what is expected and desirable in a debate. It is when these two modes of communication are confused in student minds that frustration arises and teachers become disheartened by the inability of students to conduct meaningful discussions. The items in table 4.1, based on the Socratic Seminar page at www.studyguide.org/socratic _seminar_student.htm, might help students become aware of the differences in these two methods of thinking and speaking.

Table 4.1: Dialogue Versus Debate According to the Socratic Seminar

Dialogue	Debate
• Is collaborative (participants work to gain and share understandings)	• Is oppositional (two sides try to prove each other wrong)
• Uses listening to understand, make meaning, find common ground	• Uses listening to find flaws, spot differences, counter arguments
• Possibly changes one's point of view	• Defends one's position as truth
• Creates an open-minded attitude	• Creates a closed-minded attitude
• Searches for strengths in positions	• Searches for weaknesses in positions
• Respects others, seeks not to offend	• Rebuts others, sometimes belittles
• Remains open ended	• Demands a conclusion

Source: StudyGuide.org, 2012

Small-Group Discussion Charts

The reproducibles Group Discussion Guidelines and Group Discussion Report Sheet (pages 164–165) will be useful in preparing for and evaluating the success of class discussions. First, talk over the guidelines with the whole class to see if students understand them and to determine whether or not the guidelines need tweaking for this particular class. The guidelines are as follows:

- Listen for good ideas, not "right" answers.

- Don't interrupt another speaker; be patient and respectful.

- Use the phrase *yes, and . . .* instead of *yes, but. . . .*

- Clarify what others have said: *What I hear you saying is . . . .*

- Use good body language to show you are fully listening.

- Ask for evidence of statements if necessary.

- Don't monopolize the discussion; share the talk time.

- Address each other by name when asking a question or following up.

- Aim to deepen understanding, not to agree or win a debate.

- Encourage each member to join in the discussion.

- Keep on the topic; don't wander off on other issues.

One student should take the job of recorder at the beginning and use hash marks to note how many times each member speaks. The group should turn in the report sheet after the discussion has ended. The report sheet allows each member to comment on the context of the discussion as well as on how he or she feels the discussion went in general.

Moving a Discussion to Dialogue

To have good discussions, students need practice using specific responses. A real mind changer is the guideline to use *yes, and . . .* rather than the usual *yes, but. . . .* This slight change in wording shifts the response to one that builds on the previous statement instead of immediately countering it. Instead of mentally developing how one is going to react to what the current speaker is saying, the student must actually listen to be able to add to that comment. Students could practice beginning every comment they make with this phrase for an entire discussion, until it becomes second nature to elaborate on others' statements. This elaboration technique serves to broaden and deepen the discussion.

Another guideline stem that students need to be trained to use is the summarizing/clarifying stem *What I hear you saying is . . .* followed by what else they think about that idea. Students also need to ask each other "Why do you think that?" to solicit reasons and evidence to support their statements. Students will more easily incorporate these kinds of stems in their discussions if they consistently hear their teachers ask the same sorts of questions. Teachers need to make a conscious effort to change their questions from those that have a single correct answer or, in regard to evidence in the texts, require a simple seek-and-find motion from their students. Higher-order questions require students to explain the reasoning behind an answer, and can be followed up with questions like, "How did you come to that conclusion?" or "What evidence has brought you to that statement, and why do you think it is valid?" When students expect to be asked to give reasons for their answers, they begin looking for those reasons beforehand. When they find out that giving answers such as "I don't know" or "I just think that way" aren't considered acceptable, they begin thinking.

What do you do when a student doesn't answer with anything except a shrug and "I don't know"? We don't let him off the hook by simply deflecting the question to another student. Too many students have gone year after year without being held responsible for that "I don't know" answer. One way of handling this might be to first ask the student what he would say if he *did* know the answer! Some students actually respond to that one. Another would be to tell the student to think about it, that you will be coming back to ask him again later. If he still doesn't come up with a response, tell him to choose a statement one of the other students gave that seems pretty correct. What we are doing is gently demanding active engagement and effort of everyone, no exceptions—no one can get away with zoning out and not being mentally present.

Students usually refuse to answer because of fear—fear of looking or sounding stupid in front of their peers. A suggestion offered during the 2012 ASCD Annual Conference by Rick Smith (2012), author of *Conscious Classroom Management*, which creates an environment that is more fearless, is his 8 Raised Hands strategy. In this strategy, the teacher requires that eight hands be raised before calling on someone to answer. Then, each of the eight students gives an answer followed only by a "thank you" from the teacher. After this, the teacher gives the correct answer. This process dissolves the fear factor associated with being singled out.

If these expectations are made clear at the beginning of the term and repeated with consistency, it is far easier to harness students' attention and cooperation and sustain it throughout the year. When a student has not been required to participate for long periods of time and this exchange of expectation has not been woven into the fabric of the student-teacher interchanges, if that student is asked to cooperate, there will often be resistance. Thinking is work. It takes effort. It's much easier for students to sit and entertain their own thoughts and choose not to mentally engage in the subjects and ideas others want them to engage in. This is one reason why it is important to present the material in as pleasant and interesting a context as possible. When a class has repeatedly tuned out the teacher and habitually refused to participate in any thoughtful exchanges, turning this behavior around is really difficult—not impossible, but difficult.

Purposeful Talk as Rehearsal for Writing

How interesting it would be to walk down a school hallway and instead of hearing the teacher loudly directing the class to stop talking, to hear her just as loudly urge them all to start talking! We have been conditioned to accept the quiet classroom as a sign of studious, hard-working boys and girls who are well disciplined and absorbed in their lessons. Sometimes this is indeed the case, but all too often it is not. Active learning—where students are involved in the construction of meaning by interacting with peers on cognitively engaging problem-solving tasks within a collaborative learning environment—is in my experience the most effective setting for deep, sustained learning. Researchers Leonard Rivard and Stanley Straw's (2000) study of the effects of talk and writing on the learning of science could be applied to any subject. They conclude:

> The results suggest that talk is important for sharing, clarifying, and distributing scientific ideas among peers while asking questions, hypothesizing, explaining, and formulating ideas together all appear to be important mechanisms during discussions. The use of writing appears to be important for refining and consolidating these new ideas with prior knowledge. These two modalities appear to be dialectical: talk is social, divergent, and generative, whereas writing is personal, convergent, and reflective. Moreover, writing appears to enhance the retention of co-constructed knowledge over time. Gender and ability are important variables that may be mediating the effects of talk and writing that should be investigated in a more robust future study. (p. 588)

When both talk and writing are integrated consistently in the instructional plan, the rate of retention and the depth and elaboration of thought increase dynamically. How would this look in the classroom? If students are given the opportunity to rehearse the ideas and information they have chosen to use in a written paper by talking them through before drafting, the results will be impressively better. When given the chance to use both the divergent modality (talking) and the convergent modality (writing), our students experience a whole-brain effort that they find both engages and satisfies.

Rehearsal opportunities for your students before they write is only one way of providing meaningful short discussions. Students could rehearse oral presentations, summaries of lessons previously taught, possible methods of solving problems, homework assignments, and more—before the formal class discussion actually begins. Using talk as rehearsal doesn't take long, but it can have a long-lasting effect on student retention and understanding of material.

The Power of Questions

Tony Wagner (2008), of the Harvard Graduate School of Education, shared a conversation on a flight to Minneapolis in 2006 with Clay Parker, president of the Chemical Management Division of BOC Edwards about the qualities most wanted in new employees. Parker's remarks seemed to take Wagner by surprise. Parker explains:

> First and foremost, I look for someone who asks good questions. Our business is changing, and so the skills our engineers need change rapidly, as well. We can teach them the technical stuff. But for employees to solve problems or to learn new things, they have to know what questions to ask. (as cited in Wagner, 2008, p. 2)

He continues:

> I want people who can engage in good discussion—who can look me in the eye and have a give and take . . . all of our work is done in teams. If you can't engage others, then you won't learn what you need to know. (as cited in Wagner, 2008, p. 2)

Questions, discussion, true engagement by listening and considering another's point of view—these are all skills that need to be exercised within the classroom setting. Conveying to students the understanding that a good question is as, or even more, important than a right answer can cause a major shift in the traditional classroom environment. We can help students respect and recognize the value of good questions in multiple ways—not least by giving them opportunities to create questions about what they are reading.

Practice in Making Questions

Ask students to label a sheet of paper in their working folders with the words *My Own List of Questions*. They are to add any questions that come up as the days go by, but they are also to add questions prompted by short exercises meant solely to generate questions. An example of one such exercise uses National Geographic's (2009) *Weird But True: 300 Outrageous Facts*. At least four books in this specific series work well with all ages of children. These books are filled with facts and colorful photographs that easily bring questions up in the minds of the readers. For this exercise, tear up these small books into sets of about three to four pages each stapled together. Hand out a set to each student, asking him or her to read through the pages and come up with at least two or three interesting questions. A typical set might include facts such as these:

- New York City's Empire State Building was built with ten million bricks.

- A coffin was once designed to look like a lobster.

- Peanut butter can be converted into a diamond.

- If you could travel the speed of light, you would never get older.

- An eleven-year-old girl named the dwarf planet Pluto.

- The world's biggest flower—found in an Indonesian rain forest—can grow wider than a car.

- Hotdogs can last up to twenty years in landfills.

Students share their facts and questions with the class and are then reminded to write down their questions on their personal question sheets. They are also free to write down questions that prove interesting to them that come from other students.

One pragmatic purpose of this exercise is the opportunity it offers students to research the answers. These miniresearch opportunities will be based on personal choice and contain a built-in engagement factor, since they are the products of each student's curiosity. They can thus be used as a foundation for teaching skills associated with online research.

Modeling to Demonstrate a Reader's Questioning Mind

Since our current educational culture with its emphasis on standardized tests places such a premium on finding the right answer, we need to consistently make a conscious effort to develop an understanding in our students that much of life does not fit in a multiple-choice construct, that many questions are coated with a thick layer of ambiguity, and that what appears to be a black-and-white question can usually be probed and expanded. We do not want them to fear asking questions or not coming up with the right answer. We want them to have experiences that show *many* answers can be right. One way to help alleviate a student's lack of confidence in his or her reading comprehension ability is for the teacher to verbally model the questions that arise in the mind as a person begins to read an unfamiliar text. The exercise in the next section describes an activity teachers can use to accomplish this.

"The Carnival"

Students sit in a semicircle with the teacher in the middle. All have a copy of the material to be studied in class. Today, the text is a short story by Michael Fedo (1980) titled "The Carnival." Instead of asking students to start reading silently or to take turns reading, the teacher asks them to listen to her. She is not going to simply read the story aloud; she is going to add the inner commentary that she feels the reading might bring up in her students' minds. Here are the first three paragraphs followed—in italics and brackets—by the same text with the teacher's commentary on them:

> The chartered bus stopped at the corner of Fourteenth and Squire. Jerry smiled nervously, turned and waved to his mother who stood weeping a few feet away, and boarded the bus.
>
> He returned the driver's silent nod and settled himself in the only remaining seat—near the front—next to a poorly dressed middle-aged woman.
>
> Jerry tingled with excitement. He glanced around, eager for conversation, but the other passengers were strangely silent. This puzzled Jerry, for he was looking forward with great anticipation to the carnival. (Fedo, 1980, p. 36)

Here is the text plus commentary.

> [Well, this sounds like a cool story, better than the last one we read. At least I know what a carnival is like.]
>
> The chartered bus stopped at the corner of Fourteenth and Squire. Jerry smiled nervously, turned and waved to his mother who stood weeping a few feet away, and boarded the bus.

[Why would his mother be crying? Why would going to a carnival make a kid nervous? Already this story is sounding weird.]

He returned the driver's silent nod and settled himself in the only remaining seat—near the front—next to a poorly dressed middle-aged woman.

[This is a charter bus but it seems strange that he has to sit next to a poor woman. Why isn't she working? How come she is going to this carnival? Do I even have to worry about her at all? I never know what to worry about and what to just ignore at the beginning of a story.]

Jerry tingled with excitement. He glanced around, eager for conversation, but the other passengers were strangely silent. This puzzled Jerry, for he was looking forward with great anticipation to the carnival.

[Now this is getting weird. I can see how Jerry would be excited, but why isn't anyone else? He says they were all "strangely" silent. Are there any kids his age on this bus? I still can't understand why his mother was crying. I bet this isn't going to be a normal carnival.]

"Lost Face"

Let's try another one. This time we are using the first paragraph of Jack London's (1910) "Lost Face."

It was the end. Subienkow had traveled a long trail of bitterness and horror, homing like a dove for the capitals of Europe, and here, farther away than ever, in Russian America, the trail ceased. He sat in the snow, arms tied behind him, waiting the torture. He stared curiously before him at the huge Cossack, prone in the snow, moaning in his pain. The men had finished handling the giant and turned him over to the women. That they exceeded the fiendishness of the men the man's cries attested.

Here is the text plus commentary.

It was the end.

[If this is the end, what is the story going to be about? What a strange way to begin. Kind of interesting though.]

Subienkow had traveled a long trail of bitterness and horror, homing like a dove for the capitals of Europe, and here, farther away than ever, in Russian America, the trail ceased.

[Oh no! I hate names like this, I never can pronounce them or remember them, and it looks like this story is not in a place I recognize. Where is Russian America? Sounds like this guy hasn't had too good a life so far—bitterness and horror. What trail is now ceasing? Does this mean his trip is over?]

He sat in the snow, arms tied behind him, waiting the torture.

[Wow! So he's a prisoner and is going to be tortured probably to death. Wonder who'll be doing the torturing? And what he did to deserve it? Is he scared? This story might be better than I first thought after all.]

He stared curiously before him at the huge Cossack, prone in the snow, moaning in his pain. The men had finished handling the giant and turned him over to the women.

[So another guy is a prisoner, too. A Cossack. What's a Cossack? I vaguely remember hearing that word associated with Russia. Wonder what the men did to the guy.]

That they exceeded the fiendishness of the men the man's cries attested.

[Yep, I bet women would make better torturers than men. Poor guy, will that guy with the S name be able to help him? Or even help himself? Wonder what is going to happen.]

The purpose of this internal commentary modeling activity is to give a more vivid example of how good readers respond to the text in their minds, how they don't always know the answers to their own questions right away, and how some texts are written to purposely keep the reader questioning. Too often, struggling readers think that any confusion about what is occurring in a text is due to their inability to read well when this is not the case at all. This activity should help struggling readers become more aware of their own interior voices and not be afraid to listen to them.

Metacognition: Examining Our Thinking

The importance of oral commentary of the kind we have just seen lies in the discussion with the class afterward. By expressing such questions as the reading goes on, the teacher is reflecting back to the class the uncertainties that almost *everyone* feels about the facts, the place, and the possible meaning of the text when beginning something new. The teacher should ask students if any of the questions and comments she voiced might have been theirs as well. This begins an important discussion on what expectations young readers should have when beginning a reading: having a ton of unanswered questions doesn't mean that the reader is lacking proficiency. Often, the author doesn't answer the questions that rise up in the reader's mind right away. Instead, the author wants to build suspense and curiosity in the reader, and withholding information is a good way to do this.

A reader needs to be patient at the beginning of a reading and not panic. And yet panic is exactly what many of our students do when faced with questions they cannot answer. They blame this lack of ability on themselves, and instead of continuing the reading—instead of holding the ambiguity that has built up in their minds about the story—they quit or turn off, saying, "I just don't get it. I don't understand."

Teachers need to help students create judgments about which facts to pay attention to and which are not so important. In areas such as math and science, for example, it's necessary to take into account all facts, and reading pace and purpose are different. Modeling what a math or science teacher thinks while reading a passage or problem can be immensely helpful for students who still think that reading is reading and can't see how they should adjust for different texts or curricula.

Examining Your Questioning Habits

The best method for an objective check on the range and quality of your questioning habits is to have a colleague observe your teaching. Go over the following Teacher's Checklist on Questioning Habits (also on reproducible page 166), mark the areas where you may be falling into the following habits, and ask a colleague to concentrate on these areas specifically during an observation:

- Sometimes I ask a question but end up answering it myself.

- I often call on a person first, then ask the question.

- I really don't give all students enough time to think of a response.

- I start with a difficult question without warming up with easier ones.

- If a student answers incorrectly, I just find another with a right answer.

- Sometimes I let a student's wrong answer go unchallenged.

- I seldom praise the quality of the answer (phrasing, completeness).

- I don't start the class with a couple of key questions to direct the entire lesson.

- I don't require all students to write answers down before accepting responses.

- Often I ask the same kind of question again and again.

- I find myself asking too many questions at once.

- I use questions as interrogation rather than paths to deeper discussions.

- At times, I call on the same few students and ignore the rest.

- Some of my questions are actually irrelevant to the topic.

- My questioning sessions seem to stress students out and sound threatening.

- I tend to give struggling students less time to answer and move to someone else.

- My questions lead to dead ends and don't set up the activity to follow.

- I fall into a Trivial Pursuit or game-show pedagogy, only asking lower-level questions.

- Many of my questions tend to have a single right answer.

Another method is to have yourself filmed and examine your questioning skills privately. All of us could benefit from this type of self-audit again and again. What we think we are communicating is not always what we are actually communicating to students. Sifting what we think from what we do and how we are perceived is the most useful of personal examinations.

Since whole-class question-answer formats tend to be the least profitable method of soliciting good in-depth answers and follow-up discussions, why not ask a few strong, open-ended questions to the whole group and then have students move into smaller groups of four to six to answer them? These groups then report back to the whole class. By doing this, more students will have a chance to voice their ideas. If students are always in the whole group during discussions, only a few end up answering and responding.

Another suggestion for auditing and improving your question expertise is to write down key questions in advance of your lessons. The goal is to counteract the insidious effect of habitual behavior. All the good resolutions in the world won't change behavior unless one takes the time and energy to prepare for those incidents when the need for change occurs. We have all experienced going to workshops or other in-service opportunities, writing down a few wonderful ideas on how to improve our instruction, and then returning to our classrooms only to find ourselves doing exactly what we've always done. The good ideas seem to fade farther and farther into the dimness of yesterday. And we go on as usual.

Using Questioning as a Base for Instruction

Most thoughtful curriculum design specialists urge teachers to develop the questions that will set the overlying focus for the study of their material and present them up front to the students at the introduction of the unit. This positioning of questions that are broad, open-ended, and meaningful on many levels serves to set purpose and structure for both the teacher and students. We all know where we are going, what we need to consider, and what questions we will eventually be concerned about answering. The first example of this juxtaposition of questions is frame formats, and the second is an exercise that uses questioning as a class to determine up front what is to be the focus of investigation and study.

Exploring Major Texts Through the Perspective of Frame Formats

Our students never really had much respect for "store-bought tests"—our class term for standardized tests created by textbook companies or other for-profit organizations that develop prepackaged units for study of the novel. One reason is that those tests never really hone in on what our focus is during our experience with the novel. We might be more globally concerned with large issues, and many test questions ask for recall of information that didn't fit with our focus. I would give out the store-bought tests with the challenge of seeing just how well students could ace it anyway, despite the lack of attention to small detail we might have spent. It is the generic feature of these tests that brings the greatest amount of criticism from our students. The test makers haven't been privy to our rich discussions, our emphasis on specific themes or features, or our purposes in reading the book in the first place. Consequently, their tests are shallow and lack the ability to gauge the effort that is born of rigorous thought.

We would often use frame questions—a series of broad questions that fit universally over a given theme—that follow a specific line of exploration and provide focus. Sets of questions follow explorations into such forces in our lives as choices, change, power, and patterns, to name a few. After considering the entire list of possible questions, students are asked to choose one as the basis for a paper on the book being studied. Developing these types of explorations and frame questions is always a satisfying exercise in unit design for any teacher. For those who have been teaching the same novel for too many years to remember, this exercise can serve to restore the freshness and curiosity that accompanied it the first few times it was taught. Because of the generic quality of the frame questions, a diversity of texts could easily be used for each of the topics that follows. For example, texts appropriate for the topic of Exploring Choices are: Ray Bradbury's (1953/2012) *Fahrenheit 451*, John Steinbeck's (1937/2002) *Of Mice and Men*, Ken Kesey's (1962) *One Flew Over the Cuckoo's Nest*, J. D. Salinger's (1951/2001) *The Catcher in the Rye*, Kurt Vonnegut's (1999) *Slaughterhouse-Five*, Ernest J. Gaines's (1992) *A Gathering of Old Men*, Elie Wiesel's (1969) *Night*, Rodman Philbrick's (1998) *Max the Mighty*, Sampson Davis, George Jenkins, Rameck Hunt, and Lisa Frazier's (2003) *The Pact*, and Ben Carson's (1998) *Gifted Hands*.

1. Exploring Choices
    a. What choices stem from the main character's values or philosophical perspective?
    b. What choices are made by minor characters that influence the main character to act or make a significant decision?
    c. What effects of the main character's choices did he or she anticipate? What effects were unexpected?
    d. What cluster of past choices brought the main character to his or her most significant choice or choices in the novel?
    e. What choices did the main character make that would be considered universal—that is, choices that were independent of time or place?
    f. What choices did the author make when developing his or her characters that could open him or her up to criticism from outside censors?

2. Exploring Change
    a. How does the change in point of view throughout the novel solidify its themes?
    b. What internal conflicts arise because of change in the traditional social roles of the characters?

    c. What are the major causes that bring about changes in the characters' behaviors?

    d. What changes occur in the characters' lives because of challenges to traditional values?

    e. How do the external changes in society affect the internal stability of some of the characters?

3. Exploring Power

    a. What sources of power do the main characters possess, and how do they consciously or unconsciously use that power in the novel?

    b. How does the cluster of breaks with authority in a main character's past lay the groundwork for his or her major attacks on authority in the present?

    c. What types of power are at work within the novel, and which are most successful, in the eyes of the reader, at demonstrating the existence and use of power?

    d. Power infers leadership to some and force to others. Explain which element is most influential in motivating the minor characters' actions.

    e. What are the results of conflicts arising from specific instances of abuse of power?

4. Exploring Patterns

    a. What language patterns surface when characters discuss the future, and how do they differ from the characters' regular speech patterns?

    b. What repeated actions lead to predictability of plot events or serve as examples of foreshadowing?

    c. What patterns of stereotyping exist? Which of these patterns shift later in the book, and which ones don't?

    d. Trace the major pattern of a main character's behavior that leads to the tragic conclusion of the novel.

    e. What word patterns are introduced and repeated by the author to build particular types of character personalities?

Teaching Students How to Formulate Their Own Questions

Students are more likely to fully commit to the difficult process of critical thinking when they develop—and therefore care about—the questions. Dan Rothstein and Luz Santana (2011a) are co-directors of the Right Question Institute and authors of *Make Just One Change: Teach Students to Ask Their Own Questions*, which details the use of their Question Formulation Technique. Teachers I have worked with who have incorporated this strategy into their classroom instruction find that students are more engaged, take more ownership of their learning, and accomplish far more. Using this method to begin a unit on virtually any subject can create a much more dynamic focus on the issues than traditional strategies. When the students come to an agreement on the questions they want answered, a built-in purpose and higher quality of meaning permeates the work and the environment. The Question Formulation Technique is as follows:

1. The teacher designs the central question focus.

2. Students produce questions according to four essential rules.

    a. Ask as many questions as you can.

    b. Do not stop to discuss, judge, or answer the questions.

    c. Write down every question exactly as it is stated.

    d. Change any statement into a question.

3. Students improve their questions.

    a. Categorize the questions as closed or open-ended.

    b. Name the advantages and disadvantages of each type of question.

    c. Change questions from one type to another.

4. Students prioritize their questions.

    a. Choose your three most important questions.

    b. Why did you choose these three as the most important?

5. Students and teacher decide on next steps.

    a. How are you going to use your questions?

6. Students reflect on what they have learned.

    a. What ideas did you come up with that surprised you?

    b. How can you use this process outside of class activities?

    c. What changes when the emphasis is on questions instead of answers?

After presenting the focus that will be the center of the unit in step one, the teacher solicits as many questions about it as students can create. To help students free up their minds, the four essential rules are offered as guideposts. The students could be writing their questions on sticky notes and bringing them up to the teacher to place on the board, or calling them out for the teacher or another student to transcribe. If a student suggests a statement, the class decides how that statement can be moved into the form of a question. The purpose of this second step is to produce questions following a divergent pattern and to dissuade students from judging their work or that of their neighbors too soon.

The third step—improve your questions—invites students to become aware of the difference between closed and open-ended questions and to understand the benefit of each. Closed questions are those that can be answered with a "yes" or "no" or with one word. Open-ended questions require an explanation. The students are asked to mark closed questions with a C and open-ended questions with an O, and then to change each type into the other.

Step four deals with prioritizing—this is the convergent process. Students choose their three most important questions and explain to the group why they chose them, with the purpose of persuading others.

Step five sets this question-making formula apart from all the others. Here, the teachers and students work together to decide what to do with these questions: Should they be the basis for an end-of-the-unit paper or project? A Socratic seminar? Should they guide outside research? Knowing that they have had a say-so in the planning and prioritizing of the upcoming unit of study provides a feeling of autonomy and ownership that students in traditional classrooms seldom experience.

The final step—students reflect on what they have learned—is where students consider the value of questioning as a thinking process. Here they have the opportunity to trace their thinking and see how their questions developed and deepened as the process moved forward. They also have the opportunity to project possible ways to use this process in other areas of their lives.

This type of framework, with its ability to provide choice, a sense of autonomy, challenge, and a feeling of ownership of the process and the material that is to be studied, is very powerful. These characteristics are the very ones that supply and sustain engagement for our students. This framework is also an effective tool for students to use when leaving the classroom and entering a world that runs on collaboration and generation of ideas.

Conclusion

The frustrated teacher whose email I shared on page 56 has classes of students who feel very little need to become engaged in the learning. They are stuck in behaviors that are anything but proactive, with nothing in place to move them into new patterns and new forms of interaction with the material. The two elements we have found that can address this are (1) introducing questioning procedures and training students to be listeners and (2) interacting through productive class discussions after taking the time to train students through rehearsals, modeling, and role-playing activities. The opportunity for students to talk to each other in pairs, small groups, and whole-class experiences—early in the school year—will have the effect of drawing in more and more of them over time.

Chapter Five

Using Novelty for Reluctant Learners

To be successful in our efforts at bringing all students to a state of literacy competency that will serve them in our complex world, we teachers need to have more than "book knowledge"; we need to have a full palette of pedagogical methods geared toward attracting and sustaining student interest. The research substantiates the relationship between a teacher's intuitive judgment in delivering material and the acquisition and mastery of literacy—especially in the case of reluctant learners.

This chapter consists of a wide variety of common classroom activities, content, and interchanges that can be transformed by the manifestation of creative and novel methods practiced in order to promote and facilitate literacy acquisition. Novelty implies something is new, unusual, original, something with a sense of freshness and curiosity about it. For students who feel chronically bored in a school routine that offers no surprise or interest, inserting a wide and consistent dose of novelty to the delivery of curriculum is a necessary element of good teaching.

Who exactly are our reluctant learners? They are those students in our classrooms who seem to drag their educational feet when confronted with new learning. But reluctant learners should not be confused with slow learners. Most slow learners want to learn but find themselves in trouble with the process along the way. A reluctant learner, however, is one who is not motivated and whose behavior often can be described as passive aggressive, creating more problems for teachers and parents through noncooperation. While reluctant learners seldom have learning disabilities, they can fall behind because of their reluctance to try and their fear of failure. That said, we must keep in mind that each reluctant learner is unique, each an unpolished gem in need of an expert jeweler to bring out his or her finest shine and brilliance.

How can we do this? We are all aware of how fragile our students' ability to sustain their concentration is—how easily they can become distracted from their work. But instead of lamenting this fact of life, we can take advantage of it. The smallest novel act or object can grab the attention of the most distractible student. Many of the suggestions in this chapter will have just such an ingredient added to an activity—an element of novelty placed there for the purpose of dispelling boredom, freeing the activity from the dark side of routine. Routine is necessary and provides a sense of safety and comfort to students whose lives are rocked with so much uncertainty and change—who may be in a constant state of stress and working toward maintaining their own mental and emotional survival. Routine must provide a soothing backdrop for the classroom. But within the framework of this routine, there should be a generous amount of novelty to draw students' attention, awaken the brain, and stimulate curiosity. The teacher steeped in soft skills knows the art of balancing routine and novelty.

The Dice Card Reading Activity

This activity can be used with students of any age to nudge them through the reading of a chapter of a book, an article, or a few pages of a textbook. The novelty can hold the attention and ensure the participation of the most reluctant class of learners. The students will be working in small groups of three to four and will have access to the following materials: a large single die, an index card with directions, and individual copies of the text to be read. Although this appears to be a game, the purpose is for everyone to read and complete the material assigned. There are only winners in this game-like activity.

Student will take turns throwing the die and following the direction on the card that corresponds with the number thrown. The index card has six different possibilities on it:

1. Read as much as you want out loud.

2. Tell the group where to read to silently.

3. Read two inches of print (approximately the size of the index card's side.

4. Select a group member to read for one minute.

5. Summarize what has been read.

6. Ask one student a question about the reading.

All the directions are aimed to move on the reading, allow for comprehension, give opportunities for quiet as well as out loud reading, and keep all students engaged in the activity.

As a consultant modeling this activity in a classroom of sophomores, I took the lowest readers as members of my own group and urged the classroom teacher to do the same. Students who usually could not concentrate on whole-class or an independent reading assignment for very long ended up spending the entire class period on task. We stopped long enough for the class to discuss the material and noted that students who often refrain from participating in such discussions felt comfortable enough with the text to join in. Like any other strategy, it should not be used too often or it will lose its novelty. It does provide a nice mix of small-group work, oral and silent reading, questioning, and summarizing opportunities for everyone.

It's in the Cards

Another prop that has been used successfully with reluctant readers is a deck of cards, or more specifically a suit of cards from a deck minus the face cards. My favorites to use are four-by-seven-inch jumbo cards, which are available from many vendors.

1. Place students in pairs or groups of three. If the groups are any larger, the level of participation of each group member becomes degraded.

2. After students have read the text to be analyzed, give each group a suit of cards and a stack of sticky notes. The reading shouldn't be too short, and the material selected should be important for the deeper understanding of a major concept.

3. Together, students decide what events in the reading are important enough to be one of their top ten cards. They write down these events and place these sticky notes in chronological order on the cards—one per card.

4. Student groups can then match up with another group and compare cards. Together they can decide which ones to add or drop in their own sets, until both groups have come to an agreement on their top ten events.

5. Both groups are then asked to reduce the top ten to five by determining which events merit this recognition of extra importance.

6. Using a gallery-walk type of movement around the room, students check out what other groups determined their top five to be.

7. As a class, students comment on the similarities and differences they observed in each other's choices and how they arrived at compromise when necessary. They are asked to reflect on the process of collaboration and what they felt were the results of such an activity in regard to understanding the material.

Teachers of science, math, and social studies classes were able to come up with ways to use this process to have students involve themselves in discussions and decisions concerning material they had often found difficult to understand when traditional teaching methods were used. This activity should also be used sparingly, but when a teacher does set up such an activity, the message to students is that he or she trusts them to make decisions, cares enough to try something different to make learning difficult concepts easier and even enjoyable, and values their thinking ability more than their ability to memorize facts alone.

Halloween: Relevance at Its Best

One of the foundations of engagement for students is relevance—if they can relate the learning to their real-world experiences, students are more apt to get involved, put out effort, and focus on the instruction. Definitely one of the strongest of a teacher's soft skills is the ability to tap into this innate yearning to relate to the information. Over the years, Halloween has become a 2.5 billion dollar business in the United States. Adults as well as students never seem to get enough of the enjoyment of dressing up, decorating, and pretending we are someone or something else. It doesn't matter what concepts or skills a teacher is currently building in students, by dressing them in the gauze of costume, we harness one of the most appealing phenomena of this generation. The group of strategies that follows begins with a lesson in statistics over Halloween consumption itself and then moves to how teachers can use the magnetic novelty of dress-up features in their lessons to spark attention and set a positive emotional state.

Halloween and the Investigative Classroom

Students should constantly be given opportunities to dig up information on their own, to be ongoing investigative reporters searching for information that confirms, elaborates on, or questions the validity of what is being offered in the classroom. This attitude of mind is one that can be fostered and heightened with short search challenges that are offered continuously to students throughout the year in every grade and subject. Making students skillful researchers isn't something that happens only when the formal research paper is assigned. This is a habit of learning that grows when practice is infused throughout the study of curriculum at every level and is nourished by student interest. The next section is an example of a cross-discipline search challenge involving the making and then reading and analyzing of charts relating to the topic of Halloween. Reading charts is a literacy skill that crosses disciplines and functions. In fact, practice working with bar, pie, scatter, column, area, and line charts—to name just a few ways data are presented—should occur in every discipline. Having students initially make the charts from a set of statistics they find would bump up the rigor and the investigative challenge.

Bumping Up the Rigor on Halloween Research

Instead of giving students the already digested data, why not ask them to search for and find these data themselves? This small shift in procedure offers students a wider area of participation, interest, and empowerment in the investigation. Teachers could keep some control over this exploration by giving students a list of potential sites to explore, and since they would be pulling material from different sources, this activity would open itself also to comparing and contrasting both their findings and their results. Some sites that might work well for this are:

- www.marketingcharts.com/direct/halloween-spending-rises-19773

- www.zippycart.com/infographics/halloween-sales-trends-and-figures.html

- http://bg016.k12.sd.us/Graphs/halloween.htm

- www.marketingcharts.com/uncategorized/escapism-will-propel-halloween-spending-to-58 -billion-6357/nrf-big-research-halloween-spending-age-september-2008jpg

- www.nrf.com/modules.php?name=News&op=viewlive&sp_id=578

What Do We Do With the Information?

First, students are invited to begin checking out the material and making decisions on what information would lend itself to being best explained by way of a chart or graph. Then they choose which type of graph they would like to use to display their information. The most often graphed data deal with "How much money is spent at Halloween and on what?" and "How do people celebrate Halloween?" Other topics might be "What ages of people celebrate Halloween most often?" or "What are the most popular costumes over the years?" After students create their charts, groups of four to five students should discuss what they found out, what sources they used, and what conclusions they came up with. The groups should also discuss the similarities and differences that they noticed in their data. Each group then chooses a spokesperson who reports back to the class. This is a way we push the class from simply relating or comparing findings to analyzing the implications and digging for causes. The following questions might arise from information found in the student-created charts.

- What can the charts tell us about participation in Halloween?

- Why has such a surge in interest developed over the years?

- What social changes might be responsible for what was traditionally a child's holiday that has now moved into the adult realm?

- Are the media and advertising conglomerates responsible for our current involvement with Halloween? Are the media and advertising interests simply following and reflecting our behavior?

- How universal is this holiday across the world? What other countries celebrate this holiday and in what ways?

- Have there been any other effects of this growth of interest in Halloween?

- What would interviews of older people on their memories and experiences with Halloween turn up?

- Who is benefiting from this growing surge in participation?

- Are there any critics? Could you find samples of their criticism?

- Have the incidents of crime gone up or down with this surge in participation? Can you find some statistics on this? What kind of crimes? Where?

An example of a student-created bar graph showing Halloween expenditures is shown in figure 5.1.

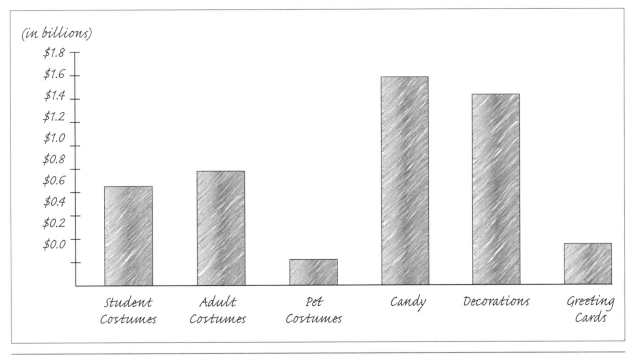

(in billions)

Figure 5.1: A student graph showing projected Halloween expenditures for 2010.

Wigs, Gowns, and Masks

At any time of the year, a wig can be all you need to transform a student into a totally new personality. I gathered a collection of such wigs over time—from relatives who owned some years ago when wearing wigs was a widespread fashion fad, from costume shops and discount department stores when after-Halloween sales lowered their prices by 75 percent, and from catalogs such as Oriental Trading. A good selection would include a white colonial man's wig (great for history classes and for Puritan-era literature), an old-lady wig with a bun in the back, a man's curly brown or black wig (all-purpose for most any use), a woman's long-haired wig, and a wig with braids. Adding role-playing to instruction always engages students both directly involved in the activity and watching it. It doesn't take much to provide a prop or costume for the participants, but this does add significantly to the memorable quality of the activity.

Graduation gowns are a wonderful costume for the judge to wear in any teacher-developed trial enactment. What is more engaging, more able to include argumentation using text-based references, and more likely to include a large number of students than a mock trial? This is also a format that most students are familiar with in some degree. It is a perfect way to integrate the information from a literary or historical work and allow students to manipulate the material and present it in their own words.

Often a text's conflict can be stretched into a public trial incident. Trials can be conducted by changing the ending of books, stories, or historical events by asking *What if . . . ?* An example might be changing the ending of Steinbeck's (1937/2002) *Of Mice and Men*. Instead of having Lennie shot, what if he were arrested and put on trial? Using the facts and information from the book as the source of evidence, how would the defense and prosecution build their cases? How would witnesses respond under questioning? What witnesses would each side call to strengthen their arguments? What would they wear? What body language would they use? The CCSS are intensely interested in having students build and defend arguments that are text-based. The trial scenario is a powerful way to showcase these very skills. This activity would blend the use of dress-up props with the use of a graduation gown, and the use of critical thinking with emotional impact to facilitate a very real higher-order thinking exercise.

With historical settings, trials could be conducted based on information that came to light later in the story and used as if it were available at the time of the trial. Many influential trials in history could be researched and presented in this more lively form rather than in a written report. There is nothing like a gavel and a black-robed judge to create a dramatic atmosphere in a classroom. Every teacher needs to have such props at his or her disposal!

Feathered masks are wonderful props for raising the formality of readers' theater presentations, and they can also be used for the chorus in Greek plays and for any character who is speaking from a spiritual dimension. A mask can represent an inner voice or two conflicting inner voices that are debating within the mind of any character or historical personality. Using such a physical symbol of an invisible reality helps our reluctant, concrete-thinking students make the jump into the world of abstraction more easily.

What Teachers Can Learn From This Phenomenon

This brief look at trends in consumerism with regard to Halloween is just a small peek at how fascinated people are with dressing up and playing pretend. The savvy teacher intent on engaging and grabbing the attention of young learners would do well to consider taking advantage of any and all such fascinations to use as hooks, props, and supplemental material when constructing lessons. The more "serious" the learning becomes—and the Common Core State Standards can be easily viewed as very serious learning indeed—the more welcome and necessary is the need for novelty, and a lightening of tone will help our students stay on a rigorous course. Chapter 7, "Outrageous Teaching" (page 107), contains many such examples of how the use of props and dress-up exercises can be initiated to engage and help scaffold the learning for all students, particularly our most reluctant ones.

Let Them Be the Book

Sometimes we need to entice our most reluctant readers and writers to keep reading, to keep writing, and to keep trying to be a part of the class and participate. In large textual commitments of class time, such as the study of a novel or thematic project, how a teacher sustains interest and engagement is paramount to success. As teachers, it is our job to not only plan what our students should do to work toward successfully reaching standards, but to plan what we will do to see that they can and will continue to make their way. This activity, heavy on props and dress up, does both.

Reading To Kill a Mockingbird

To Kill a Mockingbird by Harper Lee (1960) is one of the finest mainstays of the unwritten literary canon accessed by schools for the past fifty years. Its focus on high moral conduct despite opposition from others provides lessons in courage, empathy, and truth that have resonated in the hearts of young readers over the decades. Because of the length of this text, however, teachers find themselves needing to continually rekindle the fire of engagement while guiding their students through the book. The following activity serves as an overlay to other assignments that complement the study of this novel, such as journaling, character study, plot line development, and exploration of themes and conflicts. It is not meant to be a substitute for any of the in-depth work that usually accompanies this book.

As we begin this unit, we offer our students the opportunity to participate in photo shoots to make a documentary of Jem and Scout's experiences while the book is being read. We explain how we intend to take pictures of them dressed in period clothing in locations within the school building or close by. This pictorial documentary will be created based on what they read and select as key material to understanding the book.

As the students read, they mark passages and give reasons why these passages are important enough to be photographed and made part of the documentary. All student choices for events to be photographed are then placed on sticky notes and put on the board in chronological order. When students decide on a good scene, they are to add the caption that would be most appropriate as well. Captions should be quotes taken from the text, along with page numbers. Everyone should be responsible for offering at least five suggestions. Duplicates are discarded, and students then discuss which ones are good enough to use, based on their importance to the story and the possibility that they can be realistically caught on film. We all collaborate in these decisions. Students argue for their suggestions and defend their choices.

Because of the length of the text and the natural division of chapters, this activity will take two sessions—the first one covering chapters 1–11 and the second covering chapters 12–31 of the novel. Students are given opportunities to choose the character they want to be by putting their names in bowls, boxes, or hats labeled with the names of the main characters. There is no pressure to memorize lines or do any acting since we will be simply photographing them in a frozen tableau. Most students who are usually reluctant to volunteer are willing to participate under these low-stress conditions. Some scenes demand many characters while others have only a couple. Brainstorming what props would be necessary, what setting could most likely fit the scenes, and how the characters should be placed and dressed usually engages everyone's enthusiasm.

Another decision to be made is the format in which the documentary should be created. Does the class want to make a PowerPoint presentation? A physical exhibit on three-sided display boards? What other technologies do students want to use to present their documentary? A movie trailer? Who will be working on this? Students should have a say in how this should be presented.

An invitational gallery walk is a great way to celebrate the creation of their documentary. Move the displays to the library for a day, and invite students from other classes who have read the book. As visitors walk through, they are urged to check out the pictures and ask their student hosts any questions. If the documentary is in digital form, guests are invited to class to watch and then discuss their observations as a group. Later we all write our reflection sheets on the whole process.

Rosa Guy: High-Interest Content

The most effective lessons for students who are highly dependent on visual clues for understanding involve active participation and variation in delivery; they creatively entice students to look, think, act, and react in a new manner. Building units that place students in roles is a great way to accomplish this.

The Friends by Rosa Guy (1983) is a novel that freshmen and sophomores as well as younger students really enjoy. It is easy to develop a series of activities for this book in which the students take the roles of school counselors who deal with the characters' problems and provide alternative ways to handle conflicts common to most teenagers. They write reports, letters to parents, summaries of behavior, case studies, and simulated group counseling sessions. They can discuss scenarios in which so-called friends act any way but friendly and then judge them against a chart of what they collectively decide are qualities of true friendship. A final comparative assignment involving the analysis of material from an informational text would be to have students read sections from the book *New Kids in Town: Oral Histories of Immigrant Teens* by Janet Bode (1992). Shorter texts such as poems based on themes that run through the book also make good companion pieces. A few poems that would work well with *The Friends* might be "We Real Cool" by Gwendolyn Brooks; "Linked" by Naomi Shihab Nye; and "Hanging Fire" by Audre Lorde. One final suggestion might be pairing the book with selections from the collection in the multicultural anthology *Coming of Age in America* edited by Mary Frosch (1994).

One aim of using material that is of high interest to students no matter its complexity is to solicit much better writing, collaborating, speaking, and thinking. When students succeed in these circumstances, their expectation of what they are capable of achieving is lifted up a couple of notches. First comes success, then comes motivation and the willingness to put forth effort.

Song Lyrics: An Excellent Strategy for Reluctant Readers

For many reluctant learners, music is the ultimate novelty in the classroom. Making good use of music is one great way to ease into close-reading habits those students who have little confidence in their ability to understand complex, abstract, or metaphorical material. Today, it is easy to retrieve lyrics to most any song ever released. The ease with which a person can find Internet sites that suggest songs to fit all varieties of themes and topics is well known, and equipment is no longer an issue. Most of us have access to smartphones, tablets, iPods, and computers—there are many more ways to bring music into our classrooms than there ever were before.

Carol Lloyd Rozansky, education professor at Columbia College, Chicago, makes the point that "lyrics and music of popular songs can represent alternative perspectives to the dominant ideologies of a particular time or place. As such, they can be used effectively in classrooms to provide the voices rarely heard in textbooks" (Lloyd, 2003). Rozansky defines the term *critical literacy* as "reading the world"—being able to understand how power structures work and how to function within those structures with clarity and a sense of choice.

Song lyrics that evolve from historical times of conflict and revolution can give us a particularly vivid view and perspective. The emotional impact of music can give a student a deeper understanding of a historical event or conflict than a sterile summarized paragraph of statistics over the same event could ever do. Many of these songs arise from those who champion the causes of those on the margins of society. Many of our students can easily relate to them. Examples of songs that are appropriate for lessons dealing with the environment, history, economics, government policies and practices, racism and racial issues, and international events and situations may be found in Rozansky's article (Lloyd, 2003). This article taps artists from all music genres and eras. Table 5.1 contains a chart that lists songs and designates discipline areas that would be appropriate for their use.

The social and cultural trends and the causes and effects our human actions have put into motion are documented not only in song but also in art, movies, and all variety of media, as well as in printed articles filled with hard data. When we consider tapping into all these areas, we enrich and challenge our students to consider looking at their world through a wider lens. This inclusion of textual material that resonates so strongly with our students reflects an understanding of how important it is to draw on those areas of interest that hold students' attention. Every young person—especially one reluctant to participate—is grateful to the teacher who brings music into the usually quiet classroom and celebrates traditional learning in this novel way.

Table 5.1: Summary of Songs and Topics to Which They Pertain

Artist, Song	Topics					
	Environment	U.S. History	Economics	Government Policies, Practices	Racism, Racial Issues	International Events, Conditions
Chapman, "Rape of the World"	●					
Chapman, "Subcity"			●	●	●	
Chapman, "Nothin' Yet"		●			●	
Collins, "Another Day in Paradise"			●			
Country Joe & the Fish, "Fixin' to Die Rag"		●	●	●		
Dylan, "God on Our Side"		●		●		
Gaye, "Mercy, Mercy Me"	●					
Gaye, "What's Going On?"		●		●		
Griffith, "Trouble in the Fields"		●	●			
Guthrie, "Deportee"		●	●		●	●
Guthrie, "I Ain't Got No Home"		●	●			
Guthrie, "Ludlow Massacre"		●	●			
Hornsby, "The Way It Is"		●	●	●	●	
Lennon, "Imagine"		●		●		●
Little Village, "Do You Want My Job?"						●

CONTINUED →

Artist, Song	Topics					
	Environment	U.S. History	Economics	Government Policies, Practices	Racism, Racial Issues	International Events, Conditions
Marley, "Buffalo Soldier"		●		●	●	
Marley, "Get Up, Stand Up"				●	●	●
Mellencamp, "Rain on the Scarecrow"		●	●			
Mitchell, "Big Yellow Taxi"	●		●			
Public Enemy, "Fight the Power"					●	
Rage Against the Machine, "Without a Face"		●	●		●	●
Robertson, "Ghost Dance"		●		●	●	
Sainte-Marie, "My Country . . ."		●	●	●	●	
Stevens, "Where Do the Children Play?"	●					
Sting, "They Dance Alone"				●		●
They Might Be Giants, "Your Racist Friend"					●	
U2, "Sunday, Bloody Sunday"				●	●	●

Source: Carol Lloyd Rozansky, 2003.

Many more current lyrics could be added to this list, but it is a good starting place for teachers who might be more familiar with many of these artists than they will be with those currently at the top of the charts. Asking students to add to the list throughout the school year is a great ongoing challenge many of them would love to take. Many hip-hop lyrics are some of the strongest and most sincere about social issues available today.

Music is by nature an organic engagement tool that easily leads students to accept the challenge of tackling more difficult material. Its ability to serve as a scaffolding mechanism cannot be overstated.

Scaffolding Strategies for Reluctant Learners

The purpose of scaffolding students' reading and writing experiences is to help them bridge gaps in their ability to make comprehensive connections. Using scaffolding for literacy efforts is like using training wheels to help a child learn to ride a bicycle. Problems arise when the training wheels are given too much emphasis and status, when we don't help students get over their fear they will fall without them, and when we don't recognize the temporary quality in their usefulness. The seasoned teacher knows how to select and use scaffolding strategies when they are warranted and helps students see how these strategies are good for some situations and not for others.

If we are to build flexibility into student approaches to a reading or writing assignment for later transfer, we need to present students with a wide variety of ways to attack the material and avoid crowning one method king over another. The five-paragraph essay format is just one of those scaffolding approaches that has been royally and often rigidly accepted as the premier structure to teach students how to write, despite all the research showing its ineffectiveness. Much has been written about the artificiality of the five-paragraph essay and its inability to reflect any real writing we read in and outside the classroom. Yet, it persists in part due to its formulaic nature, which makes it easy to teach, grade, and use for testing purposes. We should teach it, but we shouldn't allow our students to think that this is the essence of writing and communicating in print. So that we don't confuse our students with what real writing and reading actually are, we need to provide ample time and opportunity for unencumbered reading and writing to occur during the class period. Decisively, we need to put away our helpful sheets with boxes or columns to fill in, outlines to be constructed, and specific formats and formulas to follow at the proper time, and let them read and write.

How Scaffolding Can Speed Progress

All students need to understand what they are asked to do in class and how best to do it. Years of experience has brought me to see the importance of leading students through their senses first when introducing any new material, moving them from the concrete to the abstract. Our teaching habits tend to do this backward. For example, research suggests using word problems as a basis for teaching addition and subtraction concepts rather than teaching computational skills first and then applying them to solve problems (Carpenter & Moser, 1983). Being exposed to a large variety of addition and subtraction situations (compare, combine, equalize, change added to, and change taken from) before moving to the rote memorization of computation formulas would lead to a stronger base of understanding.

Expressive Reading: A Nonjudgmental Fluency Builder

One area of importance to literacy success that we've often found marginalized in the upper grades is reading with expression—reading with the emotion that fits the words. Frequent repeated practice and feedback of expressive reading are found to have a significant impact on accuracy, fluency, and comprehension (Broaddus & Worthy, 2002; Rasinski, 2003). This isn't easy to embed into the middle and high school class periods. The teacher possessing a sense of humor and the ability to express encouragement while providing a safe environment has the best chance of seeing this effort produce results.

Dramatic reading also helps students feel more confident, focus longer on the material, and sharpen their decision-making skills. Opportunities to record their reading and listen to see if their reading does actually sound like their spoken language are valuable experiences at every stage of student growth.

Steve Peha (2003), president of the education consulting company Teaching That Makes Sense, publishes a website by the same name (www.ttms.org) that is a great free resource for many effective literacy strategies that apply to every content area. The link between expressive reading and comprehension has been well documented (Rasinski, 2003) but seldom emphasized, because as students grow older, most reading is assigned as quiet reading. Peha (2011) identifies and discusses strategies that students can use to make their reading more expressive:

- Go slow (slow down your normal reading pace—just because you know the words doesn't mean you should go fast)

- Repeat until it's complete (if you mess up, repeat the entire sentence until it's correct)

- Start high then go low (begin a sentence on a high pitch and gradually lower it as you get to the end)

- Character high, narrator low (when reading dialogue, read the spoken parts by raising your volume and pitch then lower your voice on the "he said, she said" parts)

- Use a big pause at a period, small pause at a comma

- Emphasize a key word

Students should be encouraged to pull favorite passages from their independent reading to use on Book Talk Day, a periodically scheduled activity during which students select passages from books they like and read them with expression. By doing this, they are not only practicing their own reading skills; by selecting a memorable short selection they are providing the class with suggestions of good books some might want to read in the future. This is a great shift from the old-fashioned oral book report, in which students simply tell the story to the class.

An even faster approach at moving students from droning away at a passage to making the words come alive is the Dynamic Daisy. To introduce this strategy, have students pair up and give them copies of a short piece of writing and a Dynamic Daisy Clapper or a Bobby Blowout. Of course, you could use other items similar to these, so long as they are novel to the usual classroom situation, able to make noise, and have a movable part. Tell them we are all going to read the passage in our robot voices. Then have students follow along as you read the passage in a deadpan, uninflected voice. When you are finished, show them your Dynamic Daisy Clapper and explain that once a person hears this sound, the robot voice dissolves and the alive voice kicks in. Have a student clap the Daisy next to you and then read the passage with feeling, life, and expression! Here is an example of how a teacher's humor, energy, and effort to get across a point at his or her own expense—a teacher's soft skills—makes it comfortable for students to appear silly in order to experience the physical and cognitive difference between expressive and unexpressive reading, a very effective key to comprehension.

After you've modeled this exercise, ask the students to read the passage out loud to their partners in their robot voices and to change voices only when their partners clap their Daisies. After both members of the pairs have had a chance to practice both their robot voice and their dynamic voice, ask for volunteers to show the class the difference between their own robot and dynamic voices. Discuss how much better it is to read with expression. Hang Dynamic Daisy in a place of honor somewhere in your room to use when a student needs to be reminded to read with more expression.

First Chapters Reading Day

First Chapters Reading Day is the best way we have found to help reluctant students decide what books they would like to read independently. In preparation for this day, we visit with our school librarian and request that a cart be filled with thirty to forty books, both fiction and nonfiction, that are considered the highest-interest books in our school's collection. We are not concerned as much about reading level as we are about interest level. We will be using these books for one class period with as many classes as we have determined to be appropriate for this activity. All books will be returned by the end of the day.

Go to reproducible page 167, First Chapters Reading Day, to view the cards that students can use to document their reading. During this class period, students are invited to test out some of the books available in the library and to make a few judgment statements about them. They can choose any book they like, but they may only read the first chapter! Afterward, they must fill out the recommendation card and put the book back on the cart or table and pick up another to review. The groans that erupt when students must put the books back is the sweetest music to a teacher's ears. And, the requirement to read only the first chapter appeals to reluctant readers, who feel overwhelmed at times when confronted with the responsibility of reading an entire book. Anyone can get through one chapter! If you like it you can go back later and check it out, but if you don't like it, who cares? It's no skin off your nose as they say! The opportunity to choose a skinny book over a fat one or nonfiction over fiction are other reasons reluctant readers find this activity to their liking.

The review card has many functions other than just documenting the fact students are on task. By asking students to evaluate and judge what they feel about the book, they are gently using those higher-order thinking skills that are so necessary when addressing more difficult activities. They are asked to judge the book's difficulty in Goldilocks fashion—"too easy," "too hard," "just right!" They are asked to suggest who would be interested in it. They are asked if they would like to read more. Then they are asked to briefly summarize what they found out in the first chapter. By being asked to comment on the book's strengths and weaknesses, students often find themselves commenting on author style, tone, point of view, diction, and so forth. These sheets give the teacher a wealth of information about the student as a reader as well as his or her reading tastes and abilities.

Unpacking a Poem Visually

Tapping into the visual strengths of our students is the fast track to helping them deal with literary terms, academic vocabulary, and abstract concepts—especially for our reluctant learners. Often, certain genres appear daunting and mysterious to many of our students, and poetry is certainly one of those genres. Many students come to us with the conviction that they will never be able to figure out what poems mean and so see no reason for even trying. Offering them the tool of visualizing what they are reading will always be of value for struggling readers, especially when it comes to the challenge of unpacking poetry. Here it serves as a lifesaver for many a floundering student.

My poem "Egg Cartons" (Schreck, 2006) shown in figure 5.2 on page 89 is structured around a central metaphor. By having students draw the metaphor and label the connections—in other words, play with the poem by sketching and questioning—the teacher's job of explaining how an extended metaphor can work is made much more enjoyable and successful. I suggest teachers pull out the poems from their static position in textbooks and make "opportunity sheets" like the one shown in the figure. The opportunity sheet allows students to mark up, label, draw, and comment on the poems or text selections in a much more hands-on manner than simply looking at a page in a book or at a screen. Teachers can make these by copying the poem or short passage they want students to study and pasting it on another piece of paper that allows for plenty of white space. Making these for students is not really time consuming, and provides a much more engaging vehicle for studying the piece than a traditional textbook or company-produced worksheet does.

Finding Metaphors, Similes, and Details in a Nonfiction Piece

The transfer of learning from one context to another is the goal of all educators. One way to help this process along is to give examples of how concepts common to one discipline can be found in another—in this case, literary terms. Usually students associate literary terms with language arts classes and seldom think that a metaphor or simile can turn up in biology, history, math, or any other discipline's material. Our goal in the next activity is to show how effective literary devices can be used to clarify meaning outside the parameters of poetry and fictional writing. The following is a selection from an article written for *Missouri Conservationist* magazine (Nelson, 1996) on the topic of hummingbirds, followed by suggested directions for demonstrating how metaphors can bring subjects to life most vividly:

> There are over 300 different kinds of hummingbirds. Most live in Central or South America, but about 17 kinds live in North America.
>
> In Missouri, the most common hummingbird is the ruby-throated, although you may see others when they come through Missouri on north and south migrations.
>
> The ruby-throated hummingbird is just under 4-inches long and weighs 3 grams, or slightly more than a dime. You could mail nine hummingbirds for the price of a single first-class stamp.
>
> Male ruby-throated hummingbirds have special feathers on their throat, called a gorget (gore-jet'). The gorget looks black in the shade, but when the sun shines on it, it turns a brilliant ruby red. It is used to impress and attract females. Both males and females have bright green backs and white breasts.
>
> Hummingbirds build a walnut-sized nest using soft plant fibers, moss and lichens (like-ins), all held together with spider web. Using spider web allows the nest to stretch, so it grows right along with the growing babies. A female hummingbird usually lays only two eggs, mostly because that's all there's room for in the tiny nest. Also, she would have a difficult time feeding more than two babies.
>
> The eggs are about the size of the eraser on the end of a pencil, and newly hatched babies are about the size of a pea. They grow so quickly that they are ready to leave the nest when only 3 or 4 weeks old.
>
> Hummingbirds have really long beaks and tongues. In fact, their tongues are twice as long as their beak. They use their tongues to reach deep into flowers to soak up the sweet liquid, called nectar. On an average day, a hummingbird will visit about 1,500 flowers. They will also eat tiny insects for protein. . . .

According to *The Hummingbird Book* by Donald and Lillian Stokes (as cited in Nelson, 1996):

- Hummingbirds beat their wings about 78 times per second. During a display dive, their wings can beat up to 200 times per second.
- They take about 250 breaths per minute.

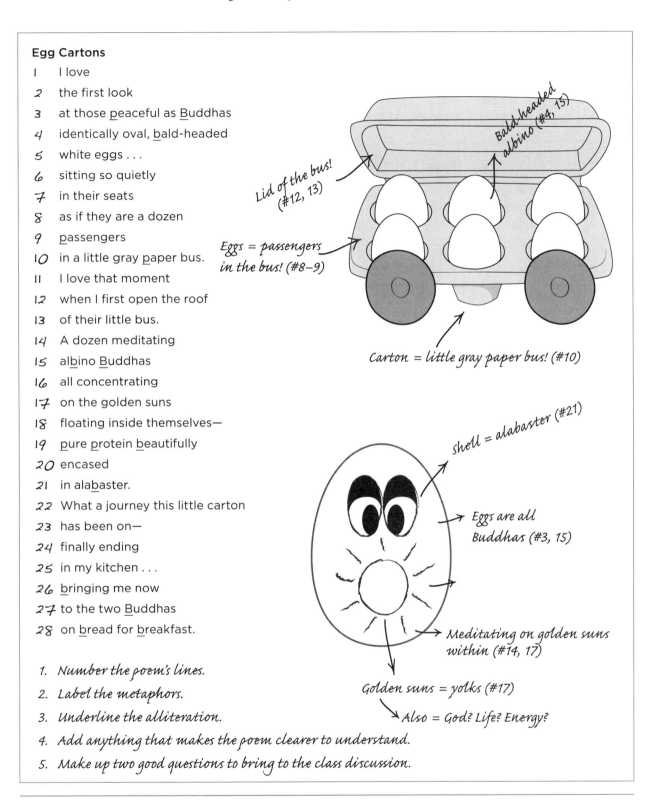

Egg Cartons

1. I love
2. the first look
3. at those <u>peaceful</u> as <u>Buddhas</u>
4. identically oval, <u>bald-headed</u>
5. white eggs . . .
6. sitting so quietly
7. in their seats
8. as if they are a dozen
9. <u>passengers</u>
10. in a little gray <u>paper</u> bus.
11. I love that moment
12. when I first open the roof
13. of their little bus.
14. A dozen meditating
15. al<u>b</u>ino <u>B</u>uddhas
16. all concentrating
17. on the golden suns
18. floating inside themselves—
19. <u>p</u>ure <u>p</u>rotein <u>b</u>eautifully
20. encased
21. in ala<u>b</u>aster.
22. What a journey this little carton
23. has been on—
24. finally ending
25. in my kitchen . . .
26. <u>b</u>ringing me now
27. to the two <u>B</u>uddhas
28. on <u>b</u>read for <u>b</u>reakfast.

1. *Number the poem's lines.*
2. *Label the metaphors.*
3. *Underline the alliteration.*
4. *Add anything that makes the poem clearer to understand.*
5. *Make up two good questions to bring to the class discussion.*

Bald-headed albino (#4, 15)

Lid of the bus! (#12, 13)

Eggs = passengers in the bus! (#8–9)

Carton = little gray paper bus! (#10)

shell = alabaster (#21)

Eggs are all Buddhas (#3, 15)

Meditating on golden suns within (#14, 17)

Golden suns = yolks (#17)

Also = God? Life? Energy?

Figure 5.2: Unpacking the egg-carton poem.

- Their hearts beat about 1,260 times per minute.
- They have 1,500 feathers.
- They consume half their body weight in food every day. That would be like an average kid eating about 40 to 50 pounds of food a day.

- During migration, they must fly 500 miles nonstop over the Gulf of Mexico to reach their wintering grounds in Mexico and Central America. To make the trip, they must eat enough so they weigh 1½ times their usual weight.

- They can fly at speeds of 60 miles per hour and can fly forward, backward, up, down, sideways, and even upside down, briefly, but they can't walk.

Here is the exercise:

1. Ask students to read the piece to themselves silently.

2. Ask them to turn the paper over when finished and jot down anything that they remember having read about hummingbirds.

3. As we share what students remembered, we write those facts on the board or overhead.

4. Review what metaphors, similes, and descriptive details are and how they function to clarify an idea or fact with their comparisons. Ask the class if any of the facts it wrote down were examples of these terms.

5. We return to the article, circle all the examples of these literary terms, and discuss how they help us more vividly understand the facts the author is relating to us.

6. With the class, work at coming up with more metaphors and similes that could have been used in the piece to make the material even more memorable.

Conclusion

Every year when we are given our class rosters, it is as if we are also given a velvet bag that is filled with uncut, unpolished jewels—our eager and reluctant learners. They are in all stages of brilliance when they come to us. It is our responsibility and delight to activate our soft skills and use them as a polishing cloth to help bring out their best. This way we will supply new, novel ways to hook our students' attention, make connections to the material they are studying, and provide a fresh approach to old exercises. If we don't utilize our creativity and passion for our work—our soft skills—to counteract the effects of boredom and misunderstanding, the jewels in that velvet bag will never reveal their full luster.

Chapter Six

Creative and Critical Thinking Approaches to Literacy

There is an urgent necessity to develop problem-solving skills in our students using both creative, or divergent, and critical, or convergent, techniques when responding to or manipulating written or spoken materials. The pressure to develop such skills is changing the way we teach and the way we move toward understanding how students learn. Here we will take a closer look at these higher-order thinking skills and see how they relate to our customary assignments and expectations for student products. Many teachers are surprised when confronted with examples of what rigorous, higher-order thinking assignments actually look like in the classroom and are eager for methods to systematically strengthen both creative and critical thinking abilities in our students.

Creative thinking can be defined as a process of exploring multiple avenues of actions or thoughts. It is often described as "divergent" or "lateral" thinking. Edward de Bono (1967) is considered a renowned expert in the field of creativity and a staunch proponent of the deliberate teaching of thinking as a subject in school. He coined the phrase "lateral thinking" in his book *The Use of Lateral Thinking*, which urges thinkers to give more attention to many possibilities and approaches to an issue instead of following a single one. From Rudolf Flesch (1955), writing consultant and author of *Why Johnny Can't Read—And What You Can Do About It*, we get the sage viewpoint that the essence of creative thinking resides in the understanding that just doing things one way because that's the way they've always been done isn't such a great idea. This viewpoint touches on the role of creative thought in the act of questioning—a main focus of this chapter. Creative thinking is, most importantly, a special form of problem solving in which the solution is independently created rather than learned with assistance.

Another man who is known for popularizing a term often used when referring to creative thinking is Alex Osborn. In his 1953 book *Applied Imagination*, he first uses and defines the process we now refer to as brainstorming—where a group of people spontaneously offer a large quantity of ideas to form a working list on how to solve a problem. Most teachers who incorporate brainstorming into their instructional practices do so on a limited basis. Creative thinking is not simply brainstorming, nor is it simply lateral thinking. As it relates to student learning, creative thinking moves away from just repeating what one has read or heard and entering into the position of using what one has learned to create something new. When students take a text that is in the form of a short story or a novel and manipulate it into a new form, such as a play or a musical composition, they are thinking creatively. Visit www.brainstorming.co.uk for more information dedicated to explaining creative thinking and brainstorming techniques.

Critical thinking, on the other hand, is a more familiar term to most educators. Critical thinking has been the mainstay of our efforts to educate students to think clearly and concisely. The Foundation for Critical Thinking refers to critical thinking as a mode of thinking—about any subject, content, or problem—in which the thinker improves the quality of his or her thinking by skillfully analyzing, assessing, and reconstructing it. Critical thinking is self-directed, self-disciplined, self-monitored, and self-corrective. It presupposes assent to rigorous standards of excellence and mindful command of their use. It entails effective communication and problem-solving abilities and a commitment to overcome our native egocentrism and sociocentrism. Richard Paul, director of research and professional development at the Center for Critical Thinking and chair of the National Council for Excellence in Critical Thinking, and Linda Elder, president of the Foundation for Critical Thinking and executive director of the Center for Critical Thinking describe the attributes of a well-cultivated critical thinker as follows:

- raises vital questions and problems, formulating them clearly and precisely;
- gathers and assesses relevant information, using abstract ideas to interpret it effectively;
- comes to well-reasoned conclusions and solutions, testing them against relevant criteria and standards;
- thinks open-mindedly within alternative systems of thought, recognizing and assessing, as need be, their assumptions, implications, and practical consequences; and
- communicates effectively with others in figuring out solutions to complex problems. (Paul & Elder, 2008b, p. 4)

Students Need Both

Together, both creative and critical thinking serve as our best tools to cope with the challenges and problems that our complex world brings us. We need to help strengthen both skill sets and modes of operation in our students.

The term *imagination* is often used in place of *creativity*, as in the work of Paul and Elder (2008b), who aptly state, concerning the need for both types of skills, that "imagination and reason are an inseparable team. They function best in tandem, like the right and left legs in walking or running. Studying either one separately only ensures that both remain mysterious and puzzling, or, just as unfortunate, are reduced to stereotype and caricature" (p. 6). If our schools' instructional programs serve to strengthen one thinking leg at the expense of the other—to exercise one leg and leave the other untouched—our ability to walk well, much less to run with any speed into the future, is severely hampered. The following sections examine ways to incorporate both thinking mechanisms on this journey to ensure better literacy instruction for all.

Bloom's Taxonomy

There isn't a teacher who has gone through traditional or unconventional teacher training who is not familiar to some degree with Bloom's taxonomy. This model, which Benjamin Bloom published in 1956, classifies thinking into six levels of complexity. Since then, this system of categorizing and tiering thinking has been universally accepted as one of education's gold standards and used as a basis for curriculum writing and study.

In an effort to make Bloom's taxonomy more relevant to the 21st century learner, a student of Bloom's—Lorin Anderson—headed a group effort to update and modernize the system. Their efforts, termed the Revised Bloom's Taxonomy (Anderson, 2002), made few but significant changes to the classification, as shown in figure 6.1.

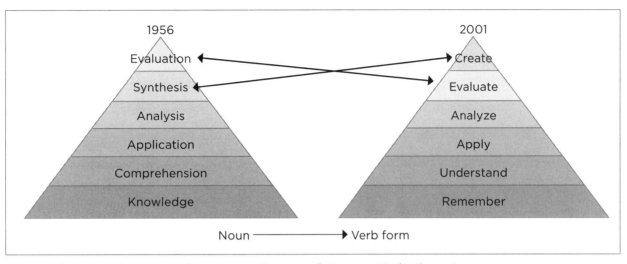

Source: *Leslie Owen Wilson, ED, Professor Emerita, University of Wisconsin. Used with permission.*

Figure 6.1: Changes to Bloom's taxonomy from 1956 to 2001.

Note the change from nouns to verbs to describe the levels of the taxonomy and the change from *synthesis* to *create*, and the exchange of the two uppermost levels, with *create* now at the top. Although we all acknowledge creativity as one of the levels of thinking we want our students to learn and to have opportunities to hone, most teachers are at a loss as to how to accomplish this. Most see this mandate to exercise student creative-thinking skills as an add-on that takes away precious time they need to ensure that content is covered sufficiently for students to score well on upcoming standardized tests.

Bloom's taxonomy isn't the only place where creative thinking, along with critical thinking, has been given a prominent place. The Partnership for 21st Century Skills (2011) states:

> Learning and innovation skills increasingly are being recognized as the skills that separate students who are prepared for increasingly complex life and work environments in the 21st century, and those who are not. A focus on creativity, critical thinking, communication and collaboration is essential to prepare students for the future.

These four elements need to run through all instruction—especially throughout literacy plans. Comprehension is built on this four-pronged foundation. But before considering how to get both of our thinking legs working on our educational track, let's check what words or phrases come naturally to us as we write out our lesson plans, orally instruct our students in what we would like them to do, or develop rubrics based on skills we would like to see measured for mastery.

Table 6.1, based in part on the work of Harris (1998), is a compilation of terms that are associated with the words *creative* and *critical* in relation to thinking activities. Using the reproducible form of this table on page 168, indicate in the yes and no columns the terms that describe the mode of thinking you use most and least often in your assignments, assessments, and oral prompting. Make a note in your plan book to employ those you marked as least used when appropriate when creating your lessons.

Table 6.1: Creative and Critical Thinking Skills

Creative Thinking Skills	Yes	No	Critical Thinking Skills	Yes	No
Flexible			Comparative		
Generative			Analytic		
Original			Classifying		
Lateral			Vertical		
Employing suspended judgment			Employing judgment		
Diffuse			Focused		
Subjective			Objective		
Right brained			Left brained		
Fluent			Sequencing		
Elaborative			Based on cause and effect		
Involving brainstorming			Involving patterning		
Modifying			Webbing		
Employing imagery			Employing analogy		
Associative			Linear		
Listing attributes			Inductive		
Metaphorical			Forecasting		
Involving forced relationships (matching things that don't usually go together to make something new)			Planning		
Stimulating curiosity			Hypothesizing		
Having no answer			Involving a specific answer		
Employing richness and novelty			Reasoning		
Using divergent thinking			Using convergent thinking		
Visual			Verbal		
Involving possibility			Involving probability		
Using the phrase *yes, and* . . .			Using the phrase *yes, but* . . .		

Dance of the Divergent and Convergent Thinker

Divergent or creative thinking is characterized by generating a quantity of ideas without stopping to judge their viability, by combining and building on already stated ideas, and by seeking out what seem to be eccentric and even wild ideas. Convergent or critical thinking, on the other hand, is a deliberate attempt to check the feasibility of ideas. In convergent thinking, we generate criteria to be used to prioritize and evaluate ideas while always attempting to improve on suggestions. Students need to see both systems of thinking as equally important and their relationship to one another as cyclic; we generate ideas and evaluate them again and again.

When reading or hearing about the desired traits that should be present in the 21st century–educated student, again and again we hear a call for students who are able to think creatively and solve problems that don't yet exist. We are urged to develop ways to prepare our students for the unknown, yet are seldom shown how. One of the hopes that rides on the implementation of the Common Core State Standards is that we will open the educational door and move away from the old factory model of the Industrial Revolution into an era of teaching that will produce flexible, critical thinkers capable of taking on challenges than no other generation has been asked to, and act upon them in creative, new ways. First, we must familiarize ourselves with the kind of thinking that nurtures and stimulates innovative thought. That is what the preceding sections have ventured to accomplish. Next, we need to set up situations where students are presented with challenges and given opportunities to try out their creative wings, to see if any of their ideas can fly. The Fun Theory, which was originated by Volkswagen and states that fun is the easiest way to change people's behavior for the better, offers just such an opportunity. Blogger Jeff Glucker (2011) explains:

> The basic premise of the theory revolves around examining if people will do the right thing if that thing is made a bit more fun. Nevena Stojanovic from Serbia came up with a new way to put the Fun Theory to use when she devised a way to make young passengers more likely to wear their seatbelts. It's a simple idea, but a rather smart one. Stojanovic proposed that rear-seat entertainment systems fail to operate unless the car senses that the seatbelt has been inserted. If a kid wants to get his Yo Gabba Gabba fix, then he or she needs to buckle up. The entire concept is so basic that we're kind of surprised no automaker has put this into practice yet.

The most popular example of fun theory in action is the piano staircase—a set of subway stairs turned into a real-life piano to encourage people to use the stairs over the escalator. The results were that 66 percent more people used the stairs than had before (Rolighetsteorin, n.d.). Another experiment tests whether making a trash can sound like a fifty-foot-deep well would make people use it more often. The Fun Theory people now sponsor a contest to see what other great ideas have turned behaviors that are hard to change into fun activities. The results of Volswagen's contests and ideas of more ways to use the Fun Theory can be found on their website (www.thefuntheory.com).

We begin to whet our students' curiosity by showing a couple of the videos that show the fun theory in action and then explain that we are going to explore such a challenge ourselves. One of our main purposes in taking on this challenge is to teach our students how to best use their creative and critical thinking skills together.

The sequence in the following section is loosely mirrored after *The Foundations of Applied Imagination: An Introduction to the Osborn-Parnes Creative Problem Solving Process (CPS)* (Creative Education Foundation, 2011). We will be using it to provide the framework of our investigation into just what problem needs solving and how to best get it done. The process is a constant dance from divergent thinking, where many ideas are gathered, to convergent thinking, where ideas are then evaluated and selected:

1. (Divergent) Determine the challenge—We ask our students to make the longest list they can that gives examples of things that need to be changed in the classroom or school for the betterment of everyone. We suggest that they use stems to get started, such as:

- I wish . . .

- It would be great if . . .

- This school would be better if . . .

- A great idea would be . . .

- What we need here is . . .

We give them enough time to move from the immediate off-the-top-of-their-heads ideas to deeper, more unusual ones. We urge them to try out the following guidelines when making their statements: write as many statements as they possibly can, don't stop to judge how good or bad an idea is, don't be afraid to write down what you think would be a wild idea. Go for *quantity*!

2. (Convergent) Review and pare down the lists—First, ask students to go over their own lists and put a mark in front of any idea jotted down that they feel could play a part in arriving at its solution. We then have them turn to a partner, compare both their lists, and make another list with all of the marked ideas that the two came up with. This time, put a check next to the ones that both partners agree are really great ideas and make them happy inside.

3. (Divergent and convergent) Develop the megalist—Now we are opening up the discussion to the entire class and asking for all the really good ideas from all pairs of students. These are written on the board. When all pairs have submitted their favorite ideas, the students are asked to speak to their ideas. As a class we now determine the best challenge and two runners-up in case our first idea comes up against insurmountable obstacles. (We teach students to do this when they are deciding on a topic to write about or an argument to explore. We also do it ourselves—always have a backup plan.)

4. (Convergent) Check the facts—Using our agreed-upon first choice, we consider the problem in more depth by investigating its history—has this always been an issue? Is it a new problem that's recently come up? What efforts to solve it have already been tried, and how do people feel about this problem? Do people get emotional about it? Do only a few feel it's a problem? And how will we know when it is solved? We come to an agreement on a strong problem statement that is important, that the class can have influence over, and that it would like an imaginative way of solving. This problem statement will clarify just what needs to be changed, why, and what the solution is. We return to the fun theory examples to see how this will appear in the concrete. Nevena Stojanovic, for example, saw a need for young students to wear seat belts consistently.

5. (Divergent) Find the *fun* solution—In accordance with the theory that fun can change behavior, we seek out the many possible ways of applying a fun solution to our challenge. We attempt to make a long list of fun ways to solve our challenge problem. The same rules apply: quantity, no judging the value of an idea, thinking fearlessly, and entertaining even crazy ideas. Fresh ideas never surface until all the obvious ones are already on the table. That is why it is so important to allow enough time and cheerleading for our students to crack through the crust of their obvious ideas to access more original ones.

If necessary, we follow steps two and three once more to come up with three possible solutions to our challenge. Once students get used to the process, it doesn't take long, but does generate better-quality thinking and more interesting results.

6. (Divergent and convergent) Turn ideas into reality—Here we consider the actions needed to make this solution happen. Again we go to list making, but this time we are jotting down all that needs to happen so that our solution will succeed. We tell our students to cover all the possible bases:

   ○ What obstacles might we encounter?

   ○ Who might help us?

   ○ Who might object?

   ○ What jobs should be distributed to students?

   ○ What permissions need to be obtained?

   ○ When will we try out our plan?

   ○ How long will it take?

   ○ Do we need supplies?

   ○ How are we going to get them?

After generating and evaluating our lists, we create an action plan as a class.

This process can be used in any content area to produce active learning projects that have their origins in real issues that are important to students and adults alike. The feeling of empowerment through collaboration that such a process fosters engages students at a much deeper level than traditional instruction could ever do.

Try This

To broaden the scope of this exercise, ask your students to make lists of what needs to be changed in their neighborhoods, towns, or cities.

Strengthening Divergent Thinking

What we practice becomes both stronger and more easily duplicated later. The "cells that fire together, wire together" principle, or Hebb's law, is also summarized in the phrase "Use it or lose it." Both point to the natural law of neuroscience that explains that when the brain's neurons fire together, the tendency for them to repeat and form a pattern is heightened and strengthened with each firing. The more cells that fire at the same time, the stronger the connection. This is the brain's behavior that forms memories and learning. Interestingly, this can't be adequately achieved if the brain is in a stressed situation, another reason to provide a motivating, highly engaging environment so students can learn more efficiently.

If we want our students to make creative thinking come more easily and readily without our prompting, we need to give them short bursts of practice. While these types of exercises don't take much time, they do help cement the process in students' minds for the long run. We also need to tell them just what these types of exercises are meant to achieve in order to boost their significance.

That's Not a Stick, It's a . . .

A good way to have students experience what their minds do when they are asked to think creatively is to have them play the stick game. This game originates from the children's book *Not a Stick* by Antoinette Portis (2008).

This little book, with its companion book *Not a Box* (Portis, 2006), displays the abundant possibilities that a small child's mind can create when given only a stick or a box to play with. We have all seen small students who were more intrigued with the wrappings gifts came in than with the gifts themselves. To use the stick exercise in this class, we bring in a dowel rod or even a small wooden skewer. The first person says, "That's not a stick, it's a . . . ," and makes the gesture or motion that that word or phrase brings to mind. For example, it's a violin bow, a fencing sword, or a toothbrush, and so on. After the student makes the motion, other students are to guess what he or she is doing. Then the stick is given to the next student, who makes up a new gesture and then passes the stick to the next. The stick keeps moving from student to student, and if possible, another full round is made, pushing their imaginations even more. We often hear students saying that the previous idea was the same one they were going to use, and wondering what they will do now!

When we are finished, we discuss how our minds reacted to the exercise. We talk about how we built on one idea—say, for example, if a person used the stick as a musical instrument, we then would think of another musical instrument to use, or perhaps we would find ourselves moving to a completely different category, such as tools, or sports, or grooming.

Christina's World

Another activity, Christina's World, comes from a five-day workshop by Siri Lynn and Donna Luther (2011). We make color copies of Andrew Wyeth's (1948) painting *Christina's World*—one for each student. We discuss what the picture and its title could possibly mean. We may give background information about Christina having polio and talk about whether that piece of information changes anyone's ideas of the picture. We have magazines, construction paper, and so on ready. We decide to create a new world for Christina by cutting her out of the picture and putting her in a new one. Travel magazines are great for this activity. Or, if possible, a digital picture could be created from the original and added to another picture with a different setting that surely might change her life. Paragraphs comparing Christina's life before and after the change in setting are a natural writing activity.

A variation on this exercise would be for a student to bring in a picture of himself or herself, place it in various settings, and write about what happens and how, when, and why, because of these changes in place and circumstances.

If/Then

A simple two-word phrase that can trigger remarkable creative or critical thinking is *What if?* With its partner *What then?* teachers can guide student thinking quickly to considerations of possibilities not yet thought about and just as quickly to considerations of the cause and effect of those possibilities. This is the territory of the imagination at work. One great resource for parents and teachers alike is *Teaching Our Children to Think* by John Langrehr (2001), a clinical psychologist and expert in the field of helping improve children's thinking processes. This book has over two hundred exercises aimed at developing core thinking processes in every discipline that all students should master. One such exercise stretches the *What if?*

concept a step further by requiring that the *if* postulate be followed by a *then* statement. Simple as this may seem, the exercise of balancing a divergent thinking process with a convergent process is a great way to show how both abilities serve to refine thinking. Here are a few examples from this exercise (Langrehr, 2001):

1. If there were no more birds in the world, then . . .

2. If the earth no longer had a moon, then . . .

3. If there were no longer any oil deposits on earth, then . . .

4. If there were no longer bees on earth, then . . .

Students should be encouraged to make up sets of their own *if/then* statements that could be shared with the whole class. These statements are the genesis of short researched pieces that require students to do fact finding to arrive at quality responses. Although they appear to be deceptively easy to complete, the end results are far from cute little sentences. They are well-researched explanations of possible physical phenomena. The steps of this exercise (followed by an example) are as follows:

1. Students select the *if* stem of their choice.

2. They then make a list of what they think could be the consequences.

3. Then they go about hunting for facts that would actually be the scientific results of their stem.

4. Now they compose their paragraphs explaining what effects would result from their chosen stem.

5. After rereading their piece, they decide on a good summarizing statement to use as the second half, or *then*, of their original sentence and have this serve as the topic sentence to their paragraphs. They also look for the best place to mention either the best or the worst possible results from their original lists.

6. At the bottom of the page, they cite and give a ranking to each source used in their piece.

For example, suppose the stem a student is working with is *If there were no longer bees on earth, then* _____. The student would write the stem at the top of a piece of paper or screen and then add as many possible results of this phenomenon as she could think of. It doesn't matters how crazy, trivial, or nonsensical these results might be, the goal at this stage is quantity. Typing the stem into Google or another search engine, the student might also come up with references to Einstein's estimate that without bees the planet would survive for only four years. The student takes notes and makes sure to jot down where the articles she is reading originate, so that they can be retrieved again if necessary. If the student further consider this provocative statement attributed to Einstein, she might find the editorial "On Einstein, Bees, and Survival of the Human Race" by the entomologist Keith S. Delaplane (n.d.). Reading this will give her a far more accurate explanation of what would happen to bee-pollinated crops. More hunting would offer up Purdue Extension's 4-H Beekeeping Project (Purdue University, n.d.), with its section on the value of the honeybee that spells out in student-friendly terms the consequences of losing our bees. Never do we allow students to visit only one source, and this assignment is no exception. Equipped now with material from at least three different sources, our student begins the work of reporting her findings. This part will vary in complexity depending on the level of the writer's competency and maturity. Whatever the student's level, we urge him or her to stretch to do a little more than he thinks possible. This is where a teacher's knowledge of her students, plus her ability to instill confidence into them, makes the most difference in the quality of achievement they reach. We also teach students how to rate the credibility of their search results and ask them to give each reference a ranking when they turn in their notes and paper. This type of exercise is a good introductory lesson on cause and effect, as well as a critical analysis of source materials.

Try This

Choose three of the following verbs to use during the coming week. Set up where you will be using them in the sequence of your lessons and what types of products, using the verbs and content you provide, you will be requiring of students. Be sure to focus on explaining to students what critical or creative thinking process they are experimenting with when using these verbs.

combine	create	adapt	reinforce
compose	formulate	anticipate	structure
generalize	integrate	collaborate	substitute
modify	rearrange	compile	intervene
invent	design	devise	negotiate
plan	speculate	express	reorganize
substitute	rewrite	facilitate	validate

Moving From Critical to Creative

One of our essential instructional tasks is to design activities and create an environment that allow students opportunities to seamlessly engage in all manner of higher-order thinking experiences within a unit or lesson. We must guide students to become not only analyzers but also producers of knowledge.

What Does a Higher-Order Thinking Prompt Look Like?

Since the 1948 Convention of the American Psychological Association when Benjamin Bloom outlined his ladder of intellectual behaviors of learning from simple recall to the ability to synthesize information—his taxonomy—teachers-to-be have been studying this classification and attempting to apply it to their newly minted lesson plans. We have all cut our educational teeth on the concepts of lower- and higher-order thinking skills.

A fundamental characteristic of higher-order questions is that the teacher can't say beforehand what responses the students should give to them. There are guidelines and rubrics to form a response's parameters, but the actual answers to higher-order thinking questions can't be encased in a predetermined response. Examine the two prompts that follow:

1. For your final assignment of the unit, write an essay in which you discuss how a variety of texts shed light on the essential question, "What is a hero?" In your discussion, be sure to reference at least three texts we have read during this unit.

2. For your final assignment of the unit, write an essay in which you discuss your views about the essential question, "What is a hero?" In your discussion, focus primarily on your own life experiences for the framework of your essay. Also make reference to at least three texts we have read during this unit, but make sure that these references are only made in support of your own ideas or claims about the question.

The first prompt is a traditional type of essay prompt asking for recall, analysis, and probably some evaluation. The student is using text-based analysis but could also be simply regurgitating the thoughts of the three authors without making a strong case for one idea over another. The second prompt has synthesis as its goal. In lower-order thinking, we deal with others' ideas—we deal with the past. In higher-order thinking, we work with the material by filtering it through our individual lens; we create the future, especially when dealing with the acts of synthesis and creativity. We use the material of the texts to form a piece that supports a personal claim or position that arises from our own experience. In this process, we also are engaged in solidifying our own thinking and supporting that thinking with the ideas released through the texts. The distinction between the two appears slight but is extremely important. Students go for years cutting and pasting together other people's ideas to do their assignments. When confronted with the question "What do *you* really think about this issue?" most are speechless. By giving students the go-ahead to think for themselves and voice those thoughts, we are empowering them to take responsibility for their own learning. This does not disregard the need to gather text-based evidence that can clarify, substantiate, or refute their opinions. It shifts the student into a position of more control and autonomy over the material.

For years, we teachers have been trained to mistrust student judgment and opinion. We have asked our students to scrape any semblance of personal opinion or comments from papers they were writing in order to produce truly "academic" papers. However, in reality, it is the reverse. Lower-level thinking prompts are great for:

- Evaluating students' preparation and comprehension

- Diagnosing students' strengths and weaknesses

- Reviewing or summarizing content

The questions at higher levels of Bloom's taxonomy, however, are usually most appropriate for:

- Encouraging students to think more deeply and critically

- Problem solving

- Encouraging discussions

- Stimulating students' desire to seek information on their own

- Manipulating information to come up with something new

We need to feel more comfortable in making assignments that probe what our students think rather than require them to repeat what they've heard from us. It's obvious that these higher-order thinking products lend themselves to formative rather than summative assessment by their very nature.

Doing What You Study

This realization—the need for students to create as well as examine—changed the way I developed my instructional pedagogy, and in the last years of my classroom career, it became the guiding principle of my teaching. I saw the need for balance between studying content and creating content, taking the foundation of the old and making something new with it. I began looking at my content with new eyes. We *did* whatever we studied! If our unit was on the short story, we took what we learned and wrote short stories; if we examined how a piece of writing could be moved into another genre—a film, a play, a poem—we took a piece and manipulated it into something else. We basically followed the original template of how young students learn. We mimicked what *was* in order to produce what *could be*. We did this with everything we learned.

I also began looking around for samples of current material that could serve as exemplars for student activities—using different formats, framing content in new ways, finding engaging student-accessible examples to inspire students to produce their own work. Instead of only writing the normal résumé and traditional autobiographical piece, why not take one of the objects near and dear to students' hearts and hands—the iPhone, for example—and have them describe themselves in its terms? This activity pulls the critical thinking mind into the process of selecting and prioritizing important segments of their life and morphing them into the creative thinking metaphor of an inanimate object. See the reproducible If You Were an iPhone: An Electronic Autobiography on page 169 for an example of how to conduct this activity.

Problem Solving With *The Hunger Games*

We all know it is not easy to find reading that engages both adolescent girls and boys equally, has them asking for the sequel only a few days after, and sparks questions of depth and significance about character motivation, thematic irony, the human condition, and societal injustices. The contemporary adolescent bestseller *The Hunger Games* by Suzanne Collins (2010) is one of those books. When such a novel grips the imaginations and interests of our students, teachers should jump at the opportunity to plan instruction that taps into and expands their growing creative and critical thinking abilities. Any teacher who is assigned to cover the short story "The Lottery" by Shirley Jackson (1948) and fails to use the first chapter of *The Hunger Games* should have his or her instructional, standard-based mind examined! This match-up instantly grabs student minds and can be used to handle a cluster of objectives in a single swoop—comparison and contrast, symbolism, close reading, prediction, inference, point of view. More importantly though, is the engagement factor that the contemporary material adds and the way in which it serves to initiate more interest into the classic piece than it would have on its own merit. Every highly effective teacher I have ever met has been one whose radar is always up and tuned into finding that perfect match of textbook with outside material. This isn't the only use a literacy-minded teacher could find for the book.

The creators of the Common Core State Standards call strongly for more argument papers to be thoughtfully written by our students. Plenty of argument pieces are simply crying to be written using material that explores the social issues of poverty, classism, the devaluation of human life, the risks of extreme entertainment and desensitization to violence on TV, reality shows that blur the lines between real human suffering and being kicked off an island, war, famine, and haves versus have-nots—that is, material that mirrors problems in our own society.

Bena Kallick (2011), program director at Eduplanet, Inc., designs social learning institutes for educators who want to develop their thinking, their skills, and their capacity to revision their schools in light of 21st century teaching and learning. She states:

> Teachers will have to learn new strategies for helping all students reach a higher level of thinking. There will be more work on interpreting, explaining, reasoning with evidence, drawing conclusions,

summarizing, and evaluating. Lessons will have to be designed that address ways for teachers to develop the curiosity, investigations, and innovative thinking that the common core standards call for.

For those not acquainted with the plot of this postapocalyptic book in the tradition of Aldous Huxley's *Brave New World*, George Orwell's *1984*, Ray Bradbury's *Fahrenheit 451*, and Lois Lowry's *The Giver*, the title—*The Hunger Games*—refers to a yearly lottery called "the reaping" held in the twelve districts of what was once North America. Two students between the ages of twelve and eighteen from each district are chosen to go to the Capitol, the seat of a heavy-handed, Big Brother–type government, to participate in a televised competition in which the twenty-four participants—called tributes—are forced to eliminate each other, literally, with all citizens required to watch.

The purpose of the games is to show that no one, not even children, are outside the power of the Capitol's control. Using children as gladiators in a televised fight to the death is definitely reality TV gone terribly bad. The main character is an endearing sixteen-year-old girl who is adept at hunting, fishing, and using a bow and arrow, and who presents a strong female role model for readers. Her male counterpart is an equally appealing character with a strong moral compass. The book is a definite page-turner that is filled with action—violent, yes, but not so over the top that it would bring out armies of censors. Because the book resonates with a generation raised on reality shows like *Survivor* and *American Gladiator* and offers human characters reminiscent of avatars in a violent video game played by any average real-world gamer, it makes readers out of nonreaders instantly.

The film version that made its debut at the end of March 2012 has been a money-making blockbuster. But before this movie came out, I was aware of the gripping ability of the novel to hook readers and keep them hooked, and I purchased thirty copies for a young teacher and her inner-city students in a Kansas City high school. A book virtually none of the students were familiar with when they first turned its pages soon became a household name among teenagers across the country. For once, these students were on the cutting edge of a national phenomenon. For once, they were set loose to use their higher-order thinking abilities in a fresh, relevant project that demanded thoughtful planning and creativity.

Using this material as the stepping-off place into literacy instruction, there is ample room to build activities that strengthen skills, engage all learners, give opportunities for all learning styles to be exercised, and put life into instruction. This portfolio project could easily be extended as the students' reading progresses to include scenarios asking for strategies that our tribute could use to get out of dangerous circumstances, examples of gifts, tools, or help he or she could request from outside mentors, reflective journals of specific situations, and products formatted in multimedia portfolios. The interviews included in this activity would make great in-class performances to be judged by a basic speech rubric. They would satisfy the objectives in school curricula for public-speaking opportunities. You could also request video representations of certain sequences.

Two of the most appealing elements of the first book of Collins's trilogy are the imagination and constant surprises that show up in the arena where the actual games take place. This is the place where the tributes are turned loose to kill each other off until only one remains to hold the title of victor. It is an artificially constructed space enclosed within a force field where everything is purposefully chosen by the Gamemakers—the environment, wildlife, weather, even time itself. The tributes have to contend with hunger, dehydration, violent fires and explosions, engineered insects like tracker jackers, wild dogs, infections, and poisons—as well as the threats posed by the other tributes.

We ask our students to construct their own version of an arena, to be Gamemakers themselves and create a possible setting—complete with booby traps and surprise changes in the environment—that would serve as a potential arena. We ask them to draw a sketch of their arena, labeling all items that will be part of their plans, and to write an explanation of what they have created and its functions. We then ask them to surprise us the way Suzanne Collins has done. The tributes in *The Hunger Games* had the chance to grab weapons, tools, backpacks with supplies, and food. We tell our students to carefully decide what to leave around the central hub of the arena, the Cornucopia, which would be necessary for their survival. We urge our students to be creative in their planning yet be able to explain in detail just how their ideas are related to the whole success of their arena project.

I guarantee this will be an assignment that will more than engage students; it will produce amazing results from students who have seldom been known for doing much by way of creative problem solving—especially boys! Too seldom are boys allowed to write about the topics they most enjoy. In his book *Boy Writers: Reclaiming Their Voices*, Ralph Fletcher (2006) makes the case that educators need to give boys a little more commonsense leeway. Most boys love action and writing about conflict. They love fight scenes and monsters. It doesn't matter that the hero in this book is female. There are enough strong male characters and enough action to entice any boy into its storytelling web. The best part of this assignment? The sharing.

To recreate a set of assignments following the motto "My students can do that," we introduce our students to the Tribute Portfolio Project. On page 170 (and online at **go-solution-tree.com/literacy**), you will find the reproducible cover sheet for the first section of their project folders.

Problem Solving for Younger Readers: *There's a Boy in the Girls' Bathroom* Meets *Ned's Declassified School Survival Guide*

There is such a strong correlation between the plot of the young adult novel *There's a Boy in the Girls' Bathroom* by Louis Sachar, about a "bad boy" who learns the benefits of changing his ways, and the Nickelodeon series *Ned's Declassified School Survival Guide*, that it begs a teacher to set up an ongoing assignment asking the class to write and assemble its own school survival guide. The Nickelodeon series aired from September 12, 2004, through June 8, 2007, and in 2009 won the Global Entertainment Award for children's programming of the millennium. Each episode takes on issues or problems normally encountered at school—academics, social problems, navigating a school day—and gives tips on how to best handle them. The fifty-five episodes are available on Netflix and iTunes and are short enough (twenty minutes) to embed into lessons that would best exemplify the unit's objectives and themes. As a parallel assignment while reading and responding to the text of the Sachar novel, this survival guide could be introduced by offering students a list of all the topics covered by the Nickelodeon series and having them circle those that they could comfortably and genuinely enjoy writing about. The entire list of topics from *Ned's Declassified School Survival Guide* can be accessed on Wikipedia (www.wikipedia.org). As these topics are negotiated in the reading, students could be drafting their own versions of experiences complete with personal episodes that describe how to survive these circumstances.

Some of the more obvious episodes from *Ned's Declassified School Survival Guide* that match up with Sachar's young adult novel would be "Guide to: Cheaters and Bullies"; "Guide to: Failing and Tutors"; "Guide to: Making New Friends and Positives and Negatives"; and "Guide to: Bathrooms and Project Partners."

Just as Sachar's main character, Bradley Chalkers, is learning to find ways to work through his problems both critically and creatively, students attack the same or similar issues as they create their own class versions of a survival guide. Class discussions on which entries to include and for what reasons add a richness and relevancy to the novel study that engage students in ways other assignments cannot.

The reproducible on page 172 contains a list of the episodes of *Ned's Declassified School Survival Guide*. There are two topics per episode. Ask students to circle any of the topics they can talk or write about, and add their own additional titles.

Conclusion

We often take our legs for granted. We walk, run, kick, climb, dance, and expect both legs to do what our minds tell them to, and we expect them to work perfectly in tandem. Our brain's legs—our critical and creative thinking engines—when in their healthiest state, work seamlessly and in concert to perform any and all tasks we assign to them. Engaging both legs, and familiarizing our students with the qualities and strengths of those legs, are two of the primary functions of an effective literacy teacher. The joy of flow experiences (Csikszentmihalyi, 2008) while reading, writing, speaking, listening, and thinking are all contingent on the blended efforts of both sides of our brains. The projects and units that engage the imagination and curiosity of the class will turn a group of students dragging their feet into a group racing to the finish line.

Chapter Seven

Outrageous Teaching

This chapter's title has its roots in the work of Stanley Pogrow (2009), professor of educational leadership at San Francisco State University and author of the book *Teaching Content Outrageously*. Pogrow states, "The Outrageous Teaching approach is designed to teach conventional content objectives more effectively and quickly than traditional approaches. It is the fusion of art, creativity, imagination, and emotion—and pragmatics" (p. viii). He has systematized what many good teachers have intuitively done to engage students and cement material and skills into instruction during their careers. This book validates and confirms the efficacy of strategies I have employed for years.

Pogrow (2009) explains that, in an outrageous lesson, the teacher uses the following elements:

- Surprise
- Characters
- Disguises, both costume and voice
- A setting that incorporates as many media and senses as appropriate
- A storyline or scenario with a dilemma, fantasy, and humor
- Props
- Eliciting of an emotional reaction (such as empathy)
- Transition to the students' learning activity
- Content materials
- Debriefing of students on the content objective of the lesson (pp. 70–71)

If any metaphor would work for this concept of presenting material to a class of students, it has to be "stepping out of the box." Creative thinking has always been portrayed as an out-of-the-box method of investigating a problem or situation. What is more like a box than the traditional classroom, complete with traditional teaching methods, procedures, environment, and expectations? So while keeping within the parameters that our educational boxes demand—curriculum, schedules, standards, physical setting, procedures—we purposefully dissolve the box of our methodology and fill the room with surprise, imagination, and intensity. We teach outrageously!

Outrageous Teaching, as explained by Pogrow (2009), "is designed to be used in lieu of rather than as an addition to conventional instruction to teach the most troublesome content objectives in your school or district's curriculum" (p. 2). In other words, it isn't an "add-on" activity but rather the major vehicle for teaching and learning a specific lesson or concept. And it is also an engaging way to get students interested in participating in assigned tasks they might have shown little interest in before.

The Blight of Boredom

Boredom is one of the most insidious states of being that hampers learning. Boredom in our schools today is a result of student passivity, lack of relevance of curriculum to our students' lives, and lack of challenge and rigor. Project director of the High School Survey of Student Engagement, Ethan Yazzie-Mintz (2009), shows in his report *Engaging the Voices of Students: A Report on the 2007 & 2008 High School Survey of Student Engagement* that there is a strong relationship between a student's feeling of boredom and thoughts of dropping out of school. Boredom could in fact help to explain the high drop-out rates in the United States. Another effect of boredom and disengagement from school is lower literacy attainment. At the other end of the spectrum, Jon Willms (2003), professor and director of the Canadian Research Institute for Social Policy at the University of New Brunswick, finds that "on average, schools with high levels of engagement tended to have high levels of literacy skills" (p. 56).

Yazzie-Mintz's (2009) report reveals some of the reasons students give for their boredom:

> "Material wasn't interesting" was cited by 82% of respondents and "Material wasn't relevant to me" by 41% of respondents. Thirty-four percent of students said that a primary source of their boredom was "No interaction with teacher." (p. 7)

Outrageous Teaching is a remedy for the disengagement and boredom that brings our efforts at educating many of our students today to a screeching halt. A more physically creative and energetic method of instruction will produce an increase in both the quantity and quality of student learning, a prolonged increase in student attention, a pronounced decrease in classroom management issues, and an increase in student and teacher enjoyment. All these benefits will serve to strengthen teacher-student relationships.

As Pogrow (2009) aptly sums up:

> It is time to recognize that this era of on-demand, individualized, and YouTubed entertainment is producing as fundamental a shift in communication and learning patterns today as the printing press did 550 years ago. The key to teaching reluctant and resistant learners who have grown up with unsurpassed access to on-demand entertainment is to transform the classroom into a highly intriguing learning environment, to make it entertaining, dramatic, visually captivating, and a multisensory experience. (p. 2)

The four scenarios of Outrageous Teaching that follow in this chapter should support any teacher willing to experiment with introducing more of these qualities into instruction. As in any learning experience, your success will be the marker that convinces and empowers you to continue trying out new strategies. Let us also emphatically state that all the deep, close reading, the thoughtful writing, and the evidence provided for statements required by the Common Core State Standards does not mean that the presentation and environment can't exist within a highly engaging context. In fact, it will exist *only if* there is a highly engaging context.

Scenario 1: Introducing Photosynthesis

Photosynthesis is often used as an example to show students' inability to grasp a major concept in their study of science. This is vividly demonstrated in a video produced by researchers at the Harvard-Smithsonian Center for Astrophysics, who sought to understand better how children learn scientific concepts.

> The researchers filmed fourth graders on the playground and MIT students on graduation day, and asked each to explain where the weight in a tree comes from. A tree starts as a seedling; it ends up as

a log; where did all that extra stuff come from? The answers that the MIT students and the fourth graders gave were almost identical, and identically wrong.

Nearly all said the added mass came from sunlight, or from water, or from the soil. When prompted with the correct answer, several of the MIT graduates expressed astonishment at the idea that most of the added weight could have come from carbon dioxide gas in the air, since "this much air wouldn't weigh this much," said one baffled student as she hefted the log. All had been introduced to the idea of photosynthesis, and knew some of the relevant words, but none really had even a basic picture of what matter is, the fact that matter is conserved, or that it can be transformed by chemical reactions. (as cited in Budiansky, 2001)

When key concepts are highlighted and pulled away from all the tons of facts and terms and material that need to be "covered" in a course, we can focus our attention on enticing the students to want to deepen their understanding. Foremost is the purposeful isolation of concepts, like photosynthesis, that are consistently misunderstood by our students. Photosynthesis is one of the primary concepts we use in setting up an Outrageous Teaching experience.

Plant Person

In this lesson, we come into class carrying a log of wood. We also have an article we wave around stating that the fourth graders and MIT seniors interviewed didn't know how trees could grow so big from tiny acorns. We also mention that it was the textbook that confused them, so we tell our students to put away their textbooks so that we can better find the answer ourselves. We tell them they are going to leave this room knowing more than those ten-year-olds and twenty-one-year-olds did! We invite a few students to pick up the log and see how heavy it feels—this is our set-up and curiosity builder.

We have designated a student as the plant photographer, and so at each stage of our process, this person takes a picture for the handmade textbook we are developing as the year progresses. This handmade textbook contains all the really important concepts and understandings that we want our class to learn.

We ask for a volunteer to become Plant Person—that is, someone who is our symbolic plant. Our volunteer is seated on a stool placed in the middle of the classroom—a version of theater-in-the-round. We empty our bag of materials on our desk and take a camouflage print shirt from the pile. The shirt has pockets, so we can fill them later during the demonstration. Now we have our volunteer wearing the shirt, and we hand him or her the branch of an artificial palm tree, if one's available.

All students have been given a paper with a photosynthesis dolly (figure 7.1, page 110) on which to label and mark notes as the demonstration proceeds. As Plant Person is given each item and told what its purpose is, students at their desks draw the items on their dolly and make notes in their own words. We will be using the following items: flashlight, headband with flowery petals, small bottle of water, small bag of M&M's, handful of green shredded Easter grass, portable hand fan, couple of little cookies, a couple of large-sized dice, a small bottle of bubbles, an apple, an artificial flower, a packet of seeds, a camouflage shirt, a log, and a branch. (A reproducible form of the photosynthesis dolly can be found on page 174.)

We ask the group what is necessary for this plant to grow strong and big. We listen to the possible replies from the group members and tell them they are all partly correct. Picking up a flashlight and headband with gold petals, we ask for a student who would be willing to serve as our sun. We place the headband on the student's head and ask him or her to shine the flashlight on our plant.

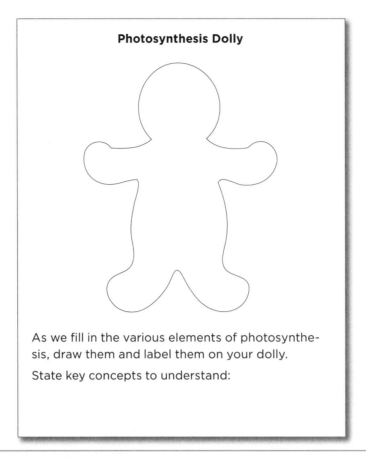

Figure 7.1: Introducing a scientific concept using the photosynthesis dolly.

Another student who says the plant probably needs water is given a small bottle of water which he offers our plant periodically during the rest of the demonstration. When a student suggests minerals, we hand that student a bag of M&M's to pour into our plant's hands to nibble on. If a student mentions chlorophyll, we give the student a handful of green Easter grass to stick in the shirt pockets.

Eventually a student will suggest or will be prompted to suggest that the plant needs air. This student has lots of props to handle, beginning with a hand fan to send air to the plant. Then we talk about what's in that air and how the plant takes in the air and breaks down its CO_2. We offer Plant Person a couple of little rice cake cookies or crackers to represent the CO_2 and have him or her swallow them with a sip of water. We explain that the CO_2 is now breaking down within the plant and making carbon, the building block of life. We ceremoniously hand our plant a couple of large dice or children's blocks to represent our building blocks, which are now filling Plant Person up. We explain that these blocks of carbon are really in the form of an invisible gas, which has plenty of mass even though you can't see it. Students have an intuitively difficult time accepting that gases have weight and mass if they are invisible. This is one of the core problems of their continued misunderstanding.

Plant Person Burps!

Handing Plant Person a bottle of bubbles, we ask him or her to blow a few. We explain that these bubbles are the plant's burps, and it burps every time it takes in air. What could those burps be made of? Someone always remembers that plants expel oxygen into the air. We talk about just what oxygen is good for. Meanwhile, all are filling up their photosynthesis dolly pages with notes, drawings, and arrows!

Oxygen isn't the only product that Plant Person releases. We place an apple in a pocket, a flower in the branch, a few packets of vegetable seeds in other pockets.

Plant Person Speaks Up

Now it's time to see how much Plant Person can tell us about himself or herself. Students are urged to ask about the props that seem to be piling up around him. Plant Person tries to remember what each one is and can ask for help from the audience whenever he or she finds the need. We go back to the wooden log we brought in and ask Plant Person to explain how this piece of his or her "brother" got to be so heavy. Students add important concepts from the lesson at the bottom of their dolly organizer.

Back to the Text

On the back of their sheets, in pairs, students are going to critique the section in their textbook on photosynthesis. They read the material, and the pairs discuss whether anything in the section differs from what they learned through the demonstration or is unclear, or if any information is missing. If a picture or drawing is included in the textbook, students are asked to rate how successful it is at explaining the process, and to comment on anything they think should have been added or changed to make it more successful. This exercise is very different from an ordinary reading of a textbook unit or lesson. In this exercise, the students are the experts and judge the validity and quality of the written work. Sometimes they suggest we go back to the dolly and add a process that might not have been added. Sometimes they take notice of different terms used in the textbook. If they have further questions that need better explanations, they add them to their critique. Students are not merely memorizing but weighing, judging, offering changes for better clarity—in other words, using higher-order thinking skills while learning the material.

Scenario 2: Finding Evidence in the Text

Many teachers feel exhausted after trying to persuade students to find evidence in the text to back up the claims they make in their papers. This effort increases as the quantity of material covered expands. When students are asked to provide textual evidence from a novel such as *The Adventures of Huckleberry Finn* (Twain, 1998) to support a theory, the very size of the book overwhelms them. Giving such an assignment to students who might have read half the book or less can doom the results from the beginning. However, instead of waiting until all have read most of the novel, you can concentrate on an early section—in particular, chapters 5 and 6. Our focus in the following exercise will be on how Huck's father treats him, and our goal is to prove that the accusations that Pap Finn is a child abuser will stand up in a court of law.

Huck Finn's Social Worker

This scenario requires a principal or other teacher to meet the students when they come into class and announce that their regular teacher will be absent. They are told they will be having a visitor in class who seems to need their help in filling out some important legal forms. They are to be on their best behavior and cooperate with this person fully. We then enter class dressed as a professional person with a briefcase. We only need to dress differently than we normally do as a teacher—a hat perhaps, a suit, fancy shoes, big fake glasses, anything that looks different than our normal appearance. We introduce ourself as Huckleberry Finn's social worker. Our job is to accumulate enough information and facts about how Huck is treated by his father to have him taken out of his custody and given to Widow Douglas.

We explain that we've heard that each of the students in this class has access to Huck's explanation of how his father has been treating him. Students only need to refer to this document (the book) to pull out proof that he might be the victim of child abuse and that Pap Finn is an unfit father. We have brought with us the papers necessary to help them find the material that will be used in the court case coming up.

We ask them to read through the various topics and detailed examples and then to see if they think any might apply to what we know of Huck's condition. We have them check those that seem most likely to be able to be proved. Then we hand them the form for documenting evidence, the Recognizing Child Abuse Checklist (reproducible page 175).

Students are then asked to go through the chapters and seek out as many examples of child abuse as they can. If they need more sheets to document their evidence, they are welcome to come up and get more. They are to copy statements from the book that prove their assumption that Huck has been abused and add the page numbers on the left side of the sheets.

Framing the Final Product

As Huck's social worker, we thank the students for all the work they are doing to help make a good case against his father. Our final request is that, using the reproducible Supporting Evidence for Child Abuse of Huck Finn (page 177), each student draft a letter to the judge that will include the information he or she has gathered and make an appeal to him to see that justice is done by way of our young friend, Huckleberry Finn. Since these letters are going to be admitted as evidence, we urge students to be as logical as possible in organizing the letters—keep all evidence of physical abuse together and all evidence of neglect and emotional maltreatment together. We then give them a date by which these letters should be completed and explain that their teacher will help them with any questions after we leave.

We gather up our briefcase and other materials, thank the students for their assistance, and leave the room. Quickly, we take off our social worker clothing and return to class. We apologize for being late and ask students for a summary of what happened when the guest was in the room. They delight in going along with the ruse and often play their roles with gusto!

Scenario 3: Meet the Characters

This scenario is adapted from a similar sequence in the book *Transformers: Creative Teachers for the 21st Century* (Schreck, 2009). As students arrive in class, they see a row of stools in front of the room with neon signs with names on them, as well as a few props such as wigs, a feather boa, a toy mouse, a cowboy hat, and a vest. This is the first day of a new unit or instructional cluster of lessons on Steinbeck's (1937/2002) novel *Of Mice and Men*. We greet the students as they enter and carefully invite our most reluctant readers to help us out in this introductory activity. We do what we need to do to see that fringe students will agree to participate—flatter, implore, tease—whatever is necessary. We let them know that this will not be difficult for them, and in fact it will be fun. There are enough stools for all the important characters in the book we will be reading. We make them comfortable and help them put on their name tags and props.

When the class is ready, we say we are going to share an important gift with the students—a gift or talent we possess that they might not have been aware of before today. We are excellent fortune-tellers. We can look into our shiny ball—a silver, extra-large Christmas tree ornament—and be able to see what hazards might occur in the future or what the deepest desires of a person's heart might be. We hand out the graphic organizer (figure 7.2) that students will fill out to capture each character's fortune, which we will use later to determine just how accurate our predictions are. A blank reproducible version of the fortune-telling chart can be found on page 178.

Fortune-Telling Chart

Curley
Don't _____
You Dream _____

Lennie
Don't _____
You Dream _____

Curley's Wife
Don't _____
You Dream _____

George
Don't _____
You Dream _____

Candy
Don't _____
You Dream _____

Figure 7.2: Fortune-telling chart.

In the corner of the room, a movie camera operated by a student volunteer captures the action. We begin our fortune-telling demonstration by standing behind or near the character who now has everyone's focused attention. The exchange that follows is typical of how the teacher as fortune-teller introduces the characters and then directs them on what to avoid in the future and what she thinks their dreams for the future might be. It usually will go something like this.

Teacher's Dialogue With Curley's Wife

We now are about to speak to the only woman on the ranch. As her sign says, she is known as Curley's Wife. She's very young—about the age of most of the girls in this class—around sixteen. When the book opens, she hasn't been married to Curley for very long.

Teacher: You are married to Curley, aren't you?

Curley's Wife: Yes.

Teacher: You look lovely in pink feathers, you know.

Curley's Wife: Thank you.

CONTINUED →

Teacher: Let me look into this crystal ball. . . . Hmmm . . . I'm beginning to see something. . . . Yes, why, you want to be in the movies, don't you?!

Curley's Wife: Yes, I do.

Teacher: Of course, I can see you clearly now. . . . Your dream is to be famous and in the movies and wear pretty clothes and have everyone take your picture, am I right?

Curley's Wife: You sure are!

Teacher: Class, write that down. Curley's Wife's dream is to be a famous movie star. You do have the makings of a beauty queen, my dear. Now let me look in this crystal ball once more. . . . Oh, my . . . yes, I'm beginning to see something that you need to look out for . . . something you definitely shouldn't do. Yes, here it is . . . don't go in the barn! Repeat after me . . . don't go in the barn.

Curley's Wife: Don't go in the barn.

Teacher: Now promise me you'll listen to what I've just told you. It's very important!

Curley's Wife: I will. I mean, I won't go in the barn.

Teacher: Thank you for coming here today. It is a pleasure to meet you.

In like fashion, we introduce each character of significance in the book, give relevant background information—terms, setting, facts about the character that will make the reading easier to follow—and ask students to write on their charts something that the character should be sure not to do and what the character's dream is. We are embedding prior knowledge into our students' minds. As Eric Jensen (1998), one of the leading translators of educational neuroscience in the world, writes, "The brain's susceptibility to paying attention is very much influenced by priming. We are more likely to see something if we are told to look for it or are prompted on its location" (p. 43). The students have an idea about what each character is like and what motivates his or her actions, as well as a hint of the conflicts each will experience in the novel.

Never, after doing this activity, has it failed to happen that when we get to chapter 5, when Curley's Wife enters the barn where she will meet her death at Lennie's hands, someone inadvertently calls out, "Oh no, she's going into the barn!" Those students who sat in wigs and held props in the front of the room follow their character throughout the book to see just what happens to him or her. They assume responsibility for that character automatically. That is why it's important to choose who will portray these characters with great care. It is an opportunity to boost the effort and engagement of those students who usually don't feel compelled to participate in the reading.

When a test comes around and students try to keep the characters straight, they will turn to one of the preliminary actors and ask, "You're Curley, aren't you?" This is the visual image that students use to identify one character from another. So, this Outrageous Teaching activity provides visual images, hints at a series of possible conflicts to look for, sets up the internal motivations of the characters that influence their behavior, and gives the students who are more challenged a reason to engage in the text. The purpose of this introductory activity is to lay sufficient groundwork for an easy transition into reading, and later into the writing.

Later, the Written Paper

After we have finished reading the novel and before we introduce the writing assignment choices, we replay the video clip from the opening fortune-telling activity. When the laughter and comic remarks subside, we take out our original chart and begin our discussion on just what these notes we took can tell us, since we are now aware of all the characters' actions. We discuss the possible significance of all the warnings we heard the fortune-teller give each character.

As a class, we speculate (another opportunity to use our *What if?* prompting) on what might have happened in the book had the characters heeded the warnings and not done what they were urged to avoid. Noting how everything we do has an influence on those around us—sometimes directly and at other times more subtly—we gently guide our students to consider how one character's avoidance could affect the actions of another character and alter the book even more profoundly.

The Characters' Dreams

We consider the relationship between a person's dream and what that person might need to do to try to reach that dream. We look for other words that might stand for a dream. We begin tracing the actions that various characters take to reach their dreams in the novel. We introduce the word *motivation*—a word that is certainly not new to these students but one that might take on a richer significance when coupled with the ideas we have shared concerning the role of dreams in a person's life. We ask our students if they feel they could say something interesting about why a specific character acted the way he or she did in the novel.

Broad Commonalities

Although there are obvious differences in the characters—age, gender, race, intelligence, to name a few—we begin to look for what all of them have in common. We spend enough time on this topic to move from the obvious statements of place and time to elements that bind them together as human beings. Two of the topics that usually emerge from this brainstorming discussion are loneliness and handicaps. All the characters seem to be suffering to some degree from each of these circumstances. Some are afflicted with physical handicaps, while others might be psychologically or intellectually handicapped. A few are victims of a host of prejudices. All seem to have reasons to feel lonely and disconnected. The conversation mixes and matches both themes as it moves along.

Choices of Writing Topics

We have now come to the point where our students are ready to choose from at least four different perspectives to write about the novel they have just read. We make a list of some of the possible topics they can use:

- What if _____ listened to the fortune-teller?

- What motivated _____ to do what he or she did, and what were the outcomes?

- How has loneliness affected the actions of the characters, specifically in the case of _____?

- What handicaps burdened the characters in the novel, or how did they function because of these handicaps?

Students are urged to choose a perspective and are free to manipulate the topic suggestions until they arrive at one that they feel they can speak to with more than a surface treatment. The time we spend helping our charges decide what they will be writing about is often proportional to the quality of the work they will produce. After everyone has settled on a topic to write about, students get into pairs with someone who has chosen a different topic from their own. Now they are asked to talk through their ideas on their chosen topic and ask their partners for additional insight. All this is done before anyone has put pen to paper or finger to key. Next, we remind the students to jot down any useful information their partner has offered as well as information they came up with while doing their talk-throughs. Now they move to drafting.

This explanation of how the written piece is generated from the opening scenario is far from complete. We go to the text itself for details and proof of assertions and narrow down the topics appropriately. We certainly do much more talking about which points will be powerful and how to deliver them to a reader. We consider format, audience, and medium. As teachers, we know what skills we are focusing on through this assignment and steer the products by this rudder as well.

Try This

Choose a text that you can adapt to a fortune-teller exercise like this one. Use the reproducible on page 178 to help concentrate your thinking while developing your own scenario.

Fortune-Telling

Name of Book: _____

First Character: _____

Don't: _____

Your Dream: _____

Good Idea for a Prop: _____

Figure 7.3: The fortune-teller exercise—using a graphic organizer.

Scenario 4: Using a Time Machine

Social studies content can be turned into Outrageous Teaching events as easily as can communication arts. One format could be a time machine that lifts a person—either an ordinary or famous person—from one era and drops him or her into our classroom. The opportunity for comparison and contrast of two distinctly different cultures or political circumstances is not difficult. Premade cheat sheets given to the time machine visitors can guide the interview and make normal note taking far more interesting for students. Comparing reasons for going to war from the point of view of a general from the North versus one from the South would be a good use of the time machine. When students have a difficult time seeing the differences between two opposing sides, or, for example, the purposes of the three branches of government, this is a technique that makes history visible.

Amnesia is also a great ploy to use. If someone like Ben Franklin appears in class—let's say his experiment with the kite and lightning went wrong and bounced him into the future—our students could use the information in their textbooks to let him know what a wonderful and remarkable statesman and inventor he was (see figure 7.4). They could share with him how much he is still emulated and remembered even now.

Ben and Me: Outrageously

- Ben Franklin tumbles down a wormhole and lands in a classroom. Students help him regain his balance!

- Ben has amnesia and must give a speech about himself as a founder and inventor.

- Students help him out by finding things that fit both categories from an article in their textbook.

- Together, they organize the material and write the speech to be given that night!

Figure 7.4: An Outrageous Teaching example using Ben Franklin.

Following is just such a sketch of Benjamin Franklin. Here's what we do: Again, we have another faculty member tell the class we will be running a little late and have the students read the section in their textbooks that deals with the biography of Ben Franklin. As they are reading, we—dressed up as best as possible as a colonial man—enter the room carrying a kite and a key. The ruse we develop is that we (like Ben) got shocked during our lightning experiment, were thrown down a galactic wormhole, and landed here in the future—specifically in this classroom. Unfortunately, we have lost our memory and need help from the students to develop a speech we will be giving about ourselves when we return to our own time period. It is our good fortune that we have landed in the future, because students studying history have access in their textbooks to just the information we need! We tell them we need facts about ourselves as founders and inventors.

Together, we gather on the SMART Board or blackboard facts that we can use in our speech and writing suggestions from class members. We cluster the best material under our two main topics. Students then are asked to individually write a draft of a speech using those facts that Ben could use on his return. We make up an appropriate audience for whom Ben needs to present this speech and make sure that students refer to them as they write their first drafts. Hopefully, these drafts are finished before the end of the class period, so that Ben can collect them to take with him. He departs with his kite and hands filled with potential speeches! The teacher then rejoins her class and asks for feedback about what has occurred in her absence.

The reproducible Outrageous Teaching Worksheet on page 179 is meant as a brainstorming apparatus for you to plan an Outrageous Teaching scenario of your own.

When Teaching Goes Terribly Wrong

A note is needed at this point about the Common Core State Standards' emphasis on cold first readings with no introduction of prior knowledge to sway the reader from making personal reading decisions and drawing inferences from the text. Not all material should be taught using the same exact method or system. A teacher's conscious shifts in strategy and emphasis when guided by a strong understanding of what goals and purpose are to be attained must be made to ensure balance and engagement as well as high achievement. Those of us who are spending the largest part of our lives with a classroom of children know the importance of using multiple approaches and variety if we wish to secure both their attention and willingness to put forth effort. By using our discretion, nurtured by our professional background and experience in the field, we will indeed use the methodology suggested to help students master the CCSS requirements. We will also know instinctively when to attack those standards from the backdoor instead of the front. The standards themselves acknowledge the need for this prerogative. When teaching goes terribly wrong, just such a backdoor, outrageous approach is necessary.

While serving as a consultant on an extended contract in a high school, I made the rounds to see how the teachers I was working with were doing. One energetic, intelligent, first-year teacher who usually greeted me with a smiling face was about to break into tears. It seems she had spent the last hour trying to do a read-aloud of a story to the whole class with no success at all. This story's assessment was to provide a baseline of her students' abilities. But the class was talking over her reading, students were moving around the room, and only a few were trying to follow along. She ended up separating these few from the whole group and reading with them, letting the rest of the class fend for themselves.

Another teacher who had joined us told this teacher that she had done what she was supposed to do, that those other kids had had their chance and simply didn't take it. Later, I told the young teacher that the advice that other teacher gave her was wrong. She *does* have the responsibility to find some way to engage those other students and should not simply dismiss them as having made a bad choice. So she asked, "What should I do now? Another class is coming in shortly, and I'm supposed to read the same story that was a disaster the first time." We brainstormed. We set up a system based on words that would appear in the story and actions students were to do when they read them.

Since the story was about a woman over the age of ninety and set around Christmastime (not the best of hooks for fourteen-year-olds in March), I suggested she first go around the room asking each student to tell the class who is the oldest person he or she knows. Then she would tell them that whenever students hear the word *green* they are to whisper it together, and when they hear the word *graft* they are to stand up. She put on a scarf and said anyone who finds out how that scarf fits the story should raise his or her hand. And so, as the students came into the room, these and other such directions graced the board instead of the usual definitions and literary notes to jot down.

The next day I asked her how it went, and she was ecstatic. Everything was awesome! She even had a volunteer—a boy!—read all of the old lady's lines. The day after that, I went back and she said she was trying to plan something for the next day and couldn't. Then she asked herself, "What would Ms. Schreck do?" and she came up with a really cool way to do the next story. She's now on autopilot! She sees it as her duty to think through the content and lesson not just for how well they match up to the objectives and standards, but equally for how effectively they will turn rebellious students into eager participants.

Of course, this teacher won't be teaching nor will she be orchestrating all of her short stories this same way next time. We don't do anything the same way all the time. But she does have another strategy to use another time, another year.

Conclusion

My hope is that after reading this chapter readers will see the need for risk taking and try out one of these scenarios or make up one on their own. The benefits by way of student engagement and emotional attention are so great, and exert so great an influence on understanding and growth of student literacy, that taking that risk is well worth it. Traditional educational practices are being questioned by—and altered based on—educational and scientific brain research. If we're intent on providing the best of all possible situations to increase our students' literacy abilities, we must join in these new practices.

Chapter Eight

Mixing Complexity and Integration Into Planning

In this chapter, we discuss the complex weaving together of standards, application, and engaging strategies as a teacher plans a block of lessons. We address the need for spacious quantities of reading and writing experiences to flow through everything we do as instructors and show how it can be done. Here we present the dance of the classroom, where the teacher is the choreographer, not the prima ballerina—where pacing, momentum, and the layering of themes combine to produce teaching as both science and art, beautifully intertwined. One of the most often-voiced complaints from students is that the content and curriculum are not interesting or meaningful. This chapter takes on that complaint and offers suggestions on how to counteract it by looking at teaching as the mix of both science and art.

When we talk about material to teach, we are referring to the *content*—the concepts, ideas, written selections, and information. This content can be found in textbooks, supplementary materials, and all other forms of media, including the Internet, art, music, and so on. *Skills*, on the other hand, are the proficiencies we target, the technical actions and strategies students need to own and access to address tasks. When we talk about *strategies* and *activities*, we are referring to the way the content is packaged, delivered, and moved from the pages of curriculum guides to the interaction between students and teacher. The teacher chooses much of what determines this interaction. In this chapter, we discuss how important these choices are for piquing student interest and ensuring achievement.

Think of pearls spread out on a table as the possible choices a teacher has concerning precise content, strategies, processes, timing, and ordering of instruction. We always have far more pearls than we can use in a single necklace. The longer a person has taught, the more pearls that person has access to, and the harder, at times, it seems to decide which to keep and which to leave in the drawer for another day or another unit. This act of choosing the precise pearls to use is an important responsibility for teachers. We are all aware of teachers who hang on to activities that really don't apply to the learning objectives and needs of their students. Many of us have also had the experience of a teacher asking to use a lesson or activity we have developed. We share graciously, while explaining how it fits into our unit. Later, we find that this teacher simply used the strategy or activity without any concern for context, simply because it seemed like a fun thing to do. This is not only a waste of time; it's a waste of a good strategy.

This brings us to the string for our necklace. The string is the purpose. It is what keeps the pearls in place and provides the continuity and context. Without a logical, ordered plan for our necklace, we are left with a handful of pearls instead of a functional piece of jewelry. When we know what we want to accomplish, choose the best material and instructional processes, and order them for the best understanding and learning, we become craftspeople, blending art and science.

The Discussion

Nothing is more satisfying and empowering in an educator's career than the ability to carefully craft a unit or lesson that plays out the way you intend it to in the classroom. That is the dual joy of teaching—the creative preparation and the manifestation of that creativity in student learning. When either of these is usurped by outside forces, teachers are disempowered and demoralized. Many of the tools available today to help teachers in their jobs are well meaning but damaging to our professional growth. When we are given a script to read and told to adhere to it with the utmost fidelity, we are being robbed of our professional judgment and self-respect. When a program is put into place to move formative assessment away from our own ability to monitor our students' progress, we are being nudged further and further away from the role of educator and more toward that of the one being monitored. Formative assessment should not be the subject of a packaged program, a set of electronic quizzes. The most important element in strong formative assessment as a tool for instruction is the teacher, and especially the teacher's intuitive ability to pick up on student confusion, misunderstanding, and need for assistance. When we are told exactly what to teach and when and what page we are to be on today and are given no latitude to make adjustments, we feel the frustration of knowing we are not meeting the needs of the students in our classes. If the string of pearls is given to us already strung, without our having any input into the decisions of what pearls to choose and how to order them, our satisfaction in our career is severely diminished—leading many of us to then choose to leave the profession.

A university adjunct professor charged with preparing teachers-to-be for the classroom finds that the lack of opportunity for teachers young and old to design flexible lessons is eroding quality teaching and the very profession itself. She expresses the following frustration:

> I think our detailed curricula are sabotaging the creative part of design. . . . I just watched a young practicum teacher teach from a PLC designed packet using *House on Mango Street* and *Funny in Farsi* leading up to a boring short-answer question. She was not allowed to talk about tone because that was the lesson for next week! How can you read either piece without tone? She found herself with her hands tied, because the students did not understand the metaphors and the point of the piece without talking about tone. They read it out loud (using popcorn for god sakes) tossing a wadded up paper to another student to begin reading without really knowing what was happening in the text at all. But the lesson was designed by a group of people for her so she ends up having no say or heart or pride or understanding or good delivery. It is like giving an actor a script without any directions or rehearsal. I want my money back . . . but the students don't know to ask for their money back. . . . They don't know what they are missing. (M. Baker, personal communication, October 24, 2011)

Students need variety, choice, challenge, input, and opportunities to relate to the content and become engaged in the products they are asked to produce. We all know that students are more engaged in learning when they are active and have some choice and control over the learning process and the curriculum is individualized, authentic, and related to their interests (Anderman & Midgley, 1998). This just isn't possible if teachers are too tightly reined in by the curriculum or by the presence of too rigid a pacing guide or by other inflexible expectations from others. There has to be a balance between a strongly focused set of standards and curriculum and the ability of teachers to infuse their instruction with self-chosen supplementary materials and strategies.

Writing on organizational culture and teacher empowerment, Paul Terry (2000) of the University of South Florida notes:

Unfortunately, many teachers go through a period of teaching under the supervision of principals who are described as authoritarian. The teacher becomes bored, resentful, and unhappy. Many wake up in the morning saying "I really don't want to go." An even larger problem arises when teachers who are not given the freedom to make appropriate choices find themselves monetarily accountable for the outcome of these decisions. Many contemplate leaving the teaching profession altogether. On the other hand, many teachers find themselves working "with" principals instead of "for" principals. Their opinion has merit. Freedom allows them to take risks in the curriculum and other areas of their job. Their teaching techniques reflect their personality as they are allowed to be empowered and creative. These teachers attribute their success in the classroom to the fact that the principal has empowered them. (p. 2)

Without this freedom, the discussion on exercising professional judgment in the areas of choosing appropriate material and deciding on the best instructional methods to arrive at precise learning goals and objectives is somewhat meaningless.

How does this issue filter down to our students? Our understanding of student engagement today is far more sophisticated and complex than it once was. As mentioned, in the previous chapter, students again and again are reporting that their lack of engagement stems from an overwhelming feeling of dissatisfaction with content that has no meaning for them now or seemingly in the future, with classroom practices that are boring and lack variety or challenge, and with teachers who show no interest in them as persons (Yazzie-Mintz, 2007). As David Zyngier (2005), an expert on student engagement as it applies to social justice, mentioned at an Australian Association for Research in Education (AARE) conference, there has been a shift in both definitions and understanding of how we used to view engagement in the past—in terms of time on task, attendance, and internal motivation; and how we tend to view it now—more in terms of cognitive, intellectual, academic, social, behavioral, participatory, and emotional considerations. With all this in mind—teacher empowerment, student engagement, a wise choice of content within the parameters of district standards, curriculum, and goals—we begin to string our necklace.

Today's Quest

If there is a quest today in the minds of quality teachers, it is the challenge and opportunity at this early initiation into the Common Core State Standards to find and solidify meaningful, engaging informational texts into their curriculum. The exemplars are just that—exemplars—not meant to be the whole basket of content from which we are allowed to make our choices. They are samples of good selections with explanations of the characteristics that make them good. Many are the same traditional pieces we have been using in our classrooms for years.

Our task, our quest, is to build a larger and more varied pool of similar materials that hit the same mark of complexity and merit. Our radar is tuned in to powerful articles, blogs, books, TED talks, and films that reach those high standards while guaranteeing that our students will be interested and curious readers, ready to intelligently react, respond, analyze, and critique. We have always delighted in finding the perfect companion pieces to highlight what we were teaching, and so find satisfaction in a document like the CCSS, which emphasizes the need to do just that—provide our students with multiple texts that enrich the instruction and learning.

One source of good material to consider adding to your repertoire comes from a thirteen-year veteran of a high school English classroom and 2010 National Teacher of the Year, Sarah Brown Wessling. During my research, her name began appearing on blogs, articles, and books dealing with the CCSS. I asked Sarah to write something for this book that touched on her experience with informational texts that engaged her students. She wrote about the experience of infusing the teaching of nonfiction with the same love and excitement that fiction generates in her, and of watching students fall into ideas the way they fall into stories. At first, she said, her students were excited, too:

> Then they started to read and discovered that these texts didn't have a beginning, middle and end the same way that their fiction did. They had facts and interviews, statistics and anecdotes—all unfamiliar territory for them, especially in book length fashion. So, their reaction was one of confusion, and through that I learned how they struggled to hold details as part of a larger argument, how they struggled to understand the difference between fact and opinion, and how they struggled to see the text attributes (e.g., statistics and anecdote) coalesce into persuasive theses.

> As is the case with everything I teach, the students taught me what they needed. They needed explicit lessons on how to read an interview, make sense of statistics, find the purpose in an anecdote. Although students were divided into five different groups, each group reading a different nonfiction text, I could do mini-lessons on these text structures for the whole class and then have them practice with their groups' text. They proceeded by creating storyboards for the chunks of their reading that highlighted the use of these text structures, they took on real-world group challenges to synthesize different portions of the text and each created a conference presentation poster as though they were the author that you might see at an academic conference.

> The reading experience was unfamiliar, but knowing that at least 70% of what they read outside of high school will be nonfiction, it was invaluable. (S. Wessling, personal communication, March 22, 2011)

Here are some of Sarah's choices for nonfiction:

- *Nickel and Dimed* (2011) by Barbara Ehrenreich
- *Geeks* (2001) by Jon Katz
- *Bitter Chocolate* (2008) by Carol Off
- *Blood Diamonds* by Greg Campbell
- *Branded* (2004) by Alissa Quart
- *Chew on This* (2007) by Charles Wilson and Eric Schlosser

One of the strongest elements in Sarah's nonfiction unit is precisely that of choice. When students feel they have some control over what they will be learning, the issues of motivation and classroom management are reduced significantly. As Sarah mentions in her thoughts about using nonfiction, although students might not all be reading the same text, they all will have common needs that should be addressed by the teacher in mini-lesson fashion. Some—though certainly not all—of the types of explicit teaching that will have to go on in classrooms introducing nonfiction are: lessons on varieties of nonfiction works; recognizing the difference between fact and opinion; evaluating source materials; reading interviews; deciphering tables, charts, and graphs and evaluating their relevance to the text; textual features (illustrations, graphic aids, organization, print), navigating a scientific journal; detecting bias in persuasive materials; and many more.

Students need practice in analyzing informational texts. Teachers can help by setting up practice sessions where a variety of such texts—websites, e-texts, trade books, journals, pamphlets, brochures, how-to instructions attached to products, newspapers, political ads, articles—can be compared and contrasted for visual appeal, text features, author's writing style, use of technical vocabulary, extent of their reliance on graphics and visuals, and students' assumptions about the targeted readers. Studying the externals of this strange bird—informational text—before dissecting him and holding him over the fire of deep analysis might be a good way to begin.

A Multigenre Edgar Allan Poe Unit

Anyone taking a quick look at the sample texts suggested by the Common Core State Standards Committee will agree they show a healthy supply of documents that we can all agree are fundamental to our American origins and foundations. In regard to American literature, the schools and districts where I taught considered Edgar Allan Poe—father of the short story—to be one of the authors who deserved coverage. In chapter 1, we already considered one of his stories as a sample of how to approach the need for close reading. That exercise is one of a series of lessons that forms a cluster or unit of study we will investigate now.

Over the years, many teachers have been amazed and saddened by local efforts across the country to strip from the curriculum the works of authors such as Poe, Mark Twain, John Steinbeck, Ernest Hemingway, Harper Lee, Toni Morrison, Kurt Vonnegut, Sherman Alexie, F. Scott Fitzgerald, and J. D. Salinger, to name a few. I was never asked to do this. Since, in literary terms, Poe is the only writer who has earned himself the title of "father" of any specific genre in the United States, my district deemed it relevant to see that teachers gave him face time. We were free to fashion our teaching of Edgar Allan Poe in any way we wished, as long as we touched upon his historical significance to American literature and introduced our students to his style and a variety of his works. Being aware that my students had already been introduced to Poe at least a few times before they arrived at my door—most had studied "The Tell-Tale Heart" and "Annabel Lee" in middle school—I knew I had to frame my unit with a fresh and intellectually interesting approach, or many would think they knew enough about Poe already. After some concentrated thinking, I figured out how to do it.

The Really Cool Frame for Examining Poe

It dawned on me that, like artists in most other fields, this father of the short story had used older forms of the short story, forms that have been used for centuries, before he began experimenting and coming up with the newer ones he is now famous for creating. I realized that I could group all of Poe's stories into four distinct formats that would allow students to see developments and patterns in his work and therefore to better appreciate his unique contribution to American literature. These four formats are described in table 8.1.

Table 8.1: Four Types of Poe Stories, With Examples From Other Authors

1. The Frame Story	2. The Gothic Horror Story
Definition: A story inside a story	Definition: The oldest form of the horror story with scary castles, grotesque figures, bizarre happenings, colors, ghosts
Example: *Canterbury Tales* by Chaucer in which all the travelers entertain each other with a story while on the a pilgrimage	Example: Scooby-Doo cartoons, which are classic Gothic horror takeoffs
Our Poe story: "The Oval Portrait"	Our Poe stories: "The Masque of the Red Death" and "The Fall of the House of Usher"

3. The Psychological Horror Story	4. The Detective Story
Definition: A story in which evil comes from the sick mind of the narrator; usually includes an obsession with an object that blocks rational thought process	Definition: A story in which (1) the detective is smarter than the police, (2) an accomplice needs everything explained, (3) a murder (or crime) is difficult to solve
Example: Stephen King's *The Shining*, *Cujo*, and *It*	Example: Sherlock Holmes and Agatha Christie stories.
Our Poe stories: "The Tell-Tale Heart" and "The Black Cat"	Our Poe story: "The Murders in the Rue Morgue" is the first detective story and prototype of many similar stories in this genre over the years. The character C. Auguste Dupin is the first true detective in literature.

In constructing a unit, not only do I have these stories as options, but I also have biographical material for research purposes and poems, for study of sound and word choice. In fact, I have too much to choose from to fit into a decent time frame—too many pearls—and I haven't even begun to list the activities available for consideration.

Developing Our Essential Questions

Before we look at the possible menu of choices we have at our disposal, we look at how we want to focus our attention. We select our essential questions to not only focus our attention but also to provide the direction we are taking as a group. Following are a few such essential questions that can provide the rudder for studying a body of work or individual selections. I use these or similar questions when teaching a unit about Edgar Allan Poe.

- How does an artist's body of work show how he or she has evolved and grown over the course of his or her career?

- What can we learn about an artist's style by mimicking his or her work?

- How does an artist's personal life influence his or her work? Does studying an artist's life help us appreciate his or her work more, or is this knowledge unnecessary?

It is important for the teacher to personally formulate essential questions rather than pull them from a manual, just as it is for students to add to or rephrase them for better comprehension. As a teacher, every summer before school started, I worked at developing a set of essential questions that would serve as the overarching focus for an entire course. Within the course would be different but complementary sets of questions that enriched those that formed the year's umbrella. Often, those questions included an embedded metaphor that would be used throughout the year—a journey, a quest, a river, a chain—a metaphor that could serve as an archetype we could return to again and again. When we take the time and thought to do this, we are able to present material with a sense of cohesiveness that satisfies a student's need to know the purpose of the activity. Even if we are in a position that is tightly structured and much is not within our control, making sense of it all *is* within our control and is a necessary gift we can offer our students.

One teacher who formulates these essential questions for the entire school year is Adam Griffin, an English teacher at Hebron High School in Carrollton, Texas. He formulates an open-house presentation for his students' parents that shows his choice of the essential questions that will guide and hold together the focus of study for the year. Here is a sample set of such questions:

1. What happens when choice results in unintended consequences?

2. What's more important—the journey or the destination?

3. How do relationships affect me?

4. What is greater—responsibility to self or responsibility to others?

5. Should there be limits on freedom?

Pulling the parents under his essential umbrella will give him a firmer foundation from which to make connections and explanations of how he teaches and how he intends to challenge their students. Visit http://prezi.com to find Adam Griffin's open-house presentation along with other wonderfully constructed presentations that he uses with his students throughout the year. Once we have decided on the focus we want to take—the essential questions that will guide our learning—we can begin to look at how we will flesh out our unit. We need to consider how much time we will be spending on this topic, how much material we want to cover, what standards will be driving our instruction, which wonderful activities we will use, and which ones we will drop. We know that variety is what keeps a course fresh, so we are careful to not duplicate a strategy or require a product that has been the basis for an earlier unit or that would be better placed in a unit later on. These are the choices that accentuate the need for a teacher's professional expertise.

Choosing Content, Activity, Skill, and Product

The longer a person teaches, especially if that person teaches in the same content area, the longer the list of choices to develop into units of study. This growing list is a double-edged sword that teachers are familiar with all too well. We want to give our students as much as we can, and we have developed wonderful ways of presenting particular texts; yet we can't possibly teach all that we have the expertise for and access to. So we must choose that which fits this particular class at this particular time. We always make these decisions with our overarching goals of what we want our students to know, to understand, and to be able to do and produce in the forefront of our minds. Following is the set of content pearls that I would need to pare down to develop a manageable Poe unit:

- The Four-Format Framework
- "The Oval Portrait" (frame story)
- "The Masque of the Red Death" (gothic horror story)
- "The Black Cat" and "The Tell-Tale Heart" (psychological horror stories)
- "The Murders in the Rue Morgue" (detective story)
- "The Fall of the House of Usher"
- "The Defamation of Edgar Allan Poe" (informational, complex text for analysis)
- Selected poetry: "The Bells," "The Raven," "Annabel Lee"
- Literary terms

Other supplementary texts might include Shakespeare's "The Seven Ages of Man," selected short biographies written over the years since Poe's death, Bradbury's "Usher II," and the third segment of *The Simpsons* "Treehouse of Horror I" episode from October, 1990, which was an adaptation of Poe's "The Raven."

The following activities and products are associated with many of these content selections:

- Make a graphic organizer of the four formats.

- Role-play a frame story. For example, ask for volunteers to pretend they are sitting around a campfire telling ghost stories. Have them each start a different story from a scary movie they know. This is an example of a frame story with the campfire as the outer frame and the individual stories as the inner portion

- Vary methods of covering the reading—individual reading, teacher reading, paired reading

- Begin reading, point out where the frame begins, move into the inner story, and then ask students to take over reading the remainder silently.

- Ask students to mimic the format of the frame story by using Poe's frame but inserting an original story.

- Have students share original stories orally in small groups, and then with the whole class.

- Ask students to draw a detailed explanation of two paragraphs describing the setting in "The Masque of the Red Death."

- With students, use little figurines (Star Wars characters, tiny dolls, LEGO people, and so on) to mark the action as the rest of the story is being read aloud.

- Guided by your questions, encourage students to discover and add the story's symbols to their drawings.

- Ask students to add the various stages of man from Shakespeare's speech to their drawings.

- Make a timeline of Poe as father of the short story, marking famous writers and artists who have followed him in writing psychological horror stories.

- Creating the illustrated version of "The Black Cat," give students a couple of blank pieces of paper and ask them to pick from a box a numbered caption to be written on the top of the paper. The captions are all visuals that could accompany the story. Ask students to draw and color with markers what the caption suggests. These are then taped to the wall in numerical order. With students' desks all pulled closely together facing the pictures and with lights out, and using a spotlight beaming on each picture in turn, the teacher reads the story to the class.

- Following this activity, have students reread the "The Tell-Tale Heart," which they have probably studied years earlier.

- Ask students to fill out a comparison and contrast chart (see the reproducible on page 180) of the two stories with a partner and then discuss as a whole class.

- Returning to the Four-Format Framework, fill in the characteristics of a detective story, and trace them in the first detective story written—"The Murders in the Rue Morgue."

- Have students choose a contemporary television detective series to trace these characteristics.

- Introduce Sherlock Holmes and compare the old stories with the contemporary movie or television series versions to Poe's characteristics

- Ask students to create and bring to class a "Poe mobile," illustrating any of the themes, stories, and formats already studied. Guidelines might include (1) doesn't contain inappropriate material, (2) must be functional—that is, it can be hung from the ceiling, and (3) it must be brought to class two to three days before the end of the unit.

- Analyze Robbins's (1975) article "The Defamation of Edgar Allan Poe" in *American History Illustrated* by pulling out the areas of conjecture Robbins exposes and listing those statements often repeated as fact that she states are lies.

- Using a preselected set of biographies of Poe that mirror the slanderous accusations made about him over the years, have students work in groups of four to five and find the questionable statements biographers make that are discussed in the Robbins's article.

- Using the group lists of evidence, ask students to discuss how untrue statements can appear year after year in print and how literary rumors can be written and reported as fact.

- Ask students to research and find other samples of biographies that repeat the same accusations.

- Introduce one of Poe's most musical poems—"The Bells." Do a close reading of the poem—first for general meaning, then for technique, then for significance.

- Discuss the use of bells during the centuries before electronics to indicate warnings, times of prayer, weddings, alarms, and the time of day.

- Prepare the class for an oral reading of the poem. Separate the class into four groups, with each group in charge of one of the poem's stanzas, with the freedom to read it any way they decide— for example, all together, assigning different lines to different people, or using a lead reader with a chorus of readers. Students choose all sorts of bells from the bags of bells we have collected over time for the groups to punctuate their recitation and capture the section's tone. Groups then decide how to present their sections and practice. We videotape the performances.

- Ask students to fill out a unit reflection sheet.

- Show *The Simpsons* "Treehouse of Horror I" episode from October, 1990 (Stanton, et al., 1990).

As any teacher can tell from examining this material, it takes too much time to do all these activities! And so the job of cutting back, making choices, and weighing options comes in. For some classes it might be important to have more writing and analysis practice, for others there needs to be more opportunity for oral presentations and group work. Some classes need more help with reading. A teacher reviews just what skills need to be stretched and strengthened at this time of the year and makes content and activity choices in this light. Constructing this unit in the fall might be very different from constructing it in the spring. The needs of the students as well as the skill levels change over the months. Developing just the right balance of activities and content with skill development and time restrictions is the creative act of lesson design. Following, a few of these strategies are explained in more detail.

Write-to-Learn Pieces

Note the absence of heavy editing of any of these writing pieces. These write-to-learn pieces are placed in students' writing folders, unedited, along with many writing pieces from previous units and will be subject to more intense scrutiny after student selection later in the course. For now, these are considered "just do it" pieces because their purpose is more on writing to learn and experiment than to produce a polished piece eligible for publication. The purpose of these pieces is to try on various authors' styles and constructions.

Complaints are rising among teachers in the field that writing instruction is becoming far too stiffly prescriptive, formulated, and overexamined—there are just too many outlines to follow, organizers to fill in, and rules to adhere to and not enough actual writing being done by students throughout the year (Stacey, 2011). Writing as it is blended into this unit is not looked upon as an isolated activity but as a vehicle for thought, practice, and creative experimentation. This does not mean that the writing isn't good—far from it. Some of my best student products come from open assignments that have not been bound up by an overabundance of teacher directives.

Trying on Poe's Style

In this unit, when given a choice of format to try out, most girls in the past have chosen the frame story format to mimic. On the other hand, my experience has been that most boys navigate toward the psychological horror story format, with a narrator who is out of touch with reality—the gory and bizarre side of Poe's stories are found to be appealing.

Following are the first two paragraphs of a piece written by a sixteen-year-old male student:

> Listen for a moment, friend, and I will tell you why I am here. Yes, that's it. Come closer. You see that man? the one wearing white? He's the one. Yes! Him along with the others! That's them. Listen now, for I assume I won't be around much longer, and you really must hear my tale.
>
> Some short time ago, I was sitting at my place of residence, my small son sleeping nearby. My wife, rest her soul, had succumbed to pneumonia this past year. This particular evening, I was enjoying a meal when my door opened. Without warning, the tall man, the man whom you see outside, entered. Not knowing who he was or what business he had with me, I got up at once. I spoke to him—yes, I believe I said "Excuse me, sir" or something to that effect, but he appeared to not understand. Seeing the look on his face, I retreated a few spaces, but he continued toward me. I raised my voice, but with no result. At this time my son awoke, and before I knew it, this white stranger with seemingly no comprehension of my words, opened his coat and removed what appeared to be a small pistol of some sort. I know it sounds unthinkable, but can you imagine what he did next? Yes! He shot me! He actually shot me! the last thing I remembered of that night was my son's innocent two-year-old look of curiosity. The wide eyes, as if to say, "What is happening father?" And with that, my world faded to black!

This particular story, which continues for some four typed pages, seems to be written in the style of a typical Poe narrator stuck in his mind's illusions. The young writer, however, gives us a twist close to the end and finishes with the following lines that make us reread his story now from a very different perspective as we begin to realize that it was the chimp narrating this story all along and not a person:

> And the cluster of men in the white coats exited without an utterance. One chimpanzee, though, with bruises on his forehead and cuts lacing his arms, continued in what seemed to be a conversation—with nobody!

Other students, intrigued by the fact that Poe concentrated on setting as the predominant feature of "The Masque of the Red Death," try their hands at reproducing that focus. Here are the first few paragraphs of another young male student's effort at capturing this particular technique:

> Somewhere during the middle ages in Italy, in the heart of the Holy Roman Empire, there was a castle—oh yes, a castle—large, unforgiving, stone, angular—a castle.

> This was no ordinary castle; upon closer inspection one might expect to see the usual fortifications of a castle—a drawbridge here, a moat there, and mere slits for windows to provide the ultimate in defense. But this castle had none of those luxuries; no, this castle had none of that, not a moat with some mythical beast in it waiting to destroy an entire army of metallic, shiny knights. No, this castle had one unique form of defense, it floated. That's it, it just floated. From a far, it would appear to be a part of the landscape, but up close it was seen that only a large chunk of land, seemingly carved out of the ground, held it up. The boulder of dirt floated a good hundred feet off the ground blackening the ground beneath it.
>
> Upon an even closer inspection, one would see that this castle was not built of many thousands of individual blocks of stone, but rather one single huge stone. One stone so large that it could not have come from any single quarry in the world; and if it were to, how would any people move it? Its walls were smooth, so smooth as to appear to shine like glass in the moonlight.

As noted before, a large percentage of the girls would rather choose to emulate the frame story format. For the most part, girls steer clear of the gory types of stories and find the frame story able to hold any kind of tale they choose to write—especially romantic ones. Here is the beginning section of a frame story written by one of my better young writers that continues in the vein of "The Oval Portrait":

> After having fallen into a troubled dream-filled slumber, I abruptly awoke thinking I heard footsteps. Pedro too awoke and checking the locks assured me that no one had entered the chateau. Thoroughly awake now, I turned my attention from the world of dreams and trespassers and focused my attention on the picture directly in front of me at the foot of my bed. Before me, bathed in the warm candlelight, was a richly framed oil painting of an aged silver maple—branches stretching out toward a midsummer sky at sunset. The deep glow of the sun's waning rays, drenching the silver-sided leaves and velvet limbs left me with an impulse to hold my breath and hush the volume of my thoughts and words in its presence. Turning from the hypnotic magnetism of the jewel-tipped leaves, I re-opened the volume and found the painting's number.

Not all of my writers have as good a grasp of vocabulary, sentence structure, and rhythm as this one does, but that doesn't matter. What matters is that students enjoy producing what they can. They write to delight, not to get a grade. They learn from each other's growth and from their own efforts and risk taking. This unit emphasizes short story formats; other units will emphasize essays, arguments, poetry, speeches, or any of the other types of writing that we will be reading. We will not ask students to write only personal pieces, nor will we ask them to write only academic argumentative pieces. We will strive for a balance both in our request for experimentation and our required products.

Multipurpose Content: *The House on Mango Street*

Many schools have been using Sandra Cisneros's *The House on Mango Street* since it was first published in 1984. It is a traditional *bildungsroman*—that is, a coming-of-age story—that focuses on the problems of being a woman in a largely patriarchal Hispanic society. The book is a collection of short vignettes—some only a few paragraphs in length—that present Esperanza's observations and experiences in the barrio throughout a year. Through the use of this material, students gain a greater understanding of the fact that many issues are not able to be resolved quickly or easily. We also want our students to come to the realization that they share many of the same problems and experiences as those from other cultures and backgrounds. We will arrive at these understandings by pulling out Cisneros's themes and topics, imitating the vignette form, and examining our own class's trends in thinking and writing. We will use our own writing, in other words, as the basis for further learning.

Pulling Out the Topics

As we examine the book with the class, students comment on the chapter headings, the strange length of some of the chapters, and the general differences from other books they have read. The fact that Cisneros has described some of her writing in this book to be more like "lazy poems" makes students wonder even more about what it is they will be reading. We share some of our plans for how we will approach the book. We tell our students we would like to eventually come up with a booklet of similarly formed vignettes but under the title of our school and our school's street. In order to do this, we will have to make a list of all the topics we encounter as we read the tiny chapters. The students' first job, then, is to decide on a topic that covers each of the vignettes as they read and to keep a list. We compare and build our lists one set at a time. Figure 8.1 shows the beginning of one list that a class agreed to use.

Set One:	Writing Topics
The House on Mango Street	My house or a house I've lived in
Hairs	Your hair; your family's hair
Boys and Girls	A best friend's, differences between boys and girls
My Name	Names; my name; I wish it were _____.
Cathy Queen of Cats	Neighbors; strange neighbors; bad neighborhoods
Set Two:	
Our Good Day	Getting people to like you; buying friendship
Laughter	Sisters; types of laughs; like-minded people
Gil's Furniture Bought & Sold	The small neighborhood store; desired items in stores
Meme Ortiz	A tree; an important tree; accident
Louie, His Cousin and His . . .	The show-off; trouble with the law; teen boy drivers
Set Three:	
Marin	Restlessness of teenagers; the older, wiser teenager
Those Who Don't	Fear of other neighborhoods; afraid of things that are different
There Was an Old Woman . . .	Families with kids out of control; large families
Alicia Who Sees Mice	Fears; trying to make a better life
Darius and the Clouds	Clouds; lack of beauty in poor parts of town
Set Four:	
And Some More	Names kids call each other; our many names
The Family of Little Feet	Scared of abusive men; danger in "dressing up"
A Rice Sandwich	School lunch time; scary nuns
Chanclas	Embarrassed by clothes; new outfit (almost)
Hips	Changing bodies

Figure 8.1: Vignette topics for *The House on Mango Street*.

There are nine such sets of vignettes in the book. As we deal with the content, we can also employ some of the following strategies:

- Ask students to silently read a set of vignettes and pick one of the topics to write on.

- Give students one of the topics beforehand to write on before they have read the selections.

- Ask for volunteers to read the next day's pieces (this gives them practice time to read the material silently first).

- Have students read and tape record a section beforehand in groups of five (each student gets one piece to read). Use the recordings for absent students and for class listening.

- Use a big sheet of paper on the wall to begin drawing the neighborhood based on the descriptions they read (use cutout houses, stores, and so on).

- Use a huge cutout of a child on which to write all the descriptions we get about Esperanza as the book goes on.

- Do as much work with rewriting good sentences, mimicking good descriptions, and so on as you can fit in.

- Have students circle the best sentence in each of their own essays. Read these aloud.

- Teach what a vignette is. Give them background information about where the book takes place.

- Select vignettes with lots of dialogue and ask students to read the different parts as you read the exposition.

The preceding list consists of only a few of the strategies that we could use to deliver the content. Since our main product, as we explained to the students in the beginning of this unit, is the production of our own "School on [your school's street] Booklet, we are all intent on choosing topics we can really consider genuine. We continue to build our personal collection of vignettes as we proceed with the reading. Some of these vignettes might be ones we all write on, while others are chosen by the students. By the end of the book, each student has a collection of around a dozen vignettes in his or her folder. Students are then asked to choose the two they feel are their best writing, their favorite pieces, or ones others could best relate to. These two are then typed up and combined with the favorites from the other students. A complete set with a cover page designed by a volunteering student is printed for each student. This sounds like a lot of paper, but we will be using these booklets for far more than simply reprinting a set of student pieces, as we will explain soon.

Nothing is more enjoyable for students than reading each other's work. The day we distribute these booklets is one filled with more than the usual engaged reading and quiet. We ask our students to write a quick response to what they have read, telling how they feel about their classmates' topic choices and explanations. We do this before we discuss them as a group. Then we entertain comments over the whole booklet regarding the most often used topic, the scope of topics and styles, the inclusion of humor, and the seriousness of tone.

Math Meets the Vignette Booklet

We then ask our students to find partners to work with for this particular assignment. They are to think up an area to analyze concerning the student work, such as:

- What is the length of these essays?

- Do boys or girls write longer or shorter narratives? What is The average? the mean?

- What observations can we make concerning the setting of the narratives?

- What categories did most students write about?

- Did these categories differ from girls to boys?

- What was the age of the subject in the narratives?

- What emotions do boys most often express?

- What do girls write about?

Since sometimes the booklets contain the essays of two or more classes of students, some teams decide to compare differences in the classes and discuss how the time that a class was scheduled might affect the writing itself.

Students decide what their questions will be and then begin the task of charting or graphing their findings. A written explanation of their results accompanies their data sheets. Each pair will give an oral report to the class. Most students find this mix of math and student writing a very interesting and unusual assignment—definitely one they hadn't been asked to do before.

Figure 8.2 and figure 8.3 are examples of graphics that students working in pairs have created using the essays as the base of their investigation. They were free to choose their topics and their method of illustrating their results. This activity was done in one class period with students working on the drawings and explanations as a homework assignment. A pair of tenth-grade girls summarized the graph this way:

> We found that girls generally have longer stories than boys. Most people wrote between eleven and forty typed lines. On average, girls have ranges from eleven to twenty-one and thirty lines [*sic*] whereas boys created stories that range from eleven to twenty lines. Only one girl and one boy typed more than forty lines. Finally, three boys and two girls wrote pieces of ten lines or less.

A pair of tenth-grade boys summarized the graph this way:

> This chart shows that people wrote vignettes about vacations the most. Many others wrote about memories that were from home or school. In our other charts (not included here) you can see that girls wrote more about vacations and boys wrote more about their relatives. Also, we recognized that most stories were in present tense or near present tense. Perhaps that's because recent events are easier to remember. Finally, girls seem to have written more than the guys, and the only explanation for that we can think of is guys seem to summarize more than girls. Both groups avoided sad topics.

As students examine these papers, many see how they could have dug deeper and not just chosen superficial items to compare. Students also recognize how little they interpreted their results and that they should have given it more thought. The second explanation of the types of topics students chose to write on is just such a rudimentary effort.

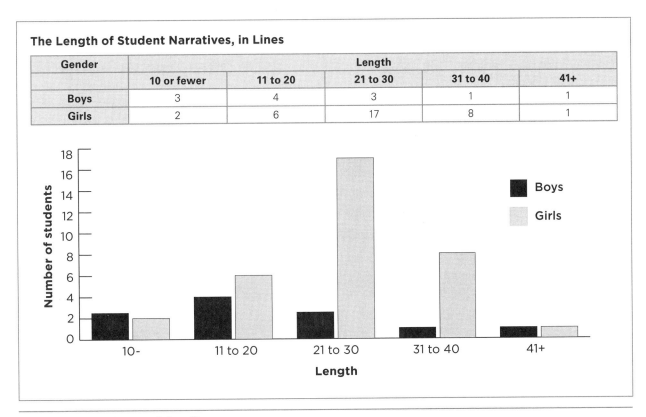

The Length of Student Narratives, in Lines

Gender	Length				
	10 or fewer	11 to 20	21 to 30	31 to 40	41+
Boys	3	4	3	1	1
Girls	2	6	17	8	1

Figure 8.2: Student writing fluency.

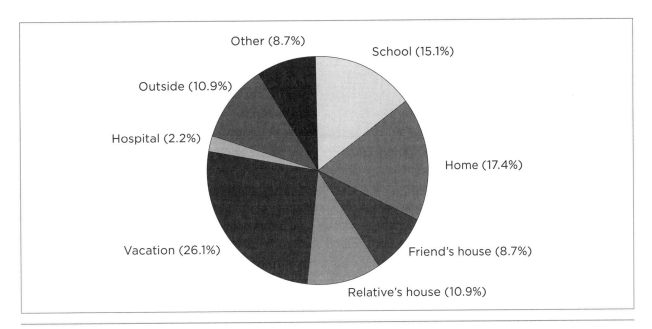

Figure 8.3: Topics chosen most frequently.

If allowed to repeat this assignment later in the year with different sets of papers, the results will be dramatically improved. We seldom give our students this opportunity to better their skills. This is one of the reasons they feel a lack of continuity in most classes; students learn a skill and are deprived of the chance to try it out again at a later date. Quality work usually needs more than a one-shot effort at a new skill or process. Spiral learning opportunities are necessary for both memory and quality performance. By spiral learning I mean the planned repetition of studying a subject at a later date, at higher levels of difficulty and in greater depth. A strong point about the Common Core State Standards is the necessity to view learning as spiraling in order for it to stick. The student work examples just examined is significant on a couple of levels: first, they are rudimentary attempts at combining the discipline of math with the discipline of language arts. With opportunities to blend what students learn in one area with material in another, students can see real-time relationships in their learning as opposed to "pigeon-holed" learning. Too often we hear students ask a teacher questions such as "Why do we have to write in history class? This isn't language arts." or "Why do I have to worry about looking at the audience or speaking up when I give my presentation in this class? It isn't a speech course, is it?" Second, the work begs for a "re-do" opportunity—a repetition of the activity so that it can improve and demonstrate greater expertise. Recognizing these types of realities in student work allows us to plan ahead so as to better cement skills and concepts and ultimately promote more substantial growth and achievement.

If you have a great assignment that both introduces and practices a new skill or process, determine how and when you will repeat this activity later in the year so that it cements the learning and offers your students an opportunity to really show improvement over their first attempts. You'll be doing yourself and them a real favor!

Vignette Booklet Becomes Grammar and Writing Craft Book

Now we can explain more fully why handing each student a copy of all the vignettes is worth the money in paper and copying. We will be using this book of students' writing to teach all the grammatical constructions that these students are responsible for mastering throughout the year. We did not edit any of the essays, vignettes, or narratives that were turned in. We have a priceless collection of their current writing complete with all their strengths and weaknesses. For ease in manipulating the material, we number each of the pages and the essays.

While introducing the craft of writing effective introductions, we select a couple of students' essays and set to work offering suggestions for different ways to begin the writings. We will also look at how our fellow classmates might have used effective beginnings already. Another day, we will focus on good titles and choose a few essays to retitle for better emphasis and appeal. When we need a review of comma use in transposed adverbial clauses starting a sentence, we comb through our booklet for sentences correctly punctuated and those that need assistance. We, as the teachers, always guide this investigation and make sure it is clear that when we use a person's essay to learn new ways to better our writing, there is no implication that the owner of the essay has done anything wrong. How can you be blamed for making a mistake about something you haven't been taught yet? Actually, most students can't wait for us to choose their essays to use as the samples we will be working on as a class.

An Interdisciplinary Unit With-High Engagement Potential

Although the lessons related to the book *The House on Mango Street* succeed in widening the scope of what can be done with a book besides simply reading it and answering questions, they are still narrow in regard to their use of complementary material. In today's world—a world that seems to have shrunk to the point that we are instantly made aware of what is happening to others many miles away—we as educators must push the parameters of our curriculum offerings to make conscious connections for our students to the events swirling around us and dramatically affecting our lives.

An example of a series of lessons that does push the parameters is *Buy, Use, Toss?* This free, downloadable, two-week unit on all phases of consumerism, which by its very nature is engaging to students, is accessible online. Our students are consumers with distinct tastes and desires. Since they were babies in front of the television, they have been massaged by the best of advertising efforts to make buying one of their highest priorities. *Buy, Use, Toss?* is produced by Facing the Future, a Seattle-based national educational nonprofit organization whose mission is to engage students in learning by making academics relevant to their lives. Its website (www.facingthefuture.org) explains that its purpose is to empower students to think critically, analyze marketers' persuasive techniques, develop a global perspective, and participate in positive solutions for a sustainable future.

For those wondering how to make learning more relevant to their students' lives while still covering standards and objectives, it is well worth examining materials that are now being developed and offered for free by organizations like Facing the Future. One of the singular benefits of access to the Internet is the ability we now have to gather rich, wide-perspective resources to lift our personal bar of course rigor while simultaneously offering authentic opportunities for student engagement. We no longer have any legitimate reason to blame the narrowness of textbook materials for stagnant learning in our classrooms. It is our obligation as professionals to utilize the wealth of supplementary resources that are literally at our fingertips.

Project Learning at the Core of Engagement

Many of the longer samples included in this book are project-oriented units. Experience has shown many great teachers over the years the benefits of clustering learning into a cause or purpose larger than the sum of its parts. The essence of rigorous learning is propelling our students' internal drive to find out, to create, to do something of value and merit. This drive is never satisfied by short pieces taken from the whole, or from an emphasis on discreet skills unrelated to each other and disjointed in the minds of the learners. I urge you as interested readers to examine the project-based learning being designed and successfully taught in classrooms all over North America. One source is Lesson Planet: The Search Engine for Teachers (www .lessonplanet.com), which provides over 400,000 teacher-reviewed lessons. Today's window of opportunity opened by the CCSS, while still in its infancy, is a boon to creative teachers. One such teacher to follow, whose classroom work bears replicating, is a twelve-year teaching veteran and California Regional Teacher of the Year, Heather Wolpert-Gawron.

Wolpert-Gawron (2011a) defines project-based writing units as "a series of constructed units built around authentic audience and authentic learning that incorporates the multiple writing genres. That is, it's all about blurring the lines between school life and the real world. The goal is: if it doesn't apply outside of school, then it isn't worthy enough to teach inside of school." Her first such unit is called the DARPA/NASA unit.

Here is Wolpert-Gawron's explanation on how inspiration knocks on the brain, walks in, and begins spinning a plan for execution. This one began when her husband told her about a conference in which participants would brainstorm ways to colonize a planet within a hundred years. She explains:

> The Conference would be segregated into 7 tracks, all focused on different aspects of what it would take to colonize: the time-distance issues, economic challenges, medical considerations, communicating and publicizing the rationale, etc. . . . As I read over the website, it occurred to me that applying to

speak at a conference was a work of a persuasive writing exercise. It also occurred to me that studying these different "tracks" and synthesizing one's research into a proposal was a sort of an executive summary. And lo, a Project Based Writing Unit was born. (Wolpert-Gawron, 2011a)

After accepting her own challenge to construct this unit, things began to come together. Students would become authorities on one of the seven tracks. They would research and complete other assignments, leading up to a mock panel discussion. What happened then was not part of the original plan. Wolpert-Gawron's students were invited to present their findings via Skype to those very scientists, futurists, ethicists, and sci-fi writers attending the conference. How much more authentic an audience could you ask for than this? To read about Wolpert-Gawron's journey and the DARPA project, go to her website (http://tweenteacher.com) or read her Edutopia blog posts (www.edutopia.org/spiralnotebook/heather-wolpert-gawron) for inspiration and insight. Here are Wolpert-Gawron's ten reasons for moving to project-based learning:

1. It is an organic way to integrate all CORE subjects: math, science, history, and language arts
2. It proves to students that imagination and creativity are connected to research and expository writing
3. It hits all the major elements of the higher level of Bloom's Taxonomy: analysis, evaluation, and creation
4. By allowing a student to choose their format of showing what they know, the buy-in for the quality of the final project is tremendous
5. Students develop projects individualized, unique, and specific from each other
6. It is a powerful way to incorporate all multiple intelligences: visual, audio, kinesthetic, musical, linguistic, logical, and so on
7. It desegregates nonfiction and fiction, blending the two
8. It integrates the CORE subjects with non-core subjects, potentially using technology, art, music, etc.
9. It is a rigorous assessment requiring high levels of thought and communication
10. It requires use of the entire writing process from brainstorm through revision, editing, and final draft regardless of the genres picked and the topic chosen (Wolpert-Gawron, 2012)

Conclusion

Only when students see a connection between one assignment and another, between one skill set and another, as the days and weeks of the school year go by do they begin to feel a sense of purpose and begin to trust our ability to design and unfold lessons. They see the string of pearls we have been meticulously preparing for them. The activities in this chapter belong to large units. For the most part, they are capable of covering a topic that can be examined from multiple perspectives. We create our string of pearls from what we have available to us, be it time, materials, standards, or observed necessity based on our students' skills or lack of skills. No matter how perfect a pearl necklace other effective teachers might construct, we need to first examine the pearls in our own context and manipulate them to fit our strings. Relinquishing the responsibility of lesson design to anyone is relinquishing the authority of our roles as professional educators to attune to our students' needs. It also relinquishes the joy and satisfaction that has kept many of us in the classroom for decades.

Chapter Nine

Standards and Assessments Fostering Literacy Growth

Everyone interested in literacy development recognizes the need to develop a balanced attitude between the assessments under the teacher's control and those that aren't. Spending the entire year trying to prepare students for that once-a-year test at the end in the spring with "test prep" regimes is not productive pedagogy. Teachers need to assume a more courageous stance against the paralyzing effects of fear, which can monopolize their thinking and conversations when dealing with the topic of high-stakes testing. We have seen testing become overemphasized and obsessed over by students, teachers, and administrators alike to the detriment of providing for our students a rich, deep program filled with a variety of experiences. This chapter is an attempt to provide a little more balance to the discussion of the role assessment plays in dictating our use of time, energy, and instruction, as well as to examine a more than superficial relationship between standards and their authentic assessments.

Let's begin by defining our terms.

Educational or academic *standards* are basically the criteria set to determine levels of student achievement, or the particular set of skills and knowledge that should be attained in specific grade levels or courses of study. According to the Common Core State Standards Initiative mission statement:

> The Common Core State Standards provide a consistent, clear understanding of what students are expected to learn, so teachers and parents know what they need to do to help them. The standards are designed to be robust and relevant to the real world, reflecting the knowledge and skills that our young people need for success in college and careers. With American students fully prepared for the future, our communities will be best positioned to compete successfully in the global economy. (Common Core State Standards Initiative, 2012)

Assessments, on the other hand, can be defined as more than appraisals, evaluations, or ratings. The Higher Learning Commission (2006), in a workshop entitled Making a Difference in Student Learning: Assessment as a Core Strategy, stated that assessment should provide data on student learning, serve to allow teachers to analyze and use data to improve both teaching and learning, provide evidence of such learning, offer areas in need of improvement and an evaluation of whether such changes have been beneficial, and provide documentation of such efforts. Formative assessments can be defined as assessments *for* learning while summative assessments are assessments *of* learning. The teacher's ability and opportunity to use formative assessment effectively will be the focus in this chapter, especially in regard to the new requirements set by the Common Core State Standards.

Assessment as a Key

A key can be used to open or to close, to free or to imprison, to safeguard or to withhold. It is just this duality that serves to make it a good metaphor for the creation and implementation of standards and

137

assessments in today's educational institutions. All too often, the purpose of assessments moves away from being a measure to enable teachers to adjust teaching, consider changes, analyze student work, and adjust for improvement. It becomes a goal in itself—a goal to rank, sort, punish, and label not only the one being assessed but the assessors and the buildings where the assessments are carried out. When this is the reality, assessment is ineffective and distorted. Standards also can become instruments of imprisonment, rather than freeing tools for better learning, if they are limited in their scope, unrealistic in their benchmarks, and restrictive, and if they tie the hands of teachers trying to follow them judiciously.

On the other hand, thoughtfully conceived standards and assessments that are open enough to allow teachers flexibility will provide a tremendous boost to the success of their efforts. So we need to carefully examine the keys of standards and assessments and use them for our benefit and not for our entrapment.

The Evolution of Standards

When we speak of academic standards, many of us have visions of three-ringed binders filled with pages and pages of carefully numbered and lettered items that serve as statements of what students should be learning. For years, these books of standards resided in the principals' offices on shelves populated with similar books of district procedures, student handbooks, and school-board declarations of rules and regulations. Ironically, those charged with the job of carrying out these standards never really had access to them.

Times have changed since then, and one can hardly find a classroom today that doesn't have a laminated list of district and state standards taped to one of the walls or stapled to a bulletin board. One will also likely find a place in the room where the day's objectives are prominently displayed for students and walk-by evaluators to access. We are genuinely moving toward becoming an educational army of standards-based instructors. Soon most states will have teachers exchanging their posted state standards for copies of the Common Core State Standards. One of the major areas that will change, besides the looks of the posters we tape to our walls, will be the way we approach and think about literacy.

How Are the Common Core State Standards Different?

Although the standards give separate consideration for the four strands of reading, writing, speaking, and listening, and language, the intent is not to address these four separately in the classroom but to integrate them throughout instruction. These dimensions are not to be considered the sole domain of the English language arts teachers any longer. Rather, they are to be spread across the curriculum and interwoven into the history, social studies, science, and technical subjects as well.

Along with this interdisciplinary emphasis, "the CCSS emphasize *rigor* and connect it with what is called *textual complexity*, a term that refers to levels of meaning, quantitative readability measures, and reader variables such as motivation and experience" (Wessling, 2011, p. 8). What this means is that our students will be guided to actually read and work from the text. They will be urged to stretch their current reading stamina and push through frustration to do deeper thinking, talking, writing, and learning. The "text" does not refer to the textbook alone. Teachers are urged to pull in a wider assortment of textual materials than was once considered adequate and to broaden the concept of text to include a wider range of media as well.

If the CCSS take hold in classrooms across the United States, there will be a tremendous shift both physically and theoretically in where the teacher stands in the room. No longer will a teacher standing in front of the room—lecturing to the class, giving questions to be answered and worksheets to be filled out, followed by a test of the information covered—be the norm. An interactive, discourse-oriented workshop approach will take its place. Students read, then make claims, assertions, and predictions, and then back these up with textual support. This teaching method is effective in pulling our students into the realms of higher-order thinking, and that is one of the main goals of the CCSS.

What's Necessary to Get to This Type of Student-Text Interaction?

Moving students from old habits of learning is at times as difficult as moving teachers from old habits of teaching. To engage students in rigorous, independent, interactive behaviors with difficult texts means that attention must be given to a student's sense of self-efficacy. What a student thinks he or she is capable of doing will dictate to a large extent how much he or she will expend motivation and effort. Those students with a low sense of self-efficacy will most likely balk at attempting work that appears difficult and will likely end in failure. These are the students who will do anything to disrupt the class in hopes of avoiding having to do the work. When we recognize the causes for much of this negative student behavior, we can better reach these students and plan ways to help them meet the new challenges.

As we have noted, the interplay of a teacher's soft skills is now of primary importance. With heightened emphasis on moving students out of their comfort zones and asking them to extend more effort than usual, teachers must provide a trusting environment, give nurturing support to struggling students, give praise for all small successes, build a relationship with each student, possess an awareness of which students are losing hope in their abilities, and offer emotional scaffolding until their self-efficacy kicks in. Because it is often difficult for students to notice that they are improving their reading or writing ability, teachers need to be constantly working on their students' sense of their own abilities, so that long-term improvement can be reached.

Dale Schunk, former dean of the School of Education at the University of North Carolina at Greensboro, points out the type of strategies and behaviors necessary to make this type of adjustment. Four of the most effective are holding consistent goal-setting conferences with students over what skills and behaviors are necessary to handle the learning, constantly modeling thinking and mental responses to text, having students perform periodic self-evaluations with teacher feedback to their progress, and giving prompts to those who are not able to do this themselves (Schunk, 2003). This is formative assessment.

Formative Assessment: Where the Rubber Hits the Road

Discussing the value of state and national assessments is not the function, nor is it within the context, of this discussion. When we speak about what it looks like in the classroom, we need to turn our collective focus to those types of assessments within our control. We look specifically at those assessments that make the most difference in student growth in literacy achievement. We look at formative assessment. Dylan Wiliam, director of the Learning and Teaching Research Center at the Educational Testing Service (ETS), has written in depth on the efficacy and essence of formative assessment in his book *Embedded Formative Assessment*. As to just what that essence is, Wiliam (2011) concludes, "Teaching is a contingent activity. We cannot predict what students will learn as a result of any particular sequence of instruction. Formative assessment involves getting the best possible evidence about what students have learned and then using this information to decide what to do next" (p. 50). It is precisely this unpredictability that should make us leery of programs and products that guarantee to do the heavy lifting of formative assessment for the teacher. This is contrary to the very nature of formative assessment. Finding out what students are or aren't understanding during the actual class period and adjusting to accommodate that information is the one most important activity that teachers can do. It is the one most important way to improve achievement.

A fundamental element of student engagement is a thorough awareness of what we are trying to achieve. When students have a clear picture of the goals they are aiming for and feel they are capable of reaching those goals, they are far more likely to expend the effort necessary to succeed. One of the many strengths of formative assessment is its ability to immediately redirect students as they work, so that they don't have to muddle through wondering if they are on the right track when in fact they might not be. Nothing satisfies the brain like feedback. Any teacher who shows a dislike for answering student questions while students are working on the tasks assigned, who shows with words or body language that he or she doesn't want to be disturbed, has not yet figured out just what the essential job of a teacher really is.

Let's look at the kinds of assessment most within our control, from answering questions, to creating complex rubrics, to setting aside time for reflection on what has been learned.

The Persuasive Argument

A cluster of lessons that emphasize the need for returning to the text to pull out evidence that will support a student-created statement or thesis are given in the following section. They all fall under the umbrella of the persuasive argument. These pieces are accompanied by samples of formative assessment activities that highlight the teacher's role in providing an environment conducive to moving students from being passive receptors of information to actively empowered independent learners. Following this section, our focus moves to self-assessment through portfolios, self-constructed tests, and building a habit of reflection.

Persuasive Writing: One Key to Incorporating Common Core Requirements

The emphasis of the Common Core State Standards from the earliest years up to the end of high school is on having students engage in writing that arises from using texts not only to prove a point or to make a case but to persuade others that their position is both logical and the best one to take. Wolpert-Gawron (2011c) points out:

> If you look through the Common Core Standards, you'll see words peppered all over the place that point to persuasive writing: *interpret, argument, analyze.* The focus isn't to provide evidence as the sole means to prove, but rather to make an argument and bring in evidence that one must then justify through argumentation.

Wolpert-Gawron (2011c) goes on to suggest that a subtle shift in purposing a writing assignment around an explanation of theme or character development to convincing the reader of the validity of a particular position would not only blend the two genres, but it would strengthen the substance of the paper considerably. I have found this to be true.

One Flew Over the Cuckoo's Nest

Ken Kesey's (1962) *One Flew Over the Cuckoo's Nest* provides a good illustration of how this works in the classroom. Students are given the task of writing a persuasive letter to the hospital board asking for either the release of the main character, Randle Patrick McMurphy, who has faked insanity to avoid serving out the remainder of a prison sentence, or for the termination of Nurse Ratched as head nurse on the men's ward. Students have the option of writing this letter from the point of view of Dr. Spivey, a ward doctor; Chief Bromden, the novel's half–Native American narrator; one of the Acutes—a patient who is considered curable; or Candy, the prostitute McMurphy brings onto the ward. Students are to be sure to choose and use enough examples from the text to bolster their claims. The style of writing should reflect the persona of the character from whose perspective they have chosen to write the letter. The arguments should be strong enough to convince the board to overturn the request of Nurse Ratched to keep McMurphy in the disturbed ward indefinitely, using unlimited electric shock therapy and the possibility of a lobotomy, or to convince the board to ask for her resignation. This type of assignment makes the following demands on the student:

1. Select the specific point of view to be used.

2. Determine in light of this persona what arguments would be feasible.

3. Choose the facts and textual information that supports this persona's arguments.

4. Focus on the purpose of the letter—persuading the board to override the decision of one of its employees regarding treatment of a patient or persuading it to terminate an employee.

5. Write in the tone and style appropriate to the chosen persona.

6. Determine and counter any arguments that might be lodged against yours.

7. Above all, be persuasive and passionate throughout the letter.

One of the most interesting aspects of using the persuasive overlay with any assignment is what happens to the work of bright students who can always cover the requirements of a paper but who seem all too often to lack the passion and deeper thought that we teachers know these students are capable of expressing. These papers are more than formulaic exercises. I have seen the shocked look of students getting back papers that didn't have the usual *A* grade on them. Immediately they are at my desk asking what possibly could have been missing. They would show how they had provided more than the minimum reasons, examples, and textual references; the required format and structure; even the fancy additional letterhead or another techy add-on. My response would be, "You didn't persuade me! Your examples and your arguments were weak and lacked much by way of validity and logic and passion. Yes, everything is there, but it isn't strong material and it doesn't make me want to override the nurse's recommendation in regard to McMurphy or fire her." This usually will happen to these bright students only once. After that, the quality rises to meet my expectations!

Freak the Mighty

These types of assignments that push students to perform over and above the usual basic requirements they might have been used to in the past are surely not for the older students alone. Many middle school teachers teach Rodman Philbrick's (1993) novel *Freak the Mighty*, about two middle school boys ostracized because of their odd physical conditions. Kevin, who is far more intelligent than most his age, suffers from Morquio syndrome and must wear leg braces and use crutches and is consequently very clumsy. Max is a sensitive, two-hundred-pound thirteen-year-old who does poorly in school and shies away from other students. Kevin tutors Max and invites him to read his favorite book on Arthurian legends. These legends of heroes provide a thematic motif that runs the length of the novel. For a persuasive paper that would serve this material, students are asked to choose a character—either Max or Kevin—whom they feel would make a good candidate to join those assembling around King Arthur's round table. They write a letter to King Arthur petitioning that their chosen character be considered and selected for knighthood.

Their letters must include at least three to five good reasons—he is loyal, fights to protect the less able, shows determination and fortitude, is brave, and so on. Then each reason must be accompanied by an example taken from the text. These examples and reasons should be written within a commentary that supports the purpose of the piece and provides enough persuasion that King Arthur himself would grant the request.

Two interesting results came from this assignment. On one occasion, I added a small but tremendously effective engagement tool: each student was given a piece of scroll stationery. Because of this simple addition, students put at least twice as much effort in writing and rewriting their rough drafts so that their final products would be as good as possible. Secondly, as just described, a bright student found that his rough draft wasn't A material and demanded to know why. He explained to me that he always got the top grades on everything he did, that he was the smartest boy in his class, and that that no one wrote as well as he did. It was only fair that he got an A. He was right that he had always been given high marks and that he was the smartest person in his class; but he was wrong that those two reasons automatically made his work quality material. I took out persuasive essays that were benchmark papers for the state assessments and showed him the difference between his paper and those considered A quality throughout the state. It was as if that proverbial lightbulb went on in that student's head. I told him his competition might not be in his small school classroom but rather outside the borders of his town. His competitive nature didn't need me to say any more. He was determined to be the best anywhere and against anyone else. My job was to show him how and not let him settle for anything less. Needless to say, his rough draft was decidedly reworked, the result was one of that student's proudest efforts, and he found the challenge exhilarating.

Bare Bones of the Persuasive Overlay

Nothing is more integrated into real-life interactions and communication than persuasion. We are bombarded at every turn with advertisements, political commercials, and efforts to have us buy things and act the way others want us to. We are constantly subjected to others' efforts at persuading us. There is little that is more of a real-life experience than this form of discourse. Wolpert-Gawron (2011c) gives a three-pronged method of writing the persuasion paper that could be adopted by anyone in any curriculum area. If we want students writing arguments, analyzing data, and synthesizing and reporting on findings across all curriculum content fields, this pattern could be of use for everyone:

- #1 Thesis Statement/Main Topic Sentence—the thesis is the map of the essay. It not only states the argument but gives an indication of the organization of the essay. All subjects must standardize the need to see one in a student's argument regardless of the content.

- #2 Evidence—Evidence is the quote, the computation, the data, the statistics, and the findings. Evidence backs up the argument made in the thesis statement. This is the content that the teacher as subject matter expert must verify. But it doesn't end there.

- #3 Commentary—Commentary is the original thought. It doesn't just translate the evidence to the layman; it brings in a new layer to the information that brings the argument home. (Wolpert-Gawron, 2011c)

Since many teachers are shifting their instruction to include more argumentative-writing experiences, small concise patterns like these are perfect for easily embedding into their lessons.

Involving Parents in a Persuasive Writing Activity

Years ago, I picked up an idea from a discussion with a few fellow English teachers while attending a writing conference. The name of the conference and the names of the fellow teachers are gone now, but the idea has stayed alive, probably because this assignment became one of the more engaging writing assignments many of my students had experienced.

To teach the process of persuasive writing, we use as our content the wishes, desires, and everyday points of contention that fill teenager-parent conversations. We write to parents or guardians and persuade them to allow their son or daughter to have a privilege, buy a product, change a house rule—anything that they could imagine wanting! This isn't a normal writing assignment, though, since we involve those parents or guardians from the very beginning. We send a letter home with each student concerning the assignment with the request that they make a list on the back of the letter of all the reasons why they won't allow their son or daughter to have their request. This list will serve as an important part of the learning process on how to handle the art of persuasion.

A Sample Letter to Parents

Teacher name:
School address:
Phone/email:

Dear Parent or Guardian of _____,

_____ is a student in my _____ hour communication arts class. We are about to learn how to best write persuasive papers. This skill is one of the cornerstones of the Common Core State Standards now adopted by most of the states of the United States. Your help is both welcome and necessary.

Your son or daughter has chosen a privilege, purchase, or change in your current household rules that he or she would like to see happen. The topic that he or she will be trying to persuade you to change your mind about is _____.

Your job is to think up as many reasons as possible why you should not grant this request to your child. The more you can think up—and don't be afraid to write down some really outrageous reasons along with reasonable ones—the better the opportunity to create a good, persuasive letter back to you. Please jot your objections down on the back of this sheet, and have your son or daughter return them to me by _____ at the latest. We are grateful in advance for your cooperation in this assignment.

When you receive the finished copy of the letter in response to your list of objections, we would appreciate your signing that letter to verify that you read it, and feel free to add any comments you would like to send back concerning how persuaded or unpersuaded you are!

Again, thank you for your cooperation in this activity. If you have any questions you would like to address to me, please feel free to email or call.

Sincerely,

To begin the process of actually writing the letter, we take plenty of time brainstorming what possible requests students might want to make of their parents. We make a list of categories and build a board full of desires that include the right to paint a room or move into a different room, the right to extend a curfew or not even have one, the right to go on a trip with another friend or drive alone to a far-off destination, the right to get a job or quit a job, the right to get a tattoo or a piercing, the right to buy a motorcycle or a car, the right to an unlimited texting package for the cell phone—the list is often quite extensive! When everyone settles on a topic, we move on.

Next, we make our own lists of why we should be allowed this particular request. We write as many reasons as we can think up and then ask our neighbors to read our lists and add any reasons we might have forgotten. Students who have a difficult time thinking up their reasons have the advantage of getting help from their peers.

Nearly all students return to class with their letters containing a list of parental objections to the specific requests. After composing our lists, we examine the reasons parents gave for not allowing this request. We then begin to find ways to respond to their objections. We fill our papers with enough material to make our claims.

Now we prioritize our lists. We decide on our strongest arguments and our best responses to parental objections, and we throw out any that seem weak or unimpressive. We begin to gather our evidence in support of our claims. If a student says that he or she should be allowed a new privilege, the student must explain why. If the answer is "because you can trust me," that student must then supply evidence that he or she has been trustworthy in the past and proceed to give strong examples. Every claim or reason must have solid evidence to support it. In this way, we build our best arguments in response to parental objections.

Peer response plays a vital part in this exercise. In small groups of three or four, students share their main points and evidence with each other, asking for feedback. Sometimes a student can offer a better example of evidence another can use; sometimes a student is shown a better way to frame his arguments or how to add more details.

Now we're ready to write the first draft and use all the material we have accumulated. Most of the work is finished, which surprises some students. Are they saving their best argument for last? Are they going to use it in the beginning? Where do they want to address their parents' objections? This is choice-making time—time to choose what order to put things in in order to have a greater impact. One of the more interesting avenues we venture down at this point is the possibility of compromise. This opens up a whole new world of potential.

Finally, after another round of peer reading and attention to transitions, structure, and polishing away errors, we write our final drafts and submit them to the parents for parental responses. (One year a father called and asked for permission to address my whole class and explain that no matter how wonderful the letter was, he still wasn't granting his son's request and wanted all of us to know why. That visit was amazing! The student had requested the right to own and ride a motorcycle. The student himself knew this wasn't a good idea but wanted to see just how well he could use his persuasive skills to make his case! The father was a good sport about participating in this assignment and proud of his son's efforts. He just wanted a chance to address us all and give his reasons why he was saying "no"!)

Many students are surprised at how well their parents receive their letters. They are surprised at how influential good, logical reasons backed by evidence can be. Because this assignment engages them with material that is so familiar, it sets the groundwork for the writing we will be doing throughout the year. Already, we have jumped the most difficult hurdle—convincing students of the power of good thinking. They are more than willing to try to convince someone else of their particular viewpoints; they are ready to take on city hall!

The Best of All Possible Tests: Those That Are Self-Created

An assignment that is capable of performing and producing multiple wonderful outcomes is the student take-home test guided by the updated version of Bloom's taxonomy, created by Lorin Anderson (2002), a former student of Bloom's, and a group of cognitive scientists. In my experience, no single assignment has had more impact on demonstrating to students just what those levels of thinking actually look and feel like in action and in developing a working understanding of just what it means to be asked higher-order thinking questions.

Here are the mechanics behind the assignment:

1. Choose a large enough block of content that makes a wide variety of questions easy to produce—a novel, a unit, or a chapter in a text.

2. Make the stakes high enough that everyone sees the importance of taking this assignment seriously—make it a large part of the quarter test grade, or the substitute for a traditional end-of-unit teacher-made test.

3. Give students enough time to construct their test and have opportunities to ask you questions about the meaning and scope of the levels and verbs—at least a week but not too much longer.

4. When assigning the test and going over the sheet, be sure to give examples of just how they can flunk their own test by misinterpreting the verb choice and not giving a full or correct answer. For example, if a student chose to compare and contrast two events, characters, or other entities and yet only explained how they are alike without mentioning the differences, this would not be a correct answer.

5. Be sure to elicit enough examples from students on what specific verbs would be required in a question in order for it to be answered appropriately before having them work on their own. Make sure everyone is initially satisfied with what he or she is being asked to do.

6. Have copies of tests manufactured by textbook companies for students to inspect for style and format. Theirs should be constructed similarly.

7. Explain that the number of the level indicates both the question's level of thinking and its weight in the grading process. For example, a level 5 (evaluating) question is worth 5 points. Students are to create one question for each of the levels. The exception is level 1 (remembering); students are to create five questions that are each worth one point. That will add up to 25 points total. The teacher multiplies the final raw score by four if she wants a test worth 100 points, and so on.

The student assignment sheet would look something like the following.

Take-Home Test Guidelines

Your challenge is to make up a test over _____. You will both compose the questions and answer them. You are to make up questions for the five levels of thinking. You will make up five questions for level 1 (remembering). After that, you are to make up one question for each of the other levels. The level number also represents the point value. (Your whole test equals 25 points, which will be multiplied by _____ to give a total test value of _____.) Be sure to label each question with its appropriate level and descriptor, use one of the verbs stated, and answer the question in clear, concise language.

Level 1: Remembering (1 point)

- Can the student recall or remember the information?

  Use recall or information process verbs such as *define, duplicate, list, memorize, repeat, reproduce,* and *state.*

Level 2: Understanding (2 points)

- Can the student explain ideas or concepts?

  Change information into a different symbolic form by using verbs such as *classify, describe, discuss, explain, identify, locate, recognize, report, select, translate,* and *paraphrase.*

Level 3: Applying (3 points)

- Can the student use the information in a new way?

  Solve a problem using knowledge and appropriate generalizations using verbs such as *choose, demonstrate, dramatize, employ, illustrate, interpret, operate, schedule, sketch, solve, use,* and *write.*

Level 4: Analyzing (4 points)

- Can the student explain ideas or concepts?

  Separate information into component parts using verbs such as *appraise, compare, contrast, criticize, differentiate, discriminate, distinguish, examine, experiment, question,* and *test.*

Level 5: Evaluating (5 points)

- Can the student justify a stand or decision?

  Make qualitative and quantitative judgments according to set standards using verbs such as *classify, describe, discuss, explain, identify, locate, recognize, report, select, translate,* and *paraphrase.*

Level 6: Creating (6 points)

- Can the student create a new product or point of view?

  Solve a problem by putting information together that requires original, creative thinking using verbs such as *classify, describe, discuss, explain, identify, locate, recognize, report, select, translate,* and *paraphrase.*

Your test is to be completed and turned in by _____.

When I first assigned this test the results were more than interesting. First, students were asking the meaning of verbs commonly found on standardized tests and often the subject of test-prep exercises. Now, though, students had a concrete reason for wanting to know their meanings and various nuisances. The discussion over why one set of verbs was of more weight than another brought up facts about the higher-order thinking levels that might have never come up in class, or at least would never have been brought up by students themselves. Most thought that it was harder to remember than to do many of the other functions and so were amazed at the ranking of these questions. Many noted and were surprised that the higher the level, the more interesting the work was—in fact, the highest level, creating, was considered the most fun to do. Explaining to students that their brains are made for those higher levels and that working with those questions actually creates more satisfaction and feelings of accomplishment than simply remembering facts caused much agreement and even more questions: How come most of our tests are in the fact and information range? Why do teachers often ask us to answer questions that fall into those lower groups?

As a result of these discussions, students begin to evaluate tests that teachers in other subjects are giving them. This might be a problem! It is best to explain that facts and memory of precise information are very important at certain times and contexts and to urge these newly awakened young scholars not to get into the business of judging their teachers. This exercise opens the eyes of most students to the wide range and variety of quality choices that exist in how standards are tested and personally assessed.

Creating Independent Judges of Standards of Quality

Often, students complain that they can't tell if they are getting any better at their attempts at literacy. They assess their growth by the grades they receive rather than their own judgment or external evidence. Any attempt at improving a student's acquisition of literacy skills must contain elements that focus on increasing self-evaluation skills as well. Making quality standards in all phases of literacy transparent to the learner and providing ample opportunities for self-reflection on completed products can offer our students the tools they need to gauge their own development. When a student is aware of his or her growing success, motivation increases and efforts at increasing engagement are much easier.

Emphasizing a Desire for Quality Work

Attached to every assignment that demands a good amount of time and work is a reflection response sheet (reproducible page 181) that asks for a student's personal judgment on the quality of that work. Some questions are general, and some more specific to the project. Figure 9.1 on page 148 is an example of a successful reflection response sheet completed by a student

Please note that in the reflection response sheet the student is asked to decide and report just what level of effort has gone into the assignment. It has been made amply clear early on in the school year that no grade will be damaged because of a student comment on any of these response sheets. We value truth over politically correct, brownnosing statements. We have discussed as a class how often students can be inundated with homework and deadlines and have to choose how much time and effort they can put into a specific project. Sometimes work in one subject has to suffer or just be good enough to get by while another class's demand is attended to. This is student time management and a fact of life. We know that every one of the assignments we require will not get a rating of effort that would be considered deeply involved. A common complaint among students is that they feel their teachers think that their subject and class should be given priority at all times. We are also aware that some students can exert little effort and still produce stellar work, while others aren't so lucky. We value effort more than innate ability. We make the connection between effort and quality far more than we make a connection between innate potential and the production of quality output. We stress that the smart student—the one who grows and becomes more and more skilled in reaching a level of quality—is the one who puts forth the effort, not just the one with a high IQ score on file.

Title of assignment: _____

1. What type of effort went into this product? (minimal, average, involved, deeply involved) Explain your choice.

    Deeply involved. _____

2. Explain what was easy about this assignment and what you considered difficult about it.

    Easy—to talk about; lots of topics to discuss. Difficult—hard to narrow down to a few topics.

3. Copy one sentence from the piece that you feel is well written and that you are pleased with. Explain why you chose this particular sentence.

    "Without stumbling blocks, it is difficult for a person to change and grow."

    This is a life lesson in one sentence! _____

4. Explain what you think the purpose in assigning this piece was. What were you expected to learn? Was it successful?

    This assignment helped us to critically examine a novel and to compare it to others.

    It helped me to understand the story and purpose better.

Name _____ Hour _____ Date _____

Figure 9.1: A student's reflection response sheet.

Another request on this sheet is for the student to decide which sentence in his or her work demonstrates quality writing. Students aren't used to being asked to do this and find it very uncomfortable at first. Giving their reasons for their choices allows the teacher to see what criteria they are using at this particular stage of the course.

Next come questions, the answers to which can be very humbling for the teacher. Why was this paper assigned? What was its purpose? What did you learn? How successful was the assignment in helping you learn? These final questions vary according to the circumstances of the assignment but are usually written along these lines. Answers to this cluster of questions can reveal who is aware of the goals and objectives and who isn't. It's the teacher's job to see that students are focused on the objectives that he or she has determined are the reason for this work. These answers can provide valuable feedback on whether or not everyone is on the same page.

Portfolios

The first suggestion on how to increase this proof of growth is to make sure that all the work that is accomplished throughout the year is available to the student for a comparison study. My first purchase of the summer for the upcoming school year has always been a ton of colored folders—usually available at dramatically discounted prices in mid-August. Instead of waiting for students to bring in folders of varying sizes, designs, and materials, I purchase enough folders to supply everyone in every class with one. Each class gets a different color to make my life easier when sorting, grading, and giving them out. I usually ask the stores for the empty boxes in which these folders had been displayed. All student work is kept in these folders. They provide the evidence for parent-teacher visits and for students to be able to monitor their growth. They are essentially portfolios of actual work that provide evidence of developing mastery seldom reflected in standardized tests.

We have created traveling portfolios of selections of student work to be given to next year's teacher and suggest this for teachers in large schools as well as in small, more intimate school settings. At the end of the school year, students are instructed to go through their year's work and select three pieces to add to their traveling portfolio that provide a good idea of the writer and reader they are becoming. These pieces are accompanied by letters from the students explaining why these specific pieces were chosen, what they felt they had learned by writing them, and what they will need help in learning in the upcoming year.

These letters are quite a profound introduction to their new teacher. A section of such a letter written by a sophomore girl—a steady *B* student—concerning her evaluation of her own writing, shows the power of such an activity:

> Now when I write my thoughts flow freely and I write with confidence. My sentence structure has immensely improved along with my vocabulary and word variation. (Yes, the vocabulary words that we got to study do seem to help me when I am writing and searching for the perfect word.) The phrasing of words and reworking my sentences now seem to be second nature, where in the past, I struggled. This class has not only improved my writing skills but has helped me when I write essays for other classes such as for American history.
>
> . . . I used to think that you were either born a writer or not but now I see that everyone is born a writer. Sometimes they need a jump-start because they got lost in the wilderness and couldn't find the path out, like me. I just needed somebody to show me the trail and then I took to it again with anything but ease. It was a rocky road but now I'm headed in the right direction and not looking back.
>
> Even though I have improved this year in my writing, I still need to work on some aspects of my writing. For instance, I can always use improvement in the grammatical area of my writing, along with getting the identifiable voice of my paper fully expressed. Details and development of my ideas also have some room for improvement. But as with anything every minute detail of my writing could use improvement no matter how small it may be. My goal for next year, as a writer, is a simple one. I would like and will keep improving my writing skills and progress as much, if not more, as I did this year. This is because I believe I have a great potential that I do not want to waste. Likewise, I need to keep my skills sharp for college and other areas of life where writing is involved.

This type of reflective exercise cannot be generated at the end of a course that has not made reflection an integral part of the classroom activities throughout the year. One of the benefits of a short reflective piece is its use as formative assessment. Feedback from those persons who are the very ones subjected day in and day out to our efforts at instructing them is valuable for us as well as for them. When a student reveals to us that he felt rushed and pressured, unable to really complete the assignment well but forced to slap something down to meet the deadline, we can reconsider just what time restrictions we are imposing on our students that might be hampering their ability to do quality work. The same goes for allowing too much time. We need to hear just how our teaching and constructing the formats for student participation is playing out. Reflection sheets can help us see more deeply into the interplay of our efforts and our students' efforts in order to fine-tune them for the better. By requiring reflection sheets consistently throughout the year, we train our students in the skill of metacognition that will serve them for a life time.

A Simpler Version

Not all calls for reflection need to be formal letters like the one just quoted. Many successful responses are initiated by a prompt from the teacher, such as the one in the feature box that follows for a creative or critical thinking project that we called our Mouse-Poet Project. Students chose an American poet from a broad and varied list. This would be a research project but with a twist. The product would be a little book relating the life and times of their poet from the point of view of a small mouse who lives with the poet for a while. All facts are biographically correct, and the book should have an ample supply of poems or poem segments logically placed. Each student is given a small 4" × 6" blank book (I purchased these from Dover Publications for around a dollar apiece). The notebook keeps all the projects uniform and allows the format requirements to be more specific and easier for students to follow.

> ### Final Self-Reflection: How Did Your Mouse-Poet Project Turn Out?
>
> Talk to me about this project as an alternative to most assessments you've taken, as a creative endeavor, and as a research project. What did you like about it, what would you suggest that I change or keep as is, and what did you learn about your poet? What did you find to be the most difficult and the easiest parts? Talk to me about how you worked through this whole thing.

Here's part of a response to this prompt from a young man who was not happy at all with the assignment:

> My book turned out bad I think because this just wasn't a good project for me. I really just didn't like it. It was a fair assessment though and I did follow the directions. Karl Shapiro, I think, should be stripped from the list because he is a bad poet and did few notable things with his life. I didn't like anything about the project and instead of changing anything, I'd dump it; but for your sake, I think that if I would change anything it would be that we need to know something about the poets before we are asked to pick one. I learned my poet was a jerk and a menace to society and hated having to spend a couple of weeks working with him and his poetry . . .

A young man with a different experience expressed it this way:

> I think my book turned out fairly well. I think that it was a good alternate assessment. It was something new that we could be creative and challenged all at once. I think we really learned a lot about our poet in our research and reading more than the couple of his poems in the textbook and looking at his life, helped me to better understand poetry. I really liked the project and wouldn't change anything. You gave us specific enough instructions and enough time so that if we worked hard enough, we were able to finish. I learned so much about Langston Hughes in my research. He had a difficult life and it is really reflected in the way he writes.

Feedback from such requests is always valuable for the constant fine-tuning of assignments that the career teacher finds herself doing. The response from the first young man is a good example. The realization that more effort needs to be put into acquainting students with what choices are available to them before they commit to a particular topic or personality to use as the content of their project came through loud and clear. This student hated the project and did poorly on it because he did not like the subject of his work. With a little effort on the teacher's part, this could be avoided. Sensitivity not only to giving students choices but also to the importance of clarifying just what those choices entail would ensure much more engagement and quality in their final products. A student's emotional cognition is a significant element to take into consideration when choosing texts. Simply offering students texts without taking into account that students need to make a personal connection with the material if engagement and quality outcomes are to be expected is one cause for students' failure to excel and their consequent apathy.

Feedback Profiting Both Teachers and Students

Students definitely benefit from the inclusion of opportunities to take stock of what they have accomplished and to consider the quality of their work. They also benefit from having the opportunity to verbalize these thoughts. Grant Wiggins, president of Authentic Education in Hopewell, New Jersey, has been the voice of authentic feedback for me since I first read articles he had written on the subject back in the 1980s. His clear definition of feedback—"helpful feedback is goal-referenced; tangible and transparent; actionable; user-friendly (specific and personalized); timely; ongoing; and consistent" (Wiggins, 2012, p. 11). This has been my gold standard for offering feedback. When students look at their own work with regard to what they tried to accomplish (goal-referenced), what they actually did (tangible and transparent) and suggest what they could have improved (actionable) on their own products (specific and personalized), and do this on a regular basis (ongoing and consistent), the results are measurable growth and depth in their learning. Giving students the opportunities to perform self-evaluations should be built into every teacher's repertoire of assignments and activities.

It is also valuable for students to give feedback about the broader scope of how they experience their learning, specifically about the course they have just taken. This helps clarify what has been learned and accomplished, not only for the students but also for the teacher. By giving students the opportunity to give thoughtful feedback on how a specific unit of study or whole course progressed, the teacher can learn a wealth of useful information. This information can help them adapt the delivery of the same material in following years, as well as adapt procedures and delivery of material coming up later in the current year. The End-of-Course evaluation (figure 9.2) is an example of how one student used such a tool. (A blank, reproducible version of this form can be found online at **go.solution-tree.com/literacy**, and on page 182.) By using a form like this and taking the responses of the entire class into consideration, patterns and insights may surface into areas of both content and pedagogy that could be better planned in the future.

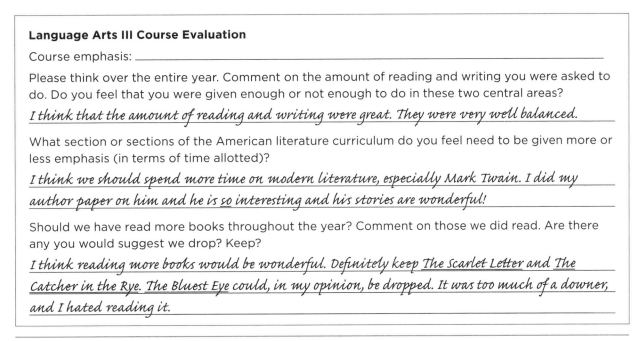

Language Arts III Course Evaluation

Course emphasis: _____

Please think over the entire year. Comment on the amount of reading and writing you were asked to do. Do you feel that you were given enough or not enough to do in these two central areas?

I think that the amount of reading and writing were great. They were very well balanced.

What section or sections of the American literature curriculum do you feel need to be given more or less emphasis (in terms of time allotted)?

I think we should spend more time on modern literature, especially Mark Twain. I did my author paper on him and he is so interesting and his stories are wonderful!

Should we have read more books throughout the year? Comment on those we did read. Are there any you would suggest we drop? Keep?

I think reading more books would be wonderful. Definitely keep The Scarlet Letter and The Catcher in the Rye. The Bluest Eye could, in my opinion, be dropped. It was too much of a downer, and I hated reading it.

Figure 9.2: A hypothetical end-of-year student evaluation of a language arts course. CONTINUED →

Are there any suggestions for changes on how the class was handled? More, less group work, whole-class activities, projects, out-of-class assignments?

I liked how the class was handled, for the most part. I prefer doing work on my own, though, so I would have less group work, but I know many people like it, so it was pretty well balanced.

What suggestions could you make to ensure that this class is challenging without being overly stressful?

Give more time for assignments, but overall the time frame was okay.

Conclusion

For both students and teachers, *standards* and *assessments* have become hot-button words charged with emotions ranging from fear, guilt, anxiety, helplessness, and anger to empowerment, satisfaction, success, and confidence. Because of all the emphasis on these two words today, the essence of their meaning can get lost in the rhetoric. Teachers can help themselves by personally examining how these powerful tools serve them in their day-to-day teaching experience. By using standards to inform planning and by using formative assessment to guide responses to student performance, teachers can more adequately assure that they are providing the well-rounded education of substance that our students deserve.

Final Thoughts

By giving concrete samples of student products, literacy-based assignments, and creative approaches meant to initiate clearer thinking and better articulation of that thinking, I have hoped to present an authentic look inside classrooms focused on effective literacy growth. As I wrote at the beginning of this book, challenging and rigorous instruction, if it is not appropriately balanced with support and materials of interest to students, can lead to overwhelmed and over-frustrated students who give up prematurely. Rigorous instruction must take place in a supportive, engaging environment, which leads to an increase in motivation that in turn builds confidence, and confidence opens the gates to student effort and focused attention on the tasks assigned. That's what these activities do.

My hope is that this will also be the effect on teachers as well. Not enough is written or spoken about the need to engage teachers in what they are asked to do. These suggested lessons and formats for designing similar lessons are intended to kindle a fire of enthusiasm in teachers that will provide the energy necessary to fill all segments of the teaching experience with joy and satisfaction as well as efficacy. We all are aware that education is considered serious business. We all feel the pressure of serious tests, evaluations, requirements, and measured outcomes inside and outside the areas of our control. If we are to keep our equilibrium and balance, we must demand of ourselves a commitment that we will teach from a position of joy and an authentic motivation that always keeps our students' welfare in the forefront. Effective, rigorous literacy teaching couched in an environment that fosters trust and equality of engaged opportunity will do this.

How Authors Pick Their Words

After reading this passage aloud, ask students to highlight the words that mean *hit* and *move* and write them in the boxed areas.

My beast had an advantage in his first hold, having sunk his mighty fangs far into the breast of his adversary; but the great arms and paws of the ape . . . had locked the throat of my guardian and slowly were choking out his life, and bending back his head and neck upon his body. . . . In accomplishing this the ape was tearing away the entire front of its breast, which was held in the vise-like grip of the powerful jaws. . . . Presently I saw the great eyes of my beast bulging completely from their sockets and blood flowing from its nostrils . . . Suddenly I came to myself and, with that strange instinct which seems ever to prompt me to my duty, I seized the cudgel, which had fallen to the floor at the commencement of the battle, and swinging it with all the power of my earthly arms I crashed it full upon the head of the ape, crushing his skull as though it had been an eggshell.

Without more ado, therefore, I turned to meet the charge of the infuriated bull ape. He was now too close upon me for the cudgel to prove of any effective assistance, so I merely threw it as heavily as I could at his advancing bulk. It struck him just below the knees, eliciting a howl of pain and rage, and so throwing him off his balance that he lunged full upon me with arms wide stretched to ease his fall. Again, as on the preceding day, I had recourse to earthly tactics, and swinging my right fist full upon the point of his chin I followed it with a smashing left to the pit of his stomach. The effect was marvelous, for, as I lightly sidestepped, after delivering the second blow, he reeled and fell upon the floor doubled up with pain and gasping for wind.

List Words That Mean *Move*:

List Words That Mean *Hit*:

Source: A Princess of Mars, by Edgar Rice Burroughs. Kindle Edition, p. 16.

Puzzling Out Meaning

After reading the passage quoted on page 9 that begins "Rudewood teemed . . ." from China Miéville's *Iron Council* and turning on your mental movie camera to *see* what the passage is describing, do the exercise that follows.

Name the beast _____.

Name the forest they are in _____.

Draw the beast *before* and immediately *after* it is shot.

Before:

After:

List five words that you don't know for certain but whose meanings you can guess:

Word	Possible Meaning
1.	
2.	
3.	
4.	
5.	

An Exercise in Close Seeing

Before we try *close reading,* we need to practice *close seeing.*

Spread out five bills of paper money in different denominations in sequential order. Find as many similarities and differences as you can by closely observing them.

Similarities	Differences

Now answer these questions:

1. What office did each man pictured on the bills hold? _____

2. Who is the oldest? _____

3. Which man is farthest away from the camera or artist? _____

4. How many times is the bill's value shown on each bill? _____
    Which bill shows the value a different number of times than the others? _____
    How many? _____

5. What war were three of the men pictured involved in? _____

6. Are the names of any women on these bills? _____

7. Which bill's value is spelled out differently on the bottom than it is on the others? _____
    How? _____

8. What is unusual about the designs around the numbers on the one dollar bill?

    _____

9. If I have a real pack of 150 bills of equal denominations, what would their value be?

    _____

10. List at least three questions that you would like answered about (real, not play money)
    bills. _____

The Storyboard: A Narrative Organizer

Making a visual representation of what has been read is a powerful tool for comprehension and summarizing. Make a list of major events in the text and draw a picture of each one with a short explanation below it. In pairs, compare and contrast what choices each of you made, and decide what changes you would make to your own storyboard as a result.

A Record Sheet for Elie Wiesel's *Night*

Keep a record of all the factual data of people, places, events, and things that you can pull from the text as you read *Night*. This record will form the basis for the factual authenticity of the narrative you will create later.

People	Places	Events	Things

Crazy 8s Brainstorming Sheet

When planning to teach important concepts or skills, an effective strategy is to determine multiple ways to present or repeat the material. These reteaching events should be spaced out over a few weeks, since students need to revisit concepts and skills if they are to cement them into their long-term memory. This worksheet allows you to plan a variety of methods for doing this. Examples of instructional variety include using manipulatives, playing to various learning styles, asking students to transfer the skill or concept to another situation, and presenting the skill or concept in other formats or across disciplines.

1. Concept or content choice: Pick a skill or content concept that is difficult for students to learn, remember, or understand.

   _____

   _____

2. Brainstorm methods of delivery: Write down as many ways you can teach this concept as possible . . . even if they sound crazy or impractical. Write them down anyway. Think up at least a dozen!

   1. _____   7. _____
   2. _____   8. _____
   3. _____   9. _____
   4. _____   10. _____
   5. _____   11. _____
   6. _____   12. _____

3. Now share your dozen with a fellow teacher and add a few more here:

   _____   _____

   _____   _____

4. From your two lists, choose the eight best ways to teach your selected material.

   1. _____
   2. _____
   3. _____
   4. _____
   5. _____
   6. _____
   7. _____
   8. _____

9. Order your eight for the best possible effectiveness over time:

1. _____   5. _____

2. _____   6. _____

3. _____   7. _____

4. _____   8. _____

6. If possible, share your final list with someone who knows how you teach for more feedback.

7. Which strategy from your sheet would be new to your normal teaching methods?

_____

_____

8. Personal debriefing: On a piece of paper, write down what you think about this process and your final results. Were there any surprises? Any new ideas? Any questions still left unanswered? What will you take to your classroom from this exercise?

X-Ray Chart

Number all the sentences in your essay. Then fill in this chart for the first ten sentences of your piece, one row at a time. Number the sentences first, then add the first four words of each sentence, and so on. Remember that your verbs are not necessarily in the first four words of your sentence and that there might be more than one verb per sentence. The last column is where you designate that a paragraph is beginning; everyone should place an asterisk in the first rows. After filling out the chart, we will diagnose our writing X-rays for strengths and weaknesses. Circle any sentences that start in a similar way. Mark your own targets for improvement at the bottom of the page and date it.

Number of Sentence	First Four Words in Each of My Sentences	Verbs Used in Each Sentence	Number of Words in Each Sentence	New Paragraph (*)
				*

My Writing Targets

Classroom Talk

Ask a fellow teacher to chart your classroom's talk for twenty minutes or more, using a stop-watch or timer to record when talking begins and ends, and noting who is doing the talking.

Person Talking	Beginning Time	Ending Time

Types of Questions Asked and by Whom

Ask a fellow teacher to record who is asking questions in your classroom, including yourself, and the kinds of questions being asked.

Person Asking a Question	Type of Question (procedural, closed, open)

Group Discussion Guidelines

Use these guidelines to facilitate effective group discussions in class.

- Listen for good ideas, not "right" answers.

- Don't interrupt another speaker; be patient and respectful.

- Use the phrase *yes, and . . .* instead of *yes, but . . .*

- Clarify what others have said: *What I hear you say is . . .*

- Use good body language to show you are fully listening.

- Ask for evidence of statements if necessary.

- Don't monopolize the discussion; share the talk time.

- Address each other by name when asking a question or following up.

- Make the goal not to agree or win a debate but to deepen understanding.

- Encourage each member to join in the discussion.

- Keep on the topic; don't wander off on other issues.

Group Discussion Report Sheet

After this report sheet is explained and discussed by the whole class, small groups should use it on their own. Distribute one sheet to each group. A volunteer takes on the responsibility of filling it in. The volunteer writes the name of each group participant next to a number. That number will remain that student's for the whole exercise. As the discussion begins, the report sheet scribe puts a hash mark next to that student's name every time he or she speaks. At the end of the discussion, each student offers an idea that he or she found important. Each student also evaluates the quality of the entire experience.

Topic: _____ **Date:** _____

Group Members' Participation

The recorder marks the number of times each member speaks to the whole group.

1. _____
2. _____
3. _____
4. _____
5. _____

Summary of Ideas Generated

Each member supplies one idea that he or she feels was important for understanding the topic.

1. _____
2. _____
3. _____
4. _____
5. _____

Members Rate the Quality of the Discussion

Use any of the following descriptors that fit the experience: *satisfying, worthwhile, great ideas, dragged at times, fun, not enough time, nothing new, lots of ideas,* or *valuable.*

1. _____
2. _____
3. _____
4. _____
5. _____

Teacher's Checklist on Questioning Habits

Following are some of the questioning habits that can keep us from achieving better results in the classroom.

- ☐ Sometimes I ask a question but end up answering it myself.
- ☐ I often call on a person first, then ask the question.
- ☐ I really don't give all students enough time to think of a response.
- ☐ I start with a difficult question, without warming the class up with easier ones.
- ☐ If a student answers incorrectly, I just find another student with a right answer.
- ☐ Sometimes I let a student's wrong answer go unchallenged.
- ☐ I seldom praise the quality of the answer (phrasing, completeness).
- ☐ I don't start the class with a couple of key questions to direct the entire lesson.
- ☐ I don't require all students to write answers down before accepting responses.
- ☐ Often I ask the same kind of question again and again.
- ☐ I find myself asking too many questions at once.
- ☐ I use questions as interrogation rather than as paths to deeper discussions.
- ☐ At times, I call on the same few students and ignore the rest.
- ☐ Some of my questions are irrelevant to the topic.
- ☐ My questioning sessions seem to stress students out and sound threatening.
- ☐ I tend to give struggling students less time to answer and move to someone else.
- ☐ My questions lead to dead ends and don't set up the activity to follow.
- ☐ I fall into a *Trivial Pursuit* or game-show pedagogy, asking only lower-level questions.
- ☐ Many of my questions tend to have a single right answer.

Source: Adapted from Brown & Wragg, 1993; Dillon, 1981; Wragg & Brown, 2001.

First Chapters Reading Day

For this "book tasting party," the school librarian provides a cart of the latest high-interest books—fiction and nonfiction—to try out. Read and critique only the first chapter (or section) of one book with regard to its readability, interest level, strengths, and weaknesses.

Name _____ Class hour _____ Date _____

Title of book _____ Author _____

Number of pages in the book's first chapter _____. This is the _____

First Chapter book you read today.

"Goldilocks" evaluation of reading level: too hard   too easy   just right

Would you recommend this book? _____ To whom? _____

Would you consider reading more? _____ Why? _____

_____

_____

Tell me what you found out in the first chapter: _____

_____

_____

_____

_____

Give a couple of this book's *strengths*: _____

_____

_____

_____

Give a couple of this book's *weaknesses*: _____

_____

_____

_____

_____

Creative and Critical Thinking Skills

Using the *yes* and *no* columns, indicate the terms that describe the modes of thinking you use most and least often. Make a note in your plan book to employ the ones in your least-used column when creating your lessons.

Creative Thinking	Yes	No	Critical Thinking	Yes	No
Flexible			Comparative		
Generative			Analytic		
Original			Classifying		
Lateral			Vertical		
Employing suspended judgment			Employing judgment		
Diffuse			Focused		
Subjective			Objective		
Right brained			Left brained		
Fluent			Sequencing		
Elaborative			Based on cause and effect		
Involving brainstorming			Involving patterning		
Modifying			Webbing		
Employing imagery			Employing analogy		
Associative			Linear		
Listing attributes			Inductive		
Metaphorical			Forecasting		
Involving forced relationships (matching things that don't usually go together to make something new)			Planning		
Stimulating curiosity			Hypothesizing		
Having no answer			Involving a specific answer		
Employing richness and novelty			Reasoning		
Using divergent thinking			Using convergent thinking		
Visual			Verbal		
Involving possibility			Involving probability		
Using the phrase *yes, and* . . . "			Using the phrase *yes, but* . . ."		

If You Were an iPhone: An Electronic Autobiography

In this activity, view the iPhone as a metaphor for yourself. Make choices, as if you were the phone, to reflect your tastes, preferences, personality, and so on.

Your outside:

- Your wallpaper would be _____

- Your accessories would look like _____

- Your ringtone would likely be _____

- Your language settings would include _____

Your other settings:

- A few of those on your speed dial would be: _____

- Your personal storage needs would be 3GB, 4GB, 8GB, 16GBs _____ because: _____

- Your volume would be (low, medium, high) _____ because _____

- Your alarm would be set at _____ because _____

Your top ten apps:

_____

_____

_____

What apps could you include that demonstrate your:

- Beliefs _____

- Behaviors _____

- Values _____

- History _____

- Family _____

- Holidays _____

If you could make up apps that fit you, what would they be? _____

Now that you have filled out your personalized iPhone settings and favorites, write a short reflection piece explaining just how well this interesting piece of technology reflects how you see yourself and what you value and find important at this point in your life.

Tribute Portfolio Project

After reading the first half of the book *The Hunger Games*, we begin work on our own portfolio. Another district, District 14, now joins the games. You are one of two tributes who have been chosen to represent this district. Complete the following tasks before the games begin.

Due: _____

1. Personal biography

    *   This piece is a narrative about yourself that includes your age, description of your physical characteristics and personality, and description of your family members and their roles in the community. You will also point out your personal strengths and any skills that will help you survive the games.

    *   Another section will give an overview of District 14—its size, number of people, its chief export (as coal is District 12's), defining characteristic, and geographic environment. Class distinctions of citizens and your family's particular position in this class structure should be noted.

    *   You can add any other information that would be good for the Capitol officers to know about you. A picture of you would also be appropriate. You can use a photo or drawing.

2. Stylist report

    *   Just as Cinna, Katniss's stylist, designed a theme for her clothing for all major events leading up to the games themselves, you too will include a report from your stylist detailing his or her similar theme and specific examples of how this theme is to be carried out in your clothing, makeup, hair, and accessories for the following events (page numbers refer to examples from Katniss's outfits for reference):

        +   Your costume for the chariot ride around the Capitol (see pp. 66–67)

        +   Your outfit for the televised interview (see pp. 119–120)

        +   Your clothing for the arena (see pp. 144–145)

    This written report should be accompanied by visuals of each of the three designs that could come from drawings, magazine pictures, digital prints, or other media of your choice.

3. Gamemakers' exhibition

    *   You are given a private opportunity to show your skills to the Gamemakers and receive points as to your potential as a survivor. Having already chosen your personal strengths and skills in your biography, explain by giving a detailed report of just how you demonstrated those strengths. Also include the ranking you earned and your evaluation on how fairly you were judged.

From Tired to Inspired © 2013 Solution Tree Press • solution-tree.com
Visit **go.solution-tree.com/literacy** to download this page.

4. Interview

- You will provide a written and audio copy of your interview with Caesar Flickerman, the official host for the past forty years. (Choose a person to be your host in the audio version of your interview, and then serve as the host in his or her audio interview.) Your interview will last exactly three minutes and can elaborate on the material you have already added in your biography.

5. Argument 1

- Choose one of the following statements. Decide if you agree or disagree with its premise. Back up each claim you make using valid reasoning and relevant and sufficient evidence not only from the initial text but from outside research as well.

    + At times the government is right to use extreme measures to curtail the rights of citizens.

    + Sacrifice of a few is necessary for the welfare of the group.

    + If a person is poor, he or she has fewer rights in society than those who are wealthy.

    + Violent video games desensitize their players to real human suffering.

    + Reality TV has negative effects on its viewers.

Episodes of *Ned's Declassified School Survival Guide*

Create a survival guide for incoming students. The short Ned episodes are valuable tools to jog your memory about what areas of school life would make good material for such a guide.

Circle which of these episodes you feel you can talk or write about:

"Guide to: The First Day and Lockers"

"Guide to: Bathrooms and Project Partners"

"Guide to: Detentions and Teachers"

"Guide to: Seating and Tryouts"

"Guide to: Crushes and Dances"

"Guide to: Sick Days and Spelling Bees"

"Guide to: Rumors and Photo Day"

"Guide to: Elections and Talent Show"

"Guide to: Computer Lab and Backpacks"

"Guide to: Notes & Best Friends"

"Guide to: Day Dreaming and Gym"

"Guide to: Cheaters and Bullies"

"Guide to: Emergency Drills and Late Bus"

"Guide to: The New Semester and Electives"

"Guide to: Pep Rallies and Lunch"

"Guide to: School Clubs and Video Projects"

"Guide to: Notebooks and Math"

"Guide to: Vice Principals and Mondays"

"Guide to: Your Body and Procrastination"

"Guide to: Gross Biology Dissection and Upperclassmen"

"Guide to: Dares and Bad Habits"

"Guide to: Substitute Teachers and the New Kid"

"Guide to: Valentine's Day and School Websites"

"Guide to: Shyness and Nicknames"

"Guide to: Asking Someone Out and Recycling"

"Guide to: April Fool's Day and Excuses"

"Guide to: Secrets and School Car Wash"

"Guide to: Spirit Week and Clothes"

"Guide to: Yearbook and Career Week"

"Guide to: Music Class and Class Clown"

"Guide to: Failing and Tutors"

"Guide to: Science Fair and Study Hall"

"Guide to: Double Dating and the Last Day"

"Guide to: A New Grade and Dodgeball"

"Guide to: Reading and Principals"

"Guide to: Popularity and Stressin' Out"

"Guide to: Dismissal and the School Play"

"Guide to: Halloween and Vampires, Ghosts, Werewolves & Zombies"

"Guide to: Art Class and Lost and Found"

"Guide to: Social Studies and Embarrassment"

"Guide to: The Bus and Bad Hair Days"

"Guide to: Revenge and School Records"

"Guide to: The Library and Volunteering"

"Guide to: Hallways and Friends Moving"

"Guide to: Boys and Girls"

"Guide to: Cellphones and Woodshop"

"Guide to: Getting Organized and Extra Credit"

"Guide to: Fundraising and Competition"

"Guide to: Making New Friends & Positives and Negatives"

"Guide to: Money and Parties"

"Guide to: Spring Fever and School Newspaper"

"Guide to: Health and Jealousy"

"Guide to: Tests and When You Like Someone Who Is Going Out With Someone Else"

"Guide to: Field Trips, Permission Slips, Signs and Weasels" (Series Finale)

Source: Adapted from List of Ned's Declassified School Survival Guide Episodes, *n.d.*

Photosynthesis Dolly

Instead of making or copying the usual notes about content material, use this sheet to follow the presentation of a live Plant Person (see pages 109–111 of the text), and draw all the elements that are used to represent the process of photosynthesis.

As we fill in the various elements of photosynthesis, draw and label them on the dolly.

What are the key concepts to understand?

Recognizing Child Abuse Checklist

When reading material that involves dysfunctional families such as the one Huck Finn finds himself in, a good way to make it relevant to the real world is to use actual forms in use today to recognize and identify child abuse. This is one such form.

Signs of Possible Abuse or Neglect

The Child

- ☐ Shows sudden changes in behavior or school performance
- ☐ Has not received help for physical or medical problems brought to the parents' attention
- ☐ Has learning problems (or difficulty concentrating) that cannot be attributed to specific physical or psychological causes
- ☐ Is always watchful, as though preparing for something bad to happen
- ☐ Lacks adult supervision
- ☐ Is overly compliant, passive, or withdrawn
- ☐ Comes to school or other activities early, stays late, and does not want to go home

The Parent

- ☐ Shows little concern for the child
- ☐ Denies the existence of—or blames the child for—the child's problems in school or at home
- ☐ Asks teachers or other caregivers to use harsh physical discipline if the child misbehaves
- ☐ Sees the child as entirely bad, worthless, or burdensome
- ☐ Demands a level of physical or academic performance the child cannot achieve
- ☐ Looks primarily to the child for care, attention, and satisfaction of emotional needs

Signs of Physical Abuse

Consider the possibility of physical abuse when the child:

- ☐ Has unexplained burns, bites, bruises, broken bones, or black eyes
- ☐ Has fading bruises or other marks noticeable after an absence from school
- ☐ Seems frightened of the parents and protests or cries when it is time to go home
- ☐ Shrinks at the approach of adults
- ☐ Reports injury by a parent or another adult caregiver

Consider the possibility of physical abuse when the parent or other adult caregiver:

- ☐ Offers conflicting, unconvincing, or no explanation for the child's injury

PAGE 1 OF 2

☐ Describes the child as "evil," or in some other very negative way

    ☐ Uses harsh physical discipline with the child

    ☐ Has a history of abuse as a child

Signs of Neglect

Consider the possibility of neglect when the child:

    ☐ Is frequently absent from school

    ☐ Begs or steals food or money

    ☐ Lacks needed medical or dental care, immunizations, or glasses

    ☐ Is consistently dirty and has severe body odor

    ☐ Lacks sufficient clothing for the weather

    ☐ Abuses alcohol or other drugs

    ☐ States that there is no one at home to provide care

Consider the possibility of neglect when the parent or other adult caregiver:

    ☐ Appears to be indifferent to the child

    ☐ Seems apathetic or depressed

    ☐ Behaves irrationally or in a bizarre manner

    ☐ Is abusing alcohol or other drugs

Signs of Emotional Maltreatment

Consider the possibility of emotional maltreatment when the child:

    ☐ Shows extremes in behavior, such as an overly compliant or demanding attitude, extreme passivity, or aggression

    ☐ Is either inappropriately adult (parenting other students, for example) or inappropriately infantile (frequently rocking or head-banging, for example)

    ☐ Is delayed in physical or emotional development

    ☐ Has attempted suicide

    ☐ Reports a lack of attachment to the parent

Consider the possibility of emotional maltreatment when the parent or other adult caregiver:

    ☐ Constantly blames, belittles, or berates the child

    ☐ Is unconcerned about the child and refuses to consider offers of help for the child's problems

    ☐ Overtly rejects the child

Source: Child Welfare Information Gateway. Available online at www.childwelfare.gov/pubs/factsheets. Used with permission.

Supporting Evidence for Child Abuse of Huck Finn

On this sheet, designate a specific type of abuse, and go to the text to validate your claim by locating and transcribing concrete examples from the text. This scaffolding sheet can be used as the basis for an essay on the material or of a role-playing trial exercise providing the prosecutor's evidence.

1. Write down the type of abuse as found in the fact sheet.

    a. Write down the page number of the evidence for this from the book and a sentence that documents the abuse.

    b. Repeat process with another example of evidence of this type of abuse.

2. Write down an additional type of abuse from the fact sheet that you can document.

    a. Write down the page number of the evidence for this from the book and a sentence that documents the abuse.

    b. Repeat process with another example of evidence of this type of abuse.

3. Write down an additional type of abuse from the fact sheet that you can document.

    a. Write down the page number of the evidence for this from the book and a sentence that documents the abuse.

    b. Repeat process with another example of evidence of this type of abuse.

From Tired to Inspired © 2013 Solution Tree Press • solution-tree.com
Visit **go.solution-tree.com/literacy** to download this page.

Fortune-Telling Chart

This exercise is meant to be an introduction to a full text. Prepare by picking out the main characters and determining what they shouldn't do (a choice or action that would help them avoid conflict or disaster in the plot) and what dream motivates their actions throughout the text. This will be the basis of your role-playing script as a fortune-teller. Consider what prior knowledge about the characters or setting might be beneficial for students to know up front and include this in your conversations with the characters.

Title of book: _____

First character: _____

Don't: _____

Your dream: _____

Good idea for a prop: _____

Second character: _____

Don't: _____

Your dream: _____

Good idea for a prop: _____

Third character: _____

Don't: _____

Your dream: _____

Good idea for a prop: _____

Fourth character: _____

Don't: _____

Your dream: _____

Good idea for a prop: _____

Outrageous Teaching Worksheet

The best and most effective "outrageous" lessons are those made up by teachers themselves. Use this form to help create your own.

Set up the *surprise* (for example, instead of your coming to class, an administrator announces a special guest). You disguise yourself as another person or thing complete with props and setting and enter the classroom:

_____

_____

_____

_____

_____

_____

_____

Decide on the *story line* (you're an explorer with amnesia who forgot what you found or where you went). You show props (maps, coins, and so on).

_____

_____

_____

_____

_____

_____

Determine the *dilemma* or *activity* (that is, what you want the students to do to help you solve the problem). This is where the *content* happens. In groups or individually, ask students to look up the material, help you figure out the answers, write a report or letter to the editor, or do whatever the activity requires. For example, the explorer with amnesia needs to know what he did and then write a speech to give at the Kennedy Center, where he is being honored.

_____

_____

_____

_____

_____

_____

Comparing Two Poe Stories

This table provides the areas of comparison that connect "The Black Cat" and "The Tell-Tale Heart," by Edgar Allan Poe. After having read or reread both stories, use the sheet as the basis for class discussion by asking students to fill it out together.

Areas of Comparison	"The Black Cat"	"The Tell-Tale Heart"
The obsession		
Murders:		
• Victim		
• Planning		
• Motive		
• Time		
• Place		
• Cause		
• Burial		
• Murderer		
• Capture		
• Remorse		
Point of view		
Setting		
Acceptance of guilt		
Time frame		
Style of story order		
Characters		
Others		

Reflection Response Sheet

All reflection sheets should be tailored to the circumstances of the class and the content. Use this sheet as a guide, and change any statement or question in order to get the feedback you are seeking from your students.

Title of assignment: _____

1. What type of effort went into this product? (minimal, average, involved, deeply involved) Explain your choice.

2. Explain what was easy about this assignment and what you considered difficult about it.

3. Copy one sentence from the piece that you feel is well written and that you are pleased with. Explain why you chose this particular sentence.

4. Explain what you think the purpose in assigning this piece was. What were you expected to learn? Was it successful?

Name _____ Hour _____ Date _____

End-of-Year Course Evaluation

Since we learn not only by doing but by reflecting on our doing, here is your opportunity to reflect on your experiences in this class over the last few months. I will use your reflections to help improve my planning for next year's course, so be as thorough as possible. Please think over the entire year.

Comment on the amount of reading and writing you were asked to do. Do you feel that you were given enough or not enough to do in these two central areas?

What section or sections of the American literature curriculum do you feel need to be given more or less emphasis (in terms of time allotted)?

Should we have read more books throughout the year? Comment on those we did read. Are there any you would suggest we drop? Keep?

Are there any suggestions for changes on how the class was handled? More or less group work, whole-class activities, projects, out-of-class assignments?

What suggestions could you make to ensure that this class is challenging without being overly stressful?

References and Resources

Alexie, S. (2005). *The Lone Ranger and Tonto fistfight in heaven*. New York: HarperCollins.

Allington, R. L. (2007). Intervention all day long: New hope for struggling readers. *Voices From the Middle, 14*(4), 7–14.

Allington, R. L., & Cunningham, P. M. (2007). *Schools that work: Where all children read and write*. Boston: Allyn & Bacon.

Anderman, L. H., & Midgley, C. (1998). *Motivation and middle school students* [ERIC digest]. Champaign, IL: ERIC Clearing-house on Elementary and Early Childhood Education. (ERIC Document Reproduction Service No. ED 421 281).

Anderson, L. W. (2002). Revising bloom's taxonomy: A special issue of theory into practice. *Theory Into Practice, 41*(4), 119–225.

Anderson, L. W., & Krathwohl, D. (Eds.). (2001). *A taxonomy for learning, teaching and assessing: A revision of Bloom's taxonomy of educational objectives* (Complete ed.). New York: Longman.

Anderson, R. C., & Pichert, J. W. (1978). Recall of previously unrecallable information following a shift in perspective. *Journal of Verbal Learning and Verbal Behavior, 17*(1), 1–12.

Archer, W., Moore, R., Silverman, D. (Directors), Swartzwelder, J., Kogen, J., Wolodarsky, W., et al. (Writers). (1990, October 25). Treehouse of horror [Television series episode]. In D. Castalleneta (Producer), *The Simpsons*. Hollywood, CA: 20th Century Fox.

Bahrick, H. P. (2005). The long-term neglect of long-term memory: Reasons and remedies. In A. F. Healy (Ed.), *Experimental cognitive psychology and its applications: Decade of behavior* (pp. 89–100). Washington, DC: American Psychological Association.

Barsade, S. G. (2002). The ripple effect: Emotional contagion and its influence on group behavior. *Administrative Science Quarterly, 47*(4), 644–675. Accessed at www.jstor.org/stable/3094912 on April 27, 2012.

Bean, M. (2011, March 29). *How to make it stick: The psychology of learning and memory* [Web log post]. Accessed at http://edcommentary.blogspot.com/2011/03/on-making-it-stick-dispatches-from.html on April 27, 2012.

BIGresearch, Consumer Intentions & Actions Survey. (2011). *BIGresearch Halloween Consumer Intentions and Actions Survey*. Accessed at www.nrf.com/modules.php?name=News&op=viewlive&sp_id=1196 on June 19, 2012.

Billmeyer, R. (2009). Creating thoughtful readers through habits of mind. In A. L. Costa & B. Kallick (Eds.), *Habits of mind across the curriculum: Practical and creative strategies for teachers*. Alexandria, VA: Association for Supervision and Curriculum Development. Accessed at www.ascd.org/publications/books/108014/chapters/Creating-Thoughtful-Readers-through-Habits-of-Mind.aspx on November 21, 2011.

Black, P., & Wiliam, D. (1998). Inside the black box: Raising standards through classroom assessment. *Phi Delta Kappan, 80*(2), 139–148.

Blackburn, B. R. (2008). *Rigor is NOT a four-letter word*. Larchmont, NY: Eye on Education.

Bode, J. (1992). *New kids in town: Oral histories of immigrant teens*. New York: Scholastic.

Bohm, D. (2004). *RC series bundle: On dialogue* (2nd ed.). London: Routledge.

Bond, S. (1981). *101 uses for a dead cat*. New York: Potter.

Bradbury, R. (2012). *Fahrenheit 451: A novel*. New York: Simon & Schuster. (Original work published in 1953).

Bransford, J. D., & Johnson, M. K. (1972). Contextual prerequisites for understanding: Some investigations of comprehension and recall. *Journal of Verbal Learning and Verbal Behavior, 11*, 717–726.

Broaddus, K., & Worthy, J. (2001). Fluency beyond the primary grades: From group performance to silent, independent reading. *The Reading Teacher, 55*, 335.

Brown, D., Galassi, J., & Alos, P. (2004). School counselors' perceptions of the impact of high-stakes testing. *Professional School Counseling, 8*(1). Accessed at http://findarticles.com/p/articles/mi_mOKOC/is_1_8/ai_n6335435/?tag+content;col1 on October 20, 2011.

Brown, G., & Wragg, E. C. (1993). *Questioning*. London: Routledge.

Bruner, J. (1986). *Actual minds, possible worlds*. Cambridge, MA: Harvard University Press.

Bruner, J. (1990). *Acts of meaning*. Cambridge, MA: Harvard University Press.

Bruner, J. (1991). The narrative construction of reality. *Critical Inquiry, 18*, 1–21.

Budiansky, S. (2001). *The trouble with textbooks*. Accessed at www.prism-magazine.org/feb01/html/textbooks.cfm on September 1, 2011.

Burchers, S. (2007). *Vocabulary cartoons: SAT word power*. Punta Gorda, FL: New Monic Books.

Burroughs, W. S. (1917). *A princess of Mars*. Kindle version. Accessed at www.amazon.com on October 1, 2012.

Campbell, G. (2004). *Blood Diamonds: Tracing the deadly path of the world's most precious stone*. New York: Basic Books.

Card, O. S. (1994). *Ender's game*. New York: Tor.

Carpenter, T., & Moser, J. (1983). The acquisition of addition and subtraction concepts. In R. Lesh & M. Landau (Eds.), *Acquisition of mathematics: Concepts and processes* (pp. 7–44). New York: Academic Press.

Carson, B. (1996). *Gifted hands: The Ben Carson story*. Cedar Rapids, MI: Zondervan.

Carter, S. L. (2002). *The emperor of Ocean Park*. New York: Knopf.

Carver, R. P. (1990). *Reading rate: A review of research and theory*. Boston: Academic Press.

Cepeda, N. J., Pashler, H., Vul, E., Wixted, J. T., & Rohrer, D. (2006). Distributed practice in verbal recall tasks: A review and quantitative synthesis. *Psychological Bulletin, 132*(3), 354–358. Accessed at http://uweb.rc.usf.edu/~drohrer/pdfs/Cepeda_et_al_2006PsychBull.pdf on August 20, 2011.

Cepeda, N., Coburn, N., Rohrer, D., Wixted, J. T., Mozer, M. C., & Pashler, H. (2008). *Optimizing distributed practice: Theoretical analysis and practical implications*. Accessed at http://laplab.ucsd.edu/articles/cepeda_exppsych_050808.pdf on August 8, 2012.

Child Welfare Information Gateway. (2007). *Recognizing child abuse and neglect: Signs and symptoms*. Accessed at www.childwelfare.gov/pubs/factsheets/signs.pdf on June 21, 2012.

Cisneros, S. (1991). *The house on Mango Street*. New York: Vintage.

Collins, S. (2010). *The hunger games*. New York: Scholastic.

Common Core Curriculum Mapping Project. (2012). Accessed at http://commoncore.org/maps on August 8, 2012.

Common Core State Standards Initiative. (2012). *Mission statement*. Accessed at www.corestandards.org on June 22, 2012.

Common core toolkit—A guide to aligning the Common Core State Standards with the Framework for 21st Century Skills. (2011). Washington, DC: Partnership for 21st Century Skills. Accessed at www.p21.org/index.php?option=com_content&view=article&id=1005&Itemid=236 on June 10, 2012.

Costa, A. L., & Kallick, B. (2009). *Learning and leading with habits of mind: 16 essential characteristics for success*. Alexandria, VA: Association for Supervision and Curriculum Development.

Costa, A. L., (200). Describing the habits of mind. In A. L. Costa and B. Kallick (Eds.), *Learning and leading with habits of mind: 16 essential characteristics for success (pp. 15–41)*. Alexandria, VA: Association for Supervision and Curriculum Development. Accessed at www.ascd.org/publications/books/108008/chapters/Describing-the-Habits-of-Mind.aspx on October 9, 2012.

Council of Chief State School Officers. (2011, April). *Interstate Teacher Assessment and Support Consortium* (InTASC) *Model Core Teaching Standards: A Resource for State Dialogue*. Accessed at www.ccsso.org/Resources/Publications/InTASC _Model_Core_Teaching_Standards_A_Resource_for_State_Dialogue_(April_2011)-x1025.html on June 10, 2012.

Creative Education Foundation. (2011). *The foundations of applied imagination: An introduction to the Osborn-Parnes creative problem solving process*. Amherst, MA: Creative Education Foundation.

Critical Thinking Community: Our concept and definition of critical thinking. (2011). Tomales, CA: The Foundation for Critical Thinking. Accessed at www.criticalthinking.org/pages/our-concept-of-critical-thinking/411 on March 2, 2012.

Csikszentmihalyi, M. (2008). *Flow: The psychology of optimal experience*. New York: Harper Perennial Modern Classics.

Davis, S., Jenkins, G., Hunt, R., & Frazier, L. (2003). *The pact: Three young men make a promise and fulfill a dream*. New York: Riverhead Books.

de Bono, E. (1967). *The use of lateral thinking*. London: Jonathan Cape.

de Bono, E. (1970). *Lateral thinking: Creativity step by step*. New York: Harper & Row.

Delaplane, K. (n.d.). *On Einstein, bees, and survival of the human race*. Accessed at www.ent.uga.edu/bees/OnEinstein BeesandSurvivaloftheHumanRaceHoneyBeeProgramCAESEntomologyUGA.html on June 20, 2012.

Dempster, F. N. (1988). The spacing effect: A case study in the failure to apply the results of psychological research. *American Psychologist, 43*(8), 627–663.

Diamond, M., & Hopson, J. (1998). *Magic trees of the mind*. New York: Dutton Books.

Dillon, J. T. (1981). To question and not to question during discussion. *Journal of Teacher Education, 32*, 6, 15ff.

Dillon, J. T. (1988). *Questioning and teaching: A manual of practice*. London: Croom Helm.

Ehrenreich, B. (2011). *Nickel and dimed: On (not) getting by in America*. New York: Picador.

Eberle, B. (1996). *Scamper: Creative games and activities for imagination development*. Waco, TX: Prufrock Press.

Fedo, M. (1980). The carnival. In M. L. Burns (Ed.), *How to read a short story: Scholastic language skills* (pp. 35–40). New York: Scholastic.

Fellows, S. (Creator). (2004). *Ned's Declassified School Survival Guide* [Television series]. Hollywood: Nickelodeon.

Fisher, D., Frey, N., & Rothenberg, C. (2008). *Content-area conversations: How to plan discussion-based lessons for diverse language learners*. Alexandria, VA: Association for Supervision and Curriculum Development.

Flesch, R. (1955). *Why Johnny can't read—And what you can do about it*. New York: Harper & Brothers.

Fletcher, R. (2006). *Boy writers: Reclaiming their voices*. Portland, ME: Stenhouse.

Flores, B., & Clark, E. (2003) Texas voices speak out about high stakes testing: Preservice teachers, teachers and students. *Current Issues in Education, 6*(3). Accessed at http://cie.asu.edu/volume6/number3/index.html on August 29, 2012.

Framework for 21st Century Learning. (2011). Washington, DC: Partnership for 21st Century Skills. Accessed at www.p21 .org/overview/skills-framework on June 10, 2012.

Frosch, M. (Ed). (1994). *Coming of age in America*. New York: The New Press.

Gallagher, K. (2009). *Readicide: How schools are killing reading and what you can do about it*. Portland, ME: Stenhouse.

Gaines, E. J. (1992). *A gathering of old men*. New York: Vintage.

Glenn, J., & Walker, R. (Eds.). (2012). *Significant objects.* Seattle, WA: Fantagraphics.

Glucker, J. (2011, September 9). *VW's "fun theory" applied to seatbelt use* [Web log post]. Accessed at www.autoblog .com/2011/09/09/vws-fun-theory-applied-to-seatbelt-use on September 12, 2011.

Godin, S. (2009). All marketers are liars: The underground classic that explains how marketing really works—and why authenticity is the best marketing of all. New York: Penguin.

Goleman, D. (1995). *Emotional intelligence: Why it can matter more than IQ.* New York: Bantam Books.

Goodreads. (n.d.). *Anaïs Nin quotes.* Accessed at www.goodreads.com/author/quotes/7190.Ana_s_Nin on October 9, 2012.

Guy, R. (1983). *The friends.* New York: Bantam Books.

Harris, R. (1998). *Introduction to creative thinking.* Accessed at www.virtualsalt.com/crebook1.htm on September 9, 2011.

Hawkins, J. (2011). *Teacher cartoon-a-day 2012.* Riverside, NJ: McMeel.

Hawthorne, N. (2011). *The scarlet letter.* Greensboro, NC: Empire Books. (Original work published 1885).

Higher Learning Commission. (2006). Paper presented at Making a difference in student learning: Assessment as a core strategy. Chandler, AZ.

Infinite Innovations. (2011). *Definitions.* Accessed at www.brainstorming.co.uk/tutorials/definitions.html on April 27, 2011.

Irvin, J. L., Meltzer, J., & Dukes, M. (2007). *Taking action on adolescent literacy: An implementation guide for school leaders.* Alexandria, VA: Association for Supervision and Curriculum Development.

Jackson, R. (2011, December 6). *Six things I look for when I visit a classroom* [Web log post]. Accessed at http://mindstepsinc .com/2011/12/six-things-i-look-for on April 27, 2011.

Jackson, S. (1948, June 26). The lottery. *The New Yorker,* pp. 25–28.

Jago, C. (2004). *Classics in the classroom: Designing accessible literature lessons.* Portsmouth, NH: Heinemann.

Jensen, E. (1998). *Teaching with the brain in mind.* Alexandria, VA: Association for Supervision and Curriculum Development.

Jensen, E. (2003). *Tools for engagement: Managing emotional states for learner success.* San Diego, CA: The Brain Store.

Johnston, P. H. (2012). *Opening minds: Using language to change lives.* Portland, ME: Stenhouse.

Jones, R. D. (2008). *Strengthening student engagement.* Rexford, NY: International Center for Leadership in Education. Accessed at www.leadered.com/pdf/Strengthen%20Student%20Engagement%20white%20paper.pdf on August 5, 2011.

Katz, J. (2001). *Geeks: How two lost boys rode the Internet out of Idaho.* Louisville: Broadway Press.

Kallick, B. (2011, January 19). *Common Core Standards call for uncommon shifts in practices* [Web log post]. Accessed at http:// blogs.sungard.com/ps_k12/2011/01/19/common-core-standards-call-for-uncommon-shifts-in-practices/ on September 13, 2011.

Kerry, T. (Ed.). (2010). *Cross-curricular teaching in the primary school: Planning and facilitating imaginative lessons.* New York: Taylor & Francis.

Kesey, K. (1962). *One flew over the cuckoo's nest.* New York: Signet.

Krashen, S. D. (1984). *Writing: Research, theory and applications.* Torrance, CA: Laredo.

Langrehr, J. (2001). *Teaching our children to think.* Bloomington, IN: Solution Tree Press.

Lee, H. (1960). *To kill a Mockingbird.* Philadelphia: Lippencott.

List of Ned's Declassified School Survival Guide episodes. (n.d.). Accessed at http://en.wikipedia.org/wiki/List_of _Ned%27s_Declassified_School_Survival_Guide_episodes on September 27, 2012.

Lloyd, C. V. (2003). Song lyrics as texts to develop critical literacy. *Reading Online, 6*(10). Accessed at www.readingonline.org /articles/art_index.asp?HREF=lloyd/index.html on April 27, 2012.

London, J. (1910). *Lost face.* New York: Macmillan. Accessed at http://london.sonoma.edu/Writings/LostFace/ on April 27, 2012.

Lynn, S., & Luther, D. (2011, June). *Creativity in the 21st century classroom.* Presented at the Creative Problem Solving Institute, Atlanta, GA.

Madaus, G., Russell, M., & Higgins, J. (2009). *The paradoxes of high stakes testing: How they affect students, their teachers, principals, schools and society.* Charlotte, NC: Information Age.

Martin, J., & Magee, C. M. (2011). *The late American novel: Writers on the future of books.* Berkeley, CA: Salt Skull Press.

McCloskey, D., & Klamer, A. (1995). One quarter of GDP is persuasion. *American Economic Review, 85*(2), 191–195.

Meyer, D. K., & Turner, J. C. (2002). Discovering emotion in classroom motivation research. *Educational Research, 37*(2). Accessed at http://150.185.184.61/profeso/vivas_m/documen/art_ie/discovering.pdf on September 25, 2012.

Miéville, C. (2004). *Iron council.* New York: Del Rey/Ballantine Books.

Myers, W. D. (1988). *Fallen angels.* New York: Scholastic.

National Council of Teachers of English. (1985). *NCTE position statement: Resolution on grammar exercises to teach speaking and writing.* Accessed at www.ncte.org/positions/statements/grammarexercises accessed 8/6/12on August 8, 2012.

National Geographic. (2009). *Weird but true: 300 outrageous facts.* Margate, FL: Author.

National Governors Association Center for Best Practices, & Council of Chief State School Officers. (2010a). *Common Core State Standards of Mathematics.* Washington, DC: Authors. Accessed at www.corestandards.org/assets/CCSSI_Math%20 Standards.pdf on November 22, 2010.

National Governors Association Center for Best Practices, & Council of Chief State School Officers. (2010b). *Common Core State Standards: Standards for English language arts 6–12.* Washington, DC: Authors.

National Research Council. (2004). *Engaging schools: Fostering high school students' motivation to learn.* Washington, DC: National Academies Press.

Nelson, M. K. (1996). Hum-dingers. *Missouri Conservationist, 57*(7). Accessed at http://mdc.mo.gov/conmag/1996/07 /hum-dingers?page=0,1 on April 27, 2012.

Nichols, M. (2006). *Comprehension through conversation: The power of purposeful talk in the reading workshop.* Portsmouth, NH: Heinemann.

Nobleman, M. (2005). *Vocabulary cartoon of the day.* New York: Scholastic Teaching Resources.

Off, C. (2008). *Bitter chocolate: The dark side of the world's most seductive sweet.* New York: The New Press.

Osborn, A. (1953). *Applied imagination.* New York: Scribner.

Palmer, E. (2011). *Well spoken: Teaching speaking to all students.* Portland, MN: Stenhouse.

Paris, S., & McEvoy, A. (2000). Harmful and enduring effects of high stakes testing. *Issues in Education, 6*(1/2), 145–160.

Partnership for 21st Century Skills. (2011). *Learning and innovation skills.* Accessed at www.p21.0rg/index.php?option=com _content&task=view&id=60&Itemid=120 on June 18, 2012.

Paul, R., & Elder, L. (2008a). *The miniature guide to critical thinking: Concepts and tools* (Updated ed.). Tomales, CA: Foundation for Critical Thinking Press.

Paul, R., & Elder, L. (2008b). *Thinker's guide to the nature and functions of critical & creative thinking.* Tomales, CA: Foundation for Critical Thinking Press.

Peha, S. (2003). *What can you say about a book?* Accessed at www.ttms.org/say_about_a_book/expression_equals _comprehension.htm on September 29, 2011.

Peha, S. (2011). *Reading allowed.* Accessed at www.ttms.org September 29, 2011.

Philbrick, R. (1993). *Freak the mighty.* New York: Scholastic.

Philbrick, R. (1998). *Max the mighty.* New York: Scholastic.

Pink, D. (2009, August 24). *The surprising science of motivation: Dan Pink on TED.com* [Video file]. Accessed at http://blog .ted.com/2009/08/24/the_surprising on July 26, 2011.

Pink, D. H. (2005). *A whole new mind: Moving from the information age into the conceptual age.* St. Leonards, Australia: Allen & Unwin.

Poe, E. A. (1845, July 19). The masque of the red death. *Broadway Journal, 2*(2), 17–19.

Pogrow, S. (2009). *Teaching content outrageously: How to captivate all students and accelerate learning, grades 4–12.* San Francisco: Jossey-Bass.

Ponsot, M., & Deen, R. (1982). *Beat not the poor desk: Writing—What to teach, how to teach it, and why.* Montclair, NJ: Boynton/Cook.

Portis, A. (2006). *Not a box.* New York: HarperCollins.

Portis, A. (2008). *Not a stick.* New York: HarperCollins.

Purdue University. (n.d.). *4-H beekeeping, division I: Understanding the honey bee.* Accessed at www.ces.purdue.edu/extmedia /4h/4-h-571-w.pdf on June 20, 2012.

Quart, A. (2004). *Branded: The buying and selling of teenagers.* New York: Basic Books.

Rasinski, T. V. (2003). *The fluent reader: Oral reading strategies for building word recognition, fluency, and comprehension.* New York: Scholastic.

Rasinski, T. V. (Ed.). (2011). *Rebuilding the foundation: Effective reading instruction for the 21st century literacy.* Bloomington, IN: Solution Tree Press.

Rasinski, T. V., Reutzel, D. R., Chard, D., & Linan-Thompson, S. (2011). Reading fluency. In M. L. Kamil, P. D. Pearson, E. B. Moje, & P. Afflerbach (Eds.), *Handbook of Reading Research* (Vol. 4, pp. 286–319). New York: Routledge.

Reynolds, J. H., & Glaser, R. (1964). Effects of repetition and spaced review upon retention of a complex learning task. *Journal of Educational Psychology, 55*(5), 297–308.

Rivard, L., & Straw, S. B. (2000). The effect of talk and writing on learning science: An exploratory study. *Science Education, 84*(5), 566–593. Accessed at http://media.kenanaonline.com/files/0020/20490/Rivardstraw.pdf on January 5, 2012.

Robbins, P. (1975). The defamation of Edgar Allan Poe. *American History Illustrated, 10*, 18–26, 27–28.

Rohrer, D., & Pashler, H. (2010). Recent research on human learning challenges conventional instructional strategies. *Educational Researcher, 39*(5), 408–412. Accessed at http://uweb.cas.usf.edu/~drohrer/pdfs/Rohrer&Pashler2010ER. pdf on April 27, 2012.

Rohrer, D., & Taylor, K. (2007). The shuffling of mathematics practice problems boosts learning. *Instructional Science, 35*(6), 481–498.

Rolighetsteorin.se. (n.d.). *Piano stairs—"TheFunTheory.com"—Rolighetsteorin.se.* Accessed at http://ukidney.com/network /62-dr-jordan-weinstein/videos/1-general-nephrology/60-piano-stairs-thefuntheorycom-rolighetsteorinse?groupid=0 on October 7, 2009.

Rosenshine, B., Meister, C., & Chapman, S. (1996). Teaching students to generate questions: A review of the intervention studies. *Review of Educational Research, 66*(2), 181–221.

Rothstein, D., & Santana, L. (2011a). *Make just one change: Teach students to ask their own questions.* Cambridge, MA: Harvard Education Press.

Rothstein, D., & Santana, L. (2011b). Teaching students to ask their own questions: One small change can yield big results. *Harvard Education Letter, 27*(5). Accessed at www.hepg.org/hel/article/507#home on September 10, 2011.

Salinger, J. D. (2001). *The catcher in the rye.* Boston: Back Bay Books. (Original work published in 1951).

Schoenfeld, A. H. (1987). What's all the fuss about metacognition? In A. H. Schoenfeld (Ed.), *Cognitive science and mathematics education* (pp. 195–196). Hillsdale, NJ: Erlbaum.

Schreck, M. K. (2006). *Crystal doorknobs.* Columbia, MO: Tigress Press.

Schreck, M. K. (2009). *Transformers: Creative teachers for the 21st century.* Thousand Oaks, CA: Corwin.

Schreck, M. K. (2011). *You've got to reach them to teach them: Hard facts about the soft skills of student engagement.* Bloomington, IN: Solution Tree Press.

Schultz, L. (2005, January 25). *Lynn Schultz: Old Dominion University: Bloom's taxonomy.* Accessed at www.odu.edu/educ /llschult/blooms_taxonomy.htm on March 28, 2012.

Schunk, D. H. (2003). Self-efficacy for reading and writing: Influence of modeling, goal setting, and self evaluation. *Reading and Writing Quarterly, 19,* 159–172.

Scieszka, J. (2005). *Guys write for guys read: Boys' favorite authors write about being boys.* New York: Viking Books.

Shakespeare, W. (2011). *As you like it.* Hollywood, FL: Simon & Brown. (Original work published 1623.)

Sleator, W. (2005). The masque of the red death. In J. Scieszka (Ed.), *Guys write for guys read: Boys' favorite authors write about being boys* (pp. 233–235). New York: Viking.

Smith, R. (2012, March). *Fifty ways to leave your lecture.* Presented at the Association for Supervision and Curriculum Development Annual Conference 2012, Pittsburgh, PA.

Stanford History Education Group. (n.d.). *Reading like a historian.* Accessed at http://sheg.stanford.edu/?q=node/45 on July 31, 2012.

Stanton, A. (Writer/Director), Andrews, M., & Chabon, M. (Writers). (2012). *John Carter* [Motion picture]. United States: Walt Disney Pictures.

Steinbeck, J. (2002). *Of mice and men* (Centennial ed.). New York: Penguin Putnam. (Original work published 1937).

Stephenson, C. (n.d.a). *Leiningen versus the ants.* Accessed at www.classicshorts.com/stories/lvta.html on August 10, 2012.

Stephenson, C. (n.d.b). *Leiningen versus the ants* [Video post]. Accessed at http://criticalpressmedia.com/2012/07/leiningen -versus-the-ants on August 10, 2012.

Sterling, L. C. (2011, May 1). *The (critical) role of storytelling in marketing* [Web log post]. Accessed at www.compellingconcepts .com/2011/05/the-critical-role-of-story-telling-in-marketing on January 8, 2012.

Stokes, D., & Stokes, L. (1989). *The hummingbird book: The complete guide to attracting, identifying, and enjoying hummingbirds.* Boston: Little, Brown.

Strong, R. W., Silver, H. F., & Perini, M. J. (2001). Teaching what matters most: Standards and strategies for raising student achievement. *Educational Leadership, 59*(3), 56–61.

StudyGuide.org. (2012). *Socratic seminars.* Accessed at www.studyguide.org/socratic_seminar_student.htm on January 8, 2012.

Taylor, B. M., Pearson, P. D., Clark, F. C., & Walpole, S. (1999). *Beating the odds in teaching all children to read: Lessons from effective schools and exemplary teachers, CIERA report 1999* (Report 2-006). Ann Arbor: University of Michigan School of Education.

Terry, P. M. (2000). Empowering teachers as leaders. *National Forum of Teacher Education Journal, 10E*(3). Accessed at www.nationalforum.com/Electronic%20Journal%20Volumes/Terry,%20paul%20M.%20Empowering%20Teachers%20As%20Leaders.pdf on April 30, 2012.

The fun theory. (2009). Accessed at www.thefuntheory.com/ on June 19, 2012.

Thornburg, D. D. (1999). *Campfires in cyberspace: Primordial metaphors for learning in the 21st century.* Lake Barrington, IL: Thornburg Center for Professional Development. Accessed at www.tcpd.org/thornburg/handouts/campfires.pdf on December 29, 2011.

Thorpe, S. (2000). *How to think like Einstein: Simple ways to break the rules and discover your hidden genius.* Naperville, IL: Sourcebooks.

Tucker, M. (2011). *Standing on the shoulders of giants: An American agenda for educational reform.* Washington, DC: National Center for Education and the Economy.

Turner, J. H., & Stets, J. E. (2005). *The sociology of emotions.* Cambridge, England: Cambridge University Press.

Turner, M. (1996). *The literary mind: The origins of thought and language.* New York: Oxford University Press.

Twain, M. (1998). *The adventures of Huckleberry Finn* (3rd ed.). New York: Norton. (Original work published 1885).

Tweney, D. (2006). Blast to the past. *Wired Magazine, 14*(7). Accessed at www.wired.com/wired/archive/14.07/start.html?pg=5 on June 10, 2012.

Van Allsburg, C. (1984). *The mysteries of Harris Burdick.* Boston: Houghton Mifflin.

Van Allsburg, C. (2011). *The chronicles of Harris Burdick: Fourteen amazing authors tell the tales.* Boston: Houghton Mifflin Harcourt.

Van Mullem, L. (2008). *Winter holiday food around the world.* Accessed at www.petergreenberg.com/2008/12/01/winter-holiday-food-around-the-world on April 27, 2012.

Vonnegut, K. (1999). *Slaughterhouse-five.* New York: Dial.

Vásquez, A. (2009). Breathing underwater: At-risk ninth graders dive into literary analysis. *Alan Review, 31*(1). Accessed at http://scholar.lib.vt.edu/ejournals/ALAN/v37n1/vasquez.html on April 30, 2012.

Wagner, T. (2008). *The global achievement gap: Why even our best schools don't teach the new survival skills our children need—And what we can do about it.* New York: Basic Books.

Ward, S. (2012). *Halloween: A really sweet business opportunity.* Accessed at http://sbinfocanada.about.com/od/business opportunities/a/halloweenopps.htm on April 30, 2012.

Warriner, J. (1982). *Warriner's English grammar and composition: Third course grade nine* (Franklin ed.). Orlando, FL: Holt McDougal.

Warriner, J. (1982a). *Warriner's English grammar and composition: Second course grade eight.* Boston: Hartcourt College

Warriner, J. (1982b). *Warriner's English grammar and composition: Second course grade seven.* Boston: Hartcourt College.

Wessling, S. B. (2011). *Supporting students in a time of core standards: English language arts grades 9–12.* Urbana, IL: National Council of Teachers of English.

Wiesel, E. (1969). *Night.* New York: Avon.

Wiggins, G. (2012). Feedback for learning. *Educational Leadership, 70,* 10–16. Accessed at www.ascd.org/publications/educational-leadership/sept12/vol70/num01/Seven-Keys-to-Effective-Feedback.aspx on October 1, 2012.

Wiggins, G., & McTighe, J. (2005). *Understanding by design* (Expanded 2nd ed.). Alexandria, VA: Association for Supervision and Curriculum Development.

Wilhelm, J. D. (1997). *You gotta BE the book: Teaching engaged and reflective reading with adolescents.* New York: Teachers College Press.

Wilhelm, J. D. (2002). *Action strategies for deepening comprehension.* New York: Scholastic.

Wiliam, D. (2011). *Embedded formative assessment.* Bloomington, IN: Solution Tree Press.

Williamson, R., & Blackburn, B. (2010). *Rigorous schools and classrooms: Leading the way.* Larchmont, NY: Eye On Education.

Willingham, D. T. (2006). The usefulness of brief instruction in reading comprehension strategies. *American Educator, 30*(4), 39–45, 50.

Willms, J. D. (2003). *Student engagement at school: A sense of belonging and participation—Results from PISA 2000.* Paris, France: Organisation for Economic Co-Operation and Development.

Wilson, C., & Schlosser, E. (2007). *Chew on this: Everything you don't want to know about fast food.* New York: Houghton-Mifflin.

Wolpert-Gawron, H. (2011a, September 6). *The power of teaching about something you don't know about* [Web log post]. Accessed at http://tweenteacher.com/2011/09/06/the-power-of-teaching-something-you-know-nothing-about on April 17, 2012.

Wolpert-Gawron, H. (2011b, September 18). *DARPA project cont'd: Research and questioning* [Web log post]. Accessed at http://tweenteacher.com/2011/09/18/darpa-project-con%E2%80%99t-research-and-questioning on April 30, 2012.

Wolpert-Gawron, H. (2011c, November 1). *Persuasive writing is a key focus in common core standards* [Web log post]. Accessed at www.edutopia.org/blog/common-core-standards-persuasive-writing-heather-wolpert-gawron December 12, 2011.

Wolpert-Gawron, H. (2012, February 13). *The power of project-based writing in the classroom* [Web log post]. Accessed at www.edutopia.org/blog/project-based-writing-real-world-heather-wolpert-gawron on April 30, 2012.

Wong, H. K., & Wong, R. T. (2009). *First days of school: How to be an effective teacher* (New 4th ed.). Mountain View, CA: Wong.

Wragg, E. C. (1994). *An introduction to classroom observation.* London: Rutledge.

Wragg, E. C., & Brown, G. (2001). *Questioning in the secondary school* (2nd ed.). London: Routledge.

Wyeth, A. (1948). Christina's World [Painting]. Accessed at www.moma.org/explore/collection/object.php?object_id=78455 on October 17, 2012.

Yazzie-Mintz, E. (2007). *Voices of students on engagement: A report on the 2006 High School Survey of Student Engagement.* Bloomington, IN: Center for Evaluation & Education Policy. Accessed at www.eric.ed.gov/PDFS/ED495758.pdf on October 20, 2011.

Yazzie-Mintz, E. (2009). *Engaging the voices of students: A report on the 2007 & 2008 High School Survey of Student Engagement.* Bloomington, IN: Center for Evaluation & Education Policy.

Zyngier, D. (2005, November). *Doing education not doing time: Engaging pedagogies and pedagogues—what does student engagement look like in action?* Presented at the AARE International Educational Research Conference, Melbourne, Australia. Accessed at http://monash.academia.edu/DavidZyngier/Papers/93298/Doing_education_not_doing_time._Engaging_Pedagogies_and_Pedagogues_-_what_does_student_engagement_look_like_in_action on April 26, 2012.

Index

You've Got to Reach Them to Teach Them
Mary Kim Schreck
Navigate the hot topic of student engagement with a true expert. Become empowered to demand an authentic joy for learning in your classroom. Real-life notes from the field, detailed discussions, practical strategies, and space for reflection complete this essential guide to student engagement.
BKF404

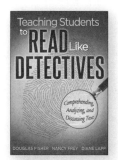

Teaching Students to Read Like Detectives
Douglas Fisher, Nancy Frey, and Diane Lapp
Prompt students to become the sophisticated readers, writers, and thinkers they need to be to achieve higher learning. Explore the important relationship between text, learner, and learning, and gain an array of methods to establish critical literacy in a discussion-based and reflective classroom.
BKF499

Common Core English Language Arts in a PLC at Work™ series
Douglas Fisher and Nancy Frey
These teacher guides illustrate how to sustain successful implementation of the Common Core State Standards for English language arts in K–12 instruction, curriculum, assessment, and intervention practices within a powerful collaborative model: Professional Learning Communities at Work™.

Joint Publications With the International Reading Association
BKF580, BKF582, BKF584, BKF586, BKF578

20 Literacy Strategies to Meet the Common Core
Elaine K. McEwan-Adkins and Allyson J. Burnett
With the advent of the Common Core State Standards, some secondary teachers are scrambling for what to do and how to do it. This book provides 20 research-based strategies designed to help students meet those standards and become expert readers.
BKF588

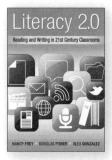

Literacy 2.0
Nancy Frey, Douglas Fisher, and Alex Gonzalez
Students in the 21st century must incorporate traditional literacy skills into a mastery of technology for communicating and collaborating in new ways. This book offers specific teaching strategies for developing students' skills related to acquiring, producing, and sharing information.
BKF373